Part 3 (pages 155–232) has been removed from TU100

Part 4 Information overload

You can find this study session online. A link is provided on the TU100 website.

The Open University

TU100
My digital life

Block 2
My stuff

This publication forms part of the Open University module TU100 *My digital life*. Details of this and other Open University modules can be obtained from the Student Registration and Enquiry Service, The Open University, PO Box 197, Milton Keynes MK7 6BJ, United Kingdom (tel. +44 (0)845 300 60 90; email general-enquiries@open.ac.uk).

Alternatively, you may visit the Open University website at www.open.ac.uk where you can learn more about the wide range of modules and packs offered at all levels by The Open University.

To purchase a selection of Open University materials visit www.ouw.co.uk, or contact Open University Worldwide, Walton Hall, Milton Keynes MK7 6AA, United Kingdom for a brochure (tel. +44 (0)1908 858793; fax +44 (0)1908 858787; email ouw-customer-services@open.ac.uk).

The Open University
Walton Hall, Milton Keynes
MK7 6AA

First published 2011. [Third edition 2014.]

Edited and designed by The Open University.

Typeset by SR Nova Pvt. Ltd, Bangalore, India.

Printed in the United Kingdom by Latimer Trend and Company Ltd, Plymouth.

ISBN 978 1 7800 7920 2

3.1

Contents

Part 1 Inside the box

You can find this study session online. A link is provided on the TU100 website.

Part 2 The vanishing computer

Part 5 'With the tears wiped off'

Part 1
Inside the box

Author: Kevin Waugh

Introduction

Welcome to the first part of Block 2 of TU100. In this part I want to explore the *hardware* and *software* that make up a modern computer system. To do this I will use the specific example of the modern desktop personal computer (PC), but the material will be applicable to most modern computing devices.

I will be looking 'inside the box' of the desktop PC, and considering how the electronics within the box represent and process data. My aim is not to give a computer engineer's view of the interior of the computer; instead I want to describe a model of how the computer works in just enough detail to give you a basic understanding of computer hardware. I will treat the computer not as an electronic calculating device, but as a device for communicating and processing symbolic representations of data.

The first two sessions of this part will consider how we use signs and symbols to communicate information and instructions that others can follow. You have already been introduced to some of these ideas in Block 1.

In later sessions I'll introduce the hardware of the computer, before briefly considering what is involved in making the computer perform *computation* – that is, how we tell the computer what to do. I'll look at how modern programming languages relate to what is happening inside the machine, and how we make programming easier by harnessing the power of the computer itself.

As discussed in the *TU100 Guide*, from this block onwards you will no longer be given any indication of how long the sessions will take to complete – it is up to you to manage your own study time. You will also not be reminded at the start of every part to make entries in your learning journal, but keeping a journal is an ongoing learning outcome of TU100 and by now you should be in the habit of making regular entries.

Note: Session 3 of this part, 'What's inside my computer, and what makes it work?', is an online study component enhanced by several animations. You should allow about 4–5 hours for this online study, which can be accessed from the resources page associated with this part on the TU100 website.

Sessions 4 and 5 also make use of a few animations on the TU100 website, but the study material for these sessions is in this printed book.

Learning outcomes

Your study of this part will help you to do the following.

Knowledge and understanding

- Explain how symbols can be used to represent data and instructions, and how these can be represented inside a computer as binary values.
- Explain the importance of standard formats and protocols for the representation and communication of symbolic data.
- Demonstrate how simple tasks can be described by instructions written in the form of algorithms using text, and be able to follow an algorithm.
- Describe the purpose of each of the major components of a computer system, and use common terminology to describe these components.
- Describe how transistors can be used to implement Boolean algebra operations, and explain how they can be used to execute machine-language instructions.
- Describe the internal features of a simple central processing unit (CPU).
- Show, in outline form, how a computer program is executed on a computer with the von Neumann architecture, and explain the importance of the program counter in controlling the flow of the program.
- Explain what a computer program is, and how low-level and high-level programming languages relate to the internal operations of the CPU.

Cognitive skills

- Analyse a simple problem and identify the operations required for a solution.

Symbolic representation

The human world is full of *signs* and *symbols* – traffic lights, telephone bells, map icons, clothes washing symbols and fire alarms are all coded representations that are intended to mean something to the people who encounter them. The computing world is also full of symbolic representations. I am going to be treating the 'inside of the box' as a place in which symbolic representations of data are communicated and processed. Computer symbols in electronic, magnetic or laser-readable forms are passed between storage and processing components within a computer system. These symbolic representations are defined by *formats* that allow them to be interpreted and processed. When the symbols are passed between computer components there will also be one or more communication protocols used to structure the message.

In this part the terms 'sign' and 'symbol' are considered to have the same meaning. I have chosen to use symbol from now on.

To set the scene, before I look at the symbolic messages being passed inside the computer I will consider some examples of message-passing systems that are used by humans. In particular I will consider a historic example of symbolic communication, the Chappe Telegraph, that allowed complex messages and instructions to be transmitted through the air – effectively a Napoleonic wireless communication network!

At the end of this session I will have laid the foundations for treating the computer as a symbolic message-passing system, dependent on standard ways of representing data and passing messages between components. This relates to the material on protocols and communication that you have already met in Block 1.

1.1   The human world of signs and symbols

A symbol can be defined as something that conveys some *information* by means other than direct representation – in other words, a symbol stands as a representation for something else. For instance, a beeping sound at a light-controlled pedestrian crossing symbolises the fact that it is safe to cross, while an arrow on a traffic sign symbolises the direction in which traffic is allowed to flow. We don't always know what a symbol means – possibly it is new to us, or perhaps we haven't encountered it in a specific location before. However, those who know what a symbol represents can act according to the meaning it carries.

When convenient, watch the five-minute video 'Symbols everywhere', which you will find in the resources page associated with this part on the TU100 website. This will give you an introduction to some of the many symbols that we may encounter in our everyday lives.

In the right situation symbols can be interpreted, giving rise to information. However, for two people to agree on what information a symbol represents they must first agree on the meaning of the symbol and then recognise the situation or context in which it is being used.
For example, consider a piece of paper on which is written 'Number 4, 2:30 p.m., Chepstow'. This could contain information that a gambler might use to place a bet on a horse race, but someone else might see it as supplying information about which bus they need to catch and when and where to catch it. The plots of detective stories often depend on the inability of the characters to make sense of data (i.e. to find the *information* in the data) until its context becomes clear.

Thus we exchange information through a process of:

* creating symbols to represent data
* agreeing on what the symbols represent
* deciding on rules for combining symbols to form messages
* communicating combinations of symbols to others.

1.2 Using symbols for communication

Communication between people relies on *conventions*. A convention is an agreement between a group of participants about what an ordered collection of symbols (a message) means. People familiar with a convention, the symbols and their structure will be able to interpret the meaning of a message.

Activity 2 (exploratory)

Give an example of:

(a) a public convention – where a large number of participants know the convention and there is an expectation of public awareness of the convention

(b) a private convention – where a small number of participants use the convention, usually to keep their messages private.

Comment

(a) There are many public conventions: music notation, written English, notations for arithmetic and so on.

(b) The secret messaging systems used extensively during wartime are a good example of private conventions. You might have thought of others.

We often have a choice as to the convention we use. For instance, I could communicate the name 'Keith' using several different conventions:

1   writing it in English – 'Keith'

2   spelling it out using one of the phonetic alphabets – Kilo, Echo, India, Tango, Hotel

3   converting the letters into Morse code – DASH DOT DASH, DOT, DOT DOT, DASH, DOT DOT DOT DOT

4   using a ROT-13 cipher – 'XRVGU'

5   using the British Sign Language spelling alphabet, as shown in Figure 1.

ROT-13 ('rotate by 13 places') is a simple substitution cipher. It is a variation of the Caesar cipher, developed in ancient Rome.

Figure 1   The name 'Keith' spelt out using British Sign Language

The above list gives five different symbolic forms of the same message content. The ability of the person receiving the communication to understand it depends on his or her awareness and knowledge of the convention being used.

It is important to appreciate that the same symbol can represent different data. For example, the symbol 'chat' means different things to a person speaking English (where it means a conversation) and a person speaking French (where it means a cat). In order to know what is meant by the symbol 'chat', we need to know which convention – in this case which language – is being used.

In our daily lives we are used to dealing with multiple conventions, often simultaneously, and translating between conventions when we need to. For example, sign language or closed-caption encoding (text) is often available alongside the soundtrack of television programmes and films. Also, simultaneous language translation is used at gatherings of international representatives such as the United Nations Assembly or the European Parliament.

Activity 3 (self-assessment)

Which of the five representations of the name 'Keith' listed above might be appropriate in the following situations:

(a) using a telephone in a noisy room

(b) sending a letter?

As you have just seen, we can usually find an appropriate convention for the circumstances in which we want to communicate. Yet our existing conventions didn't just come out of nowhere – they were developed to suit specific sets of circumstances for which a convention did not already exist. The Chappe Telegraph is an example of just such an invented symbolic convention.

1.3   The Chappe Telegraph

The Chappe Telegraph, developed in France during the Napoleonic era by an inventor called Claude Chappe, was a manually operated visual telegraph (Figure 2). Different positions of the crossbar and arms at the top of the tower represented different symbols that could be seen across long distances. A shared convention for the meaning of these symbols allowed the exchange of messages.

Chappe was not the first person to design such a system. Around 350 BC Aeneas Tacticus, an early Greek writer on the art of war, invented a hydraulic telegraph semaphore system to send messages between Sicily and Carthage.

Messages were sent along a chain of telegraph stations, with each local operator copying and repeating the message to the next in the chain. In the mid-nineteenth century a network of over 500 relay stations connecting 29 major French cities was in place (Figure 3). Messages could travel at up to 200 kilometres per hour – a speed almost inconceivable to the ordinary Frenchman.

For my purposes, the interesting thing about the Chappe Telegraph is the different conventions for message representation that were used as the system developed. Initially a convention in which one symbol replaced one character was used for message content. There was a look-up table (Figure 4) that could be printed and used by operators to encode and decode messages.

The arms of the telegraph could take 96 different positions and therefore transmit 96 different symbols, but some symbols were unused because they were easily confused with others – for instance, the symbol shown in Figure 5(a) wasn't used because at a distance it was too similar to the

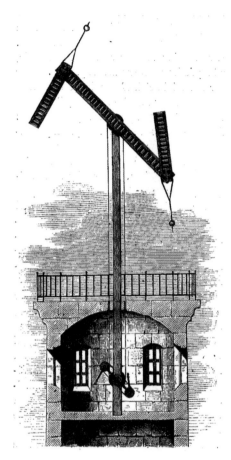

Figure 2   A Chappe Telegraph tower

symbol for 10 (shown in Figure 4). There was a convention that a
specific sequence of special 'control' symbols was used to start and end
a message; these identified who the message was to be sent to, showed
whether the message was urgent and handled errors such as the receiving
station missing symbols (due to fog, for example). Using computer
terminology we would refer to this as a *protocol* for message passing.
The control symbols, such as the one in Figure 5(b), allowed the telegraph
operators to control the messages without needing to examine the detailed
content.

Rather than representing characters, the control symbols represented
instructions on how to handle a message. Drawing on this idea, later
versions of the telegraph used a code table in which each of the arm
positions represented an entire word or phrase. The operators stationed at
each post only needed to know the control symbols, and simply recorded
or retransmitted the message symbols – which could only be deciphered
by whoever held a matching code table.

Figure 3   Chappe Telegraph coverage of France

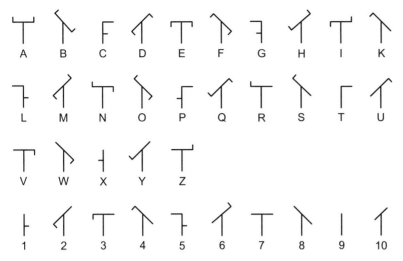

Figure 4   Some of the symbols in the Chappe Telegraph look-up table

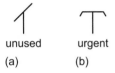

Figure 5   Two Chappe symbols: (a) an unused symbol and
(b) a control symbol

Activity 4 (exploratory)

Suppose you wanted to send both public news and private
communications over the Chappe Telegraph using code tables. How could
you ensure that some messages could be read by anyone, and others could
be read by only a small number of people?

Comment

Using a publicly available code table to encode a public message would
allow anyone with access to the same table to decode that message.

Keeping some code tables private would allow individuals to have their
own meanings for the symbols. The messages would be meaningless
without a copy of the right private table to decode the symbols.

Common control symbols could be used in both cases, as these are
unrelated to the message content.

Still later, the codes were extended to use pairs of symbols to represent
words or phrases. The first symbol in the pair represented the page of a
code book to use, while the second symbol represented the line containing
the word or phrase in the code table on that page. This allowed nearly
8000 different words or phrases to be encoded using two symbol positions.

Anyone creating a message to be sent across the telegraph didn't draw a series of pictures of the telegraph arms; instead they used a numeric representation for each word or phrase they wanted to send. For example, 53, 21 would represent the phrase on page 53, line 21 of the agreed code book, which might be the phrase 'Acknowledge completion of this task'. In other words, the positioning of the arms of the telegraph now symbolically represented a numeric value, and it was this symbolic representation that was carried in the messages passing along the chain of telegraph stations.

The Chappe Telegraph provides a good model for symbolic communication technologies. It involves:

- *choosing* an appropriate representation for the words and numbers that are to form the message (the numeric codes and their meaning)
- *combining* these with a device that is capable of being sensed by sender and receiver and capable of the symbolic representation of the message content (the telegraph towers and arms)
- *agreeing* a convention about the way in which messages, routing information, addresses and errors are to be interpreted (operating protocols and user guides).

Notice that different representation formats (written words, numeric values and telegraph arm positions) are used at different points in the message's journey.

1.4 The computer world of symbols, formats and protocols

For many years people thought of computers as fast, smart calculating devices – 'number crunchers'. Modern computers certainly began as calculating tools, but it was soon recognised that *anything* that can be symbolised using an appropriate digital code can be captured and processed by a computer. If we have the right collection of symbols, an agreement about their meaning and the right instructions for storing, processing and exchanging them, we can represent and process a huge range of things, not just numbers.

This leads to an alternative way of thinking about a computer: not as a number cruncher but as a machine for storing, communicating and processing symbolic representations of data using stored instructions. This view allows us more easily to think about the computer as having the ability to record and manipulate sound, images and video, manipulate robots, control nuclear power plants and carry out all sorts of complex activities – a long way from being simply 'a number cruncher'!

1.5 Representing symbols inside the computer

The Chappe Telegraph demonstrated that we can encode information using symbols with a numeric representation. Modern computers depend on this ability, as the internal symbolic representations used inside a computer are represented as binary numeric values.

Modern computer systems are, primarily, constructed from *electrical* and *electronic* devices such as processor and memory chips, USB sticks, LCD display panels and so on (and in addition they use magnetic and optical devices in hard drives and CDs/DVDs to store data). These devices are connected together into circuits, which control the behaviour and flow of electrical signals from device to device. Digital electronic circuits are circuits that are based on a small number of voltage levels. Most modern computer circuitry uses two voltage levels, which we can think of as being labelled 'low' and 'high'. It would be quite clumsy to talk about high and low voltages and electrical patterns on a wire when we discuss what is going on inside the computer, so instead we talk about a binary representation of these voltages: high voltage symbolised by 1 and low voltage symbolised by 0.

When a key on a computer's keyboard (an input device) is pressed, an electrical circuit is activated that causes a pattern of high and low voltages to be sent along the wires connecting the keyboard to the computer. These voltage changes are sampled by the computer system and interpreted as representing a specific key being pressed. The specific pattern of high and low voltages is the symbol that represents a specific key. We will think about this symbol in its binary form – for example, 01011111 might represent the character '?' being pressed.

You will see later in this part how electronic circuits can be used to perform symbol processing such as *Boolean algebra* and comparisons between symbolic binary representations.

1.6 Shared conventions for symbols inside the computer

Early in the development of the computer, different manufacturers developed their own internal symbolic representations of data. At that time there was no expectation that a computer would need to communicate with other computers, only with its own purpose-built input and output devices. Consequently, data stored on one manufacturer's computer systems could not be processed on another make of computer without first being translated from one internal representation to another.

In the late 1960s and early 1970s computers began to be connected to each other, and to use third-party peripherals (tape drives, disk drives, keyboards, etc.). When networking became commonplace, it became necessary for software applications to be able to exchange data between different users on different systems. Hardware and software developers expected users to share information, so they needed to ensure compatibility of the representations associated with the underlying data. This led the computer industry to develop standard formats and protocols that were publicly documented; in other words, the industry started to develop *conventions* for data representation. Standard formats and protocols permit sharing of data between computers in the same way that shared conventions permit human communication.

1.7   Computer formats for data representation

Formats are the formal descriptions used to represent the data associated with particular software applications or hardware systems. They give definitions for the symbols used by an application or hardware device and determine the structure of the data representations. For example, in a word-processing application that manipulates text documents, a format is a language that is used to express all the detail of the content and layout of the document. HTML (hypertext markup language) is a good example of this. Likewise, applications may process data representing sound or video, and these will each require their own formal description language to express the features of the sound or video that the application can process.

Data formats are necessary for several reasons:

1   to agree on the meanings of the symbols used in the data items

2   to ensure consistency – applications such as word processors need to interpret the content of a document the same way each time it is opened by a user

3   to enable sharing – if two word-processing applications use the same format then a document prepared using one application can be used with the other

4   to detect erroneous data – data that doesn't conform to a stated format cannot be interpreted using that format and therefore represents an error in the data.

You read about formats and standards in your study of Block 1. You will meet them again in Block 3.

The majority of the data formats in common use on computers today are *standard formats* – that is, they are agreed definitions that are widely known. When two applications use different formats, it is sometimes possible to build *software interfaces* that translate between the two formats. However, it is usually easier for applications to be built to use standard public formats rather than having to build new interfaces each time a user wants applications to exchange data.

1.8 Protocols in computer communication

We use the term *protocol* when we talk about the agreed conventions for communicating symbolic messages between computing devices. Protocols are similar to formats, but instead of defining a data representation they define how data can be packaged into a message to be communicated between devices. This includes definitions relating to how to express an address so that the message goes to the right device, how to mark the beginning and end of the content of the message being sent, how to handle errors and so on. Not surprisingly, computer networks depend on a lot of different protocols. You were introduced to network communication protocols in Part 4 of Block 1.

The set of rules for using control symbols in the Chappe Telegraph is an example of a protocol.

Protocols are also important when we look at communication between the components inside a computer system. Almost all desktop computer systems are constructed from components that have standard connectors and that interact using standard protocols. This avoids the need for the system manufacturer to design and build custom components. For example, most modern desktop computers contain one of two main types of hard disk system: Serial Advanced Technology Attachment (SATA) and Small Computer System Interface (SCSI). These two standards have different *hardware interfaces* with different physical forms, as shown in Figure 6.

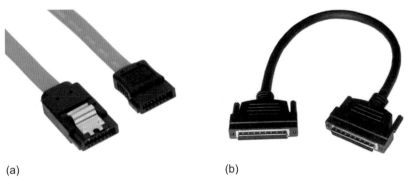

(a)   (b)

Figure 6   Physical form of (a) SATA and (b) SCSI interfaces as illustrated by their cables

Both standards connect internal hard disk drives to the other components of the system. However, the hardware interface between the main computer and the protocol that stores or retrieves data for each standard is different. Even if it were physically possible to plug a SATA hard disk into the SCSI interface connector, the different protocols for message exchange would prevent the two devices from exchanging data. These differences are hidden from the user by the operating system, which contains software routines – called *device drivers* – that translate generic requests to read and write data into specific requests that satisfy the appropriate protocol for the type of SATA or SCSI disk drive attached.

Activity 5 (exploratory)

(a) What does the acronym USB stand for?

(b) Do a Web search to find examples of different devices that have standard USB (or USB 2.0) connections and so can connect to a computer with a USB port. Do you have any devices with USB connectors in your home or workplace?

Comment

(a) USB stands for *universal serial bus*. USB quickly became a common standard for computer connectivity.

(b) If you used a search engine to look for USB devices then you were probably swamped with hits. It's the communication standard of choice for modern peripherals and external storage devices.

Activity 6 (exploratory)

The video called 'Inside the box' that is associated with this part will give you an overview of a computer from the perspectives of a computer engineer and a computer scientist. It has been divided into three ten-minute sections, which you will watch at intervals throughout the text.

Go to the resources page associated with this part on the TU100 website, where you will find the first section of the 'Inside the box' video (entitled 'Outside to inside – peripherals'). This will introduce you to a range of peripherals connected to a typical desktop PC, and show you how the computer engineer and computer scientist each view the communication between the peripherals and the main PC.

You will watch the second and third sections of this video later in the part.

1.9 Conclusion

In this session I have looked at the use of symbolic communication among humans and how symbols representing data become information when they are interpreted. I mentioned that we can use different symbolic representations to represent the same message and translate between them when required.

The inside of a computer is entirely a world of binary symbols, but to interpret and process these symbols we need an agreement about what they represent. We use formats to help define the meaning of symbols for specific purposes – word processing, web pages, spreadsheets, etc.

If we want to share symbolic data we must agree to use conventions such as common standard formats, or to translate between different formats as required.

When we communicate symbolic messages, both between computers and between the components that make up a single computer system, we need to agree a protocol so that the message is safely delivered to the correct recipient, is not damaged during exchange and is still a readable message when it arrives.

The majority of computer component manufacturers benefit by following the standard formats and protocols because this allows computer components to be interchangeable.

In a computer, as well as communicating data we also need to process it, which means processing binary symbolic representations of the data. This raises the issue of how we represent the instructions for the processing of symbols. If the inside of the computer is entirely a world of binary symbols then we need to represent the instructions in binary form as well as using binary to represent the data the instructions process. In the next session I will consider the representation of symbolic instructions.

This session should have helped you with the following learning outcomes.

- Explain how symbols can be used to represent data and instructions, and how these can be represented inside a computer as binary values.

- Explain the importance of standard formats and protocols for the representation and communication of symbolic data.

2 Symbolic instructions and algorithms

Before I start to look in detail at the internal structure and operations taking place 'inside the box', it would be useful to consider how computers know what to do. How do we instruct a computer to perform a task? To answer this question, I'll look first at how humans are familiar with producing instructions to perform many mundane tasks, and then go on to discuss how large complex calculations were performed before digital computers existed. At the end of this session you should be familiar with the idea of algorithmic instruction.

2.1 Instructing people

A cookbook is really an ordered collection of symbolic instructions, usually in a written language and sometimes with pictures. We are used to following these instructions when using a recipe – the recipe tells us the ingredients and tools we need to have available, and the steps we need to follow to combine and cook the ingredients.

A recipe is an example of something computer scientists call an *algorithm*. An algorithm is a step-by-step list of instructions, also known as a *sequence* of instructions, that when followed will solve a problem. The instructions in the algorithm should be simple enough that each step can be performed accurately and without needing to break it down into simpler steps, or such that each complex step can be described by another algorithm or standard definition.

Here's another example. Figure 7 is taken from an instruction booklet that is designed to show customers how to assemble an IKEA table. This is a good example of almost purely diagrammatic instructions that form an algorithm. The instructions are provided in a numbered sequence. Here I have shown only steps 2 and 3 of the build process – Figures 7(b) and 7(c) – which show complex detail in an expanded form. The parts and tools required are described by symbols that are easily interpreted or matched against the parts in the box (Figure 7a). This forms a *pre-condition* for the algorithm: you need to have the listed items available to be able to build this table.

You will notice that in step 3 (Figure 7c), which shows the table top being attached, repetition of an action is required. This is indicated by the 12 screws and washers shown in the main image and the symbol '12×' appearing against the expanded view. The repetition symbol '4×' is also

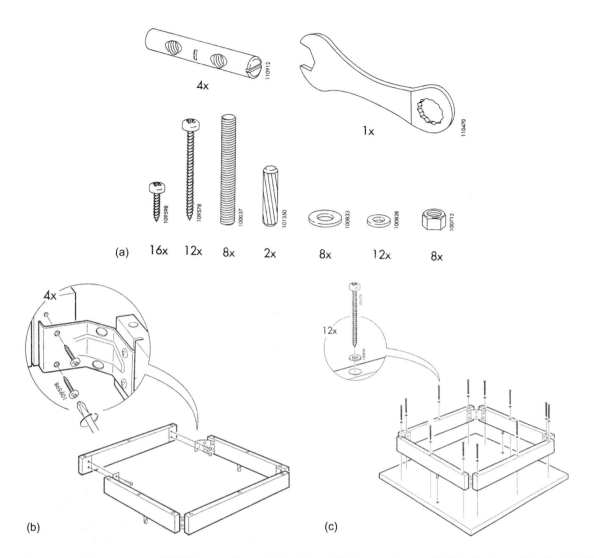

Figure 7 **Extracts from IKEA instructions: (a) tools and fixing parts supplied in the box; (b) step 2 of the build, forming the frame; (c) step 3 of the build, attaching the frame**

used in the expanded view in step 2, but here the main image shows a mixture of incomplete and complete corners of the table. This is something that can easily be interpreted as illustrating the 'before' and 'after' states, but it does break the spirit of an algorithm as the person following the instructions has to realise that the 'after' states are not steps in the instruction sequence. The 'after' state can be treated as a *post-condition* showing what the corner should look like after the step has been performed. A person building the table would use the post-condition to check that they had followed the instructions properly.

In the repetition shown in Figure 7(c) there is no specific order given for the 12 screws – provided the person building the table completes them all

When you studied Block 1 you were introduced to repetition loops in the Sense programming language.

before moving on to the next numbered diagram in the sequence, they will have completed the required task. So they could choose in which order to follow the instructions in step 3, or (assuming they had eleven friends to help) they could attempt to screw in all 12 screws at the same time. Either way, the end result would be the same. If the order of the repeated instruction was important then IKEA would have broken the diagram into smaller diagrams and arranged them in the necessary sequence.

I will now consider an algorithm that is more typical of computing algorithms, as it does the kind of task that computers do frequently – sorting things.

2.2   An algorithm to put things into categories

Below is an algorithm in textual form. It gives instructions for sorting a single pile of playing cards into four piles, each of which contains cards of a single suit.

Category-sorting algorithm

1   Pick up all the cards.

2   Choose any card from those in your hand and look at the suit of the card.

3   If there is already a pile of cards of that suit, put this card on that pile; otherwise start a new pile with this card.

4   If there is at least one card left in your hand, go back to step 2.

5   There are no cards in your hand; the cards are sorted, you are finished.

Activity 7 (exploratory)

Find a pack of playing cards and follow the above algorithm. What are the pre-conditions and post-conditions?

Comment

To be sure the algorithm will work I need to state some pre-conditions. In this case I require that:

- I have some cards at the start.
- There are no 'Jokers' in the pack.
- I am able to interpret the instructions in the way the writer intended (so that I can accurately follow them).

The post-condition for sorting a pack of 52 normal playing cards is to have four piles, each pile containing 13 cards from the same suit.

The same algorithm could be represented in many different formats: as different text representations, as different pictorial representations or (as you will see shortly) as binary instructions. These would be *different* symbolic representations of the *same* algorithm. When we implement an algorithm to execute on a computer we need to represent the algorithm in a suitable programming language – you are using Sense for TU100, but there are many other languages in common use.

The category-sorting algorithm can be made more general-purpose than simply sorting playing cards. For instance, suppose the problem I had was to sort addressed letters according to their destination towns. You should be able to see how the above algorithm could be changed to perform a category sort on addresses. The general version of this algorithm can sort anything into categories based on some distinguishing characteristic.

Activity 8 (self-assessment)

(a) Where in the card-sorting algorithm is the 'distinguishing characteristic' used to decide on categories?

(b) What causes the algorithm to finish, and how is this shown in the algorithm text?

(c) Would the algorithm work if you had only 10 playing cards, or 110 playing cards, or 1000 playing cards?

(d) How could you apply the above algorithm to group addressed letters into a pile for each town and then, within each town, into a pile for each street?

A problem can usually be solved using a range of different algorithms and combinations of algorithms. Computer science is often concerned with the efficiency of these algorithms – either their speed, or the amount of additional memory they require to store intermediate results.

Activity 9 (self-assessment)

The answer to the previous activity described two ways of using the category-sorting algorithm to group addressed letters into piles based on their street within a town. The first involves applying the sorting algorithm twice – once to group into towns, and then again to group into streets within those towns. The second involves a more complex distinguishing characteristic to group the letters into streets within towns.

For each of these two versions of the sorting activity, how many times is each letter examined? Which approach is more efficient?

2.3 Following an algorithm

Algorithms can be quite complicated, involving a lot of steps and a lot of decision points. This can make them look difficult to understand. Well, some algorithms *are* difficult to understand. However, the good news is that it is not necessary to understand an algorithm in order to follow (execute) it.

To follow an algorithm requires only that you obey one instruction at a time, and know which is the next instruction to execute after the one you have just obeyed. In the text version of the category-sorting algorithm the instruction is one of the numbered sentences, and the 'next' instruction is either the next numbered sentence or the one mentioned at the end of the instruction. It would be possible to follow the algorithm by putting your finger on the first instruction and tracing the instructions, one at a time, following the instruction numbers in the text representations.

This is exactly how a computer system executes a computer program – one instruction at a time (although with fewer fingers involved!). The computer does not understand the algorithm encoded in the computer program; it simply executes the symbolic instruction and knows how to get to the next instruction.

You will find out in a later part how to develop simple algorithms that you can program using Sense.

2.4 Computers before the age of electronics

The algorithms I have considered so far have been about following recipes, making furniture and sorting playing cards – all very physical activities. However, algorithms have long been in use for carrying out numeric calculations and data processing. Accountancy is an example of a trade with a long history that depends on numeric and data-handling algorithms.

Figure 8 shows a worksheet for calculating the amount of wallpaper needed for a rectangular room. The boxes with labels A1, A2 and A3 are where values for the height, width and length of the room can be entered. Boxes A4 through to A8 are intermediate results for the calculations. Each calculation to be performed is shown alongside the box in which the result is to be placed. Notice that this worksheet is clearly for human use – it's got lots of descriptive text explaining what is happening.

Historically the term 'computer' was used to describe a person who computes; that is, someone who performs a numeric calculation by following instructions given to them in a worksheet (such as the one in Figure 8). Human computers were used to calculate the values that appear

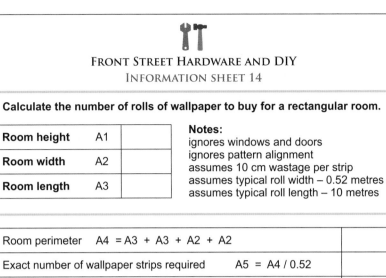

FRONT STREET HARDWARE AND DIY
INFORMATION SHEET 14

Calculate the number of rolls of wallpaper to buy for a rectangular room.

Room height	A1	
Room width	A2	
Room length	A3	

Notes:
ignores windows and doors
ignores pattern alignment
assumes 10 cm wastage per strip
assumes typical roll width – 0.52 metres
assumes typical roll length – 10 metres

Room perimeter A4 = A3 + A3 + A2 + A2	
Exact number of wallpaper strips required A5 = A4 / 0.52	
Actual number of strips required A6 = round A5 up to next whole number	
Number of strips per roll A7 = 10 / (A1 + 0.10)	
Exact number of rolls required A8 = A6 / A7	

Number of rolls to buy = round A8 up to next whole number	

Figure 8   Worksheet to calculate the number of rolls of wallpaper required to cover a rectangular room

in large mathematical tables – logarithms, trigonometric tables, ballistic trajectories for cannon shells, probabilities and so on – and were used to process large-scale calculations right through to the start of the modern computer age in the 1940s.

Activity 10 (exploratory)

It's your turn to be a computer! Using the worksheet in Figure 8, how many rolls of standard wallpaper do you need to buy in order to cover a room 2.4 metres high, 5 metres long and 2 metres wide? You may wish to use a calculator for this activity.

Comment

If you completed the worksheet accurately you should be buying 7 rolls of wallpaper. Figure 9 shows the completed worksheet.

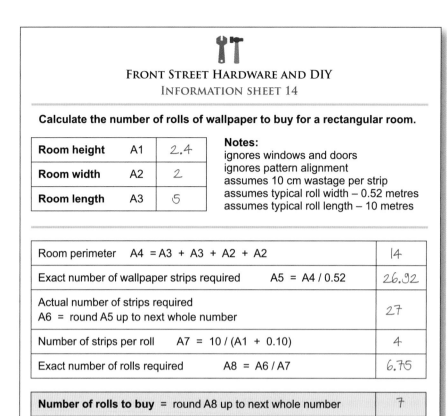

Figure 9   Completed worksheet

In the 1680s Isaac Newton and Gottfried Wilhelm Leibniz invented the *calculus* – a set of mathematical techniques that permitted scientists to analyse the motion of objects such as stars and planets. Calculus had a major drawback: the amount of time it takes a person to work through the required calculations is enormous. In 1757 a calculation to predict the date of the return of Halley's comet took three top astronomers four months. A critical scientific commentator of the day, Jean d'Alembert, described the calculations as 'more laborious than deep'.

In 1776 Adam Smith published his book *The Wealth of Nations*, which included the idea of the division of labour in the workplace. This idea led to the production-line process in manufacturing: workers specialising in small parts of a larger production task. A French civil engineer, Gaspard de Prony, applied this 'division of labour' principle to the task of preparing tables of mathematical functions.

De Prony employed two kinds of worker in his computational office. The first group of workers, few in number, were skilled mathematicians.

They converted the complicated calculations required for calculus (and other complex numeric tasks) into worksheets containing lots of simple calculations involving addition and subtraction. Completing a single calculus equation could require the completion of thousands of these worksheets.

The second group of workers, the 'computers', were ex-servants, wig makers, footmen and the like who had lost their jobs when the French Revolution made their roles obsolete. Computers were not trained in mathematics, but they could carry out simple addition and subtraction and follow instructions. Each computer would receive a number of worksheets which they would work through, being paid a small amount for each worksheet completed. In his book *When Computers Were Human*, Grier (2005, p. 36) refers to these computers as follows.

> They were little different from manual workers and could not discern whether they were computing trigonometric functions, logarithms, or the orbit of Halley's comet. One labor historian has described them as intellectual machines, "grasping and releasing a single piece of 'data' over and over again."

Today we would think of de Prony's trained mathematicians as programmers designing algorithms – and, of course, we would replace the human computers with digital electronic computers.

A de Prony-style worksheet for one of his computers involved in producing a book of pre-calculated wallpaper requirements for a range of room sizes might have looked something like Table 1.

Table 1 Extract from a worksheet

A1	A2	A3	A4	A5	A6	A7	A8	Result
			A2+A2+A3+A3	A4/0.52	Round A5	10/(A1+0.10)	A6/A7	Round A8
2.4	2.0	4.0						
2.4	2.0	4.1						
2.4	2.1	4.0						
2.4	2.1	4.1						

The 'division of labour' idea can be applied to a range of repetitive symbolic processing tasks, not just to numeric calculations. During the Second World War, the cryptographic analysis teams working at Bletchley Park in Buckinghamshire made use of human computers to apply symbol-processing algorithms to encrypted messages. One group would look to see if they could locate specific patterns of symbols in the data that showed a particular encryption method had been used; others would look for repeated patterns in all messages sent from the same location, or at the same time of day, to see if they could identify the encoded name of the sending station or how time information was being represented; still other teams performed simple frequency counts of the letters in the messages, and so on. Today all these repetitive tasks would be carried out by programmed electronic computers, but during the war they were performed by humans.

Human computers following simple algorithms were used right up until the end of the 1940s, allowing many large-scale calculation projects to be completed. They opened the way for the processing of large populations of data values, supplying the 'data processing' power required for early economists and social science statisticians to develop their field of study.

2.5 Conclusion

Humans have a long history of writing instructions – algorithms – to be followed by others. Algorithms need to be detailed, and are formed from complete lists of simple instructions showing the sequence in which they are to be performed. Algorithms typically include ways to represent the repetition of instructions ('do this series of instructions until some condition is true' or 'do this series of instructions a specific number of times') and conditional instructions ('if this is true then do this, otherwise do this') as well as simple sequences of instructions. Writing algorithms is complex, but well-written algorithms expressed in clear representations are easy to follow, provided that each of the simple instructions is within the capabilities of the person following the algorithm.

A computer spends its time carrying out sequences of symbolic instructions – algorithms – that manipulate symbolic data (binary representations of numbers, characters, etc.). Algorithms are essential for instructing (i.e. programming) a computer to solve a problem. To instruct a machine a programmer needs to have an understanding of what the machine can do, along with the symbolic notation that is used to represent the instructions and data within the machine. What the machine can do is determined by the instruction set designed into the computer processor chips (I will return to these later in this part). Writing an algorithm for a computer is more difficult than writing for humans because computers can't apply common sense to the interpretation of the instructions; they do exactly what they are told every time.

I will return in the next session to show how a computer follows symbolic instructions. To do this I first need to look 'inside the box', where I will examine how the computer is a symbolic message passing and processing device.

This session should have helped you with the following learning outcome.

* Demonstrate how simple tasks can be described by instructions written in the form of algorithms using text, and be able to follow an algorithm.

What's inside my computer, and what makes it work?

3

This session (including Figures 10–28 and Activities 11–20) is delivered online. It can be found in the resources page associated with this part on the TU100 website.

4

At the heart of a computer: CPU, memory and operating system

In Figure 11 at the start of Session 3, you saw an abstract representation of the important computing components 'inside the box'. In the second section of the 'Inside the box' video you saw how these were physically realised in a particular desktop PC.

In this session I am going to give a more detailed description of the core components – the central processing unit, main memory and buses. I will introduce internal control signals, memory addresses, instructions, data values and suchlike; however, remember what I really mean is that there is an electronic symbolic representation of data and instructions, coupled with electronic circuits that can respond appropriately – using the correct formats and protocols – when required.

In this session I will focus on the desktop computer system, but this is typical of a huge range of computing devices.

I will start by redrawing the key parts of Figure 11 to show in greater detail what is inside the central processing unit (CPU) and how the CPU connects, through the buses, to the other components in the system. This new representation is shown in Figure 29.

At the heart of a computer is the CPU, some main memory (of different types) and some wired connections (data, address and control buses) to allow electronic signals to pass between the CPU and memory and also to the outside world. In a desktop computer the CPU and memory are connected, via the buses, to various standard interfaces and through them to a range of input and output devices – typically a keyboard, monitor, disk drives and printers (collectively known as peripherals or peripheral devices). In embedded computer systems the CPU is connected via the data bus to control hardware (for example in a portable CD player or mobile phone). In supercomputer systems the CPU and memory may be connected to other computer systems to form *parallel processing* systems.

The terms 'processor', 'microprocessor' and 'CPU' are often used interchangeably. The term 'microprocessor' usually refers to the chip on which the processor is implemented.

The arrangement of the CPU, together with the way in which memory, internal communications and input/output are organised (the CPU architecture), has been established since the 1940s. This architecture was first described by the computer scientist John von Neumann, who was mentioned in Session 3. You may recall that characteristic of the von Neumann architecture is that program instructions can be stored in the same memory as the data – both are stored as binary symbols.

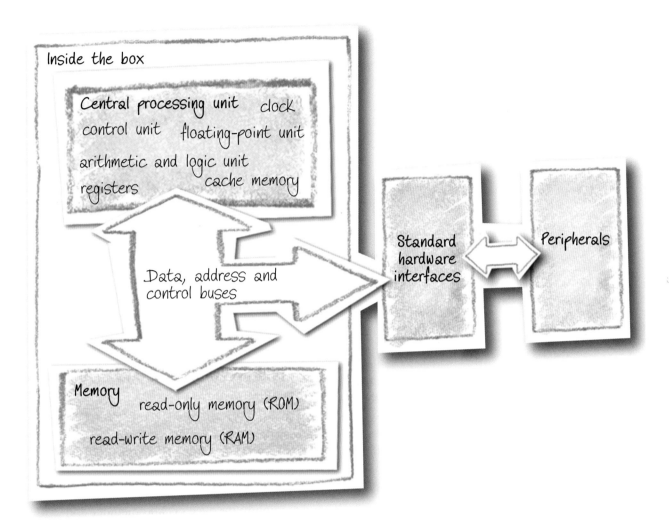

Figure 29   Another representation of the parts of a desktop computer system

4.1   The central processing unit

The CPU of a desktop computer is fabricated using a photographic etching process on a wafer of silicon that can contain several hundreds of millions of logic gates. CPUs come in 'families', such as Intel's Core, Celeron and AMD Athlon processors. Each family of processors has its own *instruction set*. The instruction set is the collection of basic instructions, called *machine-language instructions*, that a particular processor is designed to execute.

What follows is a brief description of the main components inside the CPU and their roles. In a later session I will show you how a simple machine-language program is executed by the CPU.

The terms *machine language* and *machine code* are synonymous, but I will be referring to machine language in this part.

Control unit

The *control unit* orchestrates the behaviour of the whole CPU; it activates the necessary connections between the memory, the registers, the *arithmetic and logic unit* and the *floating-point unit* as required by the execution of each instruction. The control unit manages the loading of instructions from the memory into the registers, determines the internal steps necessary to perform each instruction, loads any additional data values required, and sets up the lowest level of the hardware to execute the instruction.

Registers

Registers are fast, efficient areas of memory that are located inside the CPU. They are used as a holding area for instructions and data during the execution of a program. There are a number of different types of registers in different parts of the CPU, and each is designed to hold a particular type of information for a specific function. Some of the important registers are detailed below.

- **Accumulator**

  In the simplest model of a processor, all arithmetic operations are carried out on data stored in the *accumulator*. The accumulator is the register in the arithmetic and logic unit that is used to store intermediate values during a calculation. For example, to add two numbers together the first number would be loaded (fetched) from main memory and placed into the accumulator, the second number would then be loaded from main memory and added directly into the accumulator, and the result would remain in the accumulator until it was written to main memory. In most modern computers the CPU contains several general-purpose registers that can be used as accumulators.

- **Status register**

  The status register, sometimes called the flags register, holds information about the result of executing arithmetic or logical operations. Each bit in the register represents some description of the result of an operation – is the result zero, is the result negative, is the result too big to be stored in the accumulator, and so on. The values in the status register act as a report on the results of the recent activity in the CPU.

- **Program counter**

  The *program counter* is located in the control unit and holds the memory address of the next instruction to be executed. If a program proceeds in simple sequential steps then this register is incremented (increased by one) each time an instruction is carried out. This is because in a normal sequential program, the next instruction is located in memory immediately after the instruction just executed. However, the real power of the computer comes from the ability to place a value directly into the program counter and so choose the next instruction to

The program counter is sometimes known as the instruction pointer.

be executed. The instructions to place values directly into the program counter are usually referred to as *jump instructions*, which send the sequence of execution to a specific location, or *conditional jump instructions*, which send the sequence of execution to a location only if some condition is satisfied.

This ability to change the flow of execution of a program, by putting values directly into the program counter register, is what distinguishes a computer from a simple mechanical or electrical device.

Jumps and conditional jumps are sometimes called branches and conditional branches.

Activity 21 (self-assessment)

Consider a machine-language program that is to add one to a number in the accumulator until the accumulator contains the number 7 and then to write out the value in the accumulator. Figure 30 shows the steps in the operation of this program.

Address in memory	Meaning of instruction found there
1	Put the value 5 in the accumulator
2	Add 1 to the accumulator
3	If the value in the accumulator is 7, put 6 in the program counter
4	Put 2 in the program counter
5	Write out the value of the accumulator
6	Halt execution

Figure 30   A description of a machine-language program

(a) Describe the execution of the program by 'tracing' (following/ reporting) which instructions are executed, starting with the instruction at address 1. Complete the partially completed *trace table* shown in Figure 31 with the value of the accumulator and program counter after each instruction is executed. Assume that the halt instruction puts an undefined value in the program counter when it completes.

Address of instruction executed	Accumulator contains	Program counter contains
1	5	2
2	6	3

Figure 31   Partially completed trace table

(b) Do you think there might be an error in the above program? Can you correct it?

Activity 22 (self-assessment)

In the program above, can you identify any places where either a jump or a conditional jump instruction is part of the algorithm description?

Arithmetic and logic unit (ALU)

The arithmetic and logic unit contains the electronic circuits that perform the simple operations of binary arithmetic and logical operations. It typically also includes a range of other 'useful' circuits, such as those that compare a number with zero, test for equality between two numbers and so on.

Floating-point unit (FPU)

IEEE 754 is the most widely used standard for floating-point number representation and manipulation.

The floating-point unit is a common part of most modern CPUs. Its function is very similar to that of the ALU, but it operates on *floating-point number* representations (that is, real numbers such as 1.2 or 33322.12423534; numbers with decimal points in them, not integer numbers). In early CPUs, the CPU itself would execute algorithms to perform the basic floating-point arithmetic operations. In modern CPUs, the floating-point arithmetic operations are performed more efficiently by the specialised circuitry in the FPU. The FPU is almost a CPU in its own right, but one that is optimised for handling floating-point data and arithmetic.

Cache memory

The speed that data can be written to and read from the processor's registers is much faster than the speed of reading and writing to main memory. This could lead to a situation where the processor is forced to wait for data or instructions to be delivered from main memory. If there is a delay because of slow delivery from main memory, the processor will need to idle between instructions. To bridge this speed gap, systems use *cache memory* – memory that is faster than main memory, but slower than the registers (it is also intermediate in cost, since usually the faster the memory the more expensive the engineering required to make it). Cache memory is now routinely included on most processor microchips and is often quoted as part of the chip specification.

Cache memory is filled from main memory before the data or instructions are required by the processor. This requires some advance planning to put data that will be needed into the cache *before* it is actually required. When an instruction calls for data, the processor first checks to see if the data is in the cache. If so, the processor takes the data from the cache; if not, it fetches the data directly from main memory. The successful use of the cache to speed up execution depends on how well the cache management can predict future data use. Special instructions exist to move data efficiently between main memory and cache memory and to allow data to be 'bulk loaded' into the cache for efficient processing. Similarly, if a sequence of instructions is to be executed then pre-loading all these instructions into the cache before execution begins can improve the overall processing speed.

Activity 23 (self-assessment)

In what form are the data and instructions stored in a computer? What does the processor do?

4.2 Processor clock

Every computer has a *processor clock*, which sends out pulses at regular intervals. The purpose of this clock is to send a synchronising signal between the circuits within the CPU (and to subsystems connected to the CPU) to ensure that they remain in step. Think of a group of musicians controlled by a metronome's beat and you'll have the right idea. The number of pulses per second, or frequency, of the clock is measured in gigahertz (GHz), so a processor with a 2 GHz clock sends 2 billion pulses per second. (A 2 GHz CPU that can add 1 to a number at every clock pulse could count from 0 to 2 billion in just one second.) In modern computers, some instructions will be able to execute in a single *clock cycle* (the time between two clock pulses). Other, more complex instructions may require multiple cycles before they are complete. All other things being equal, a computer with a high clock frequency (sometimes called clock speed) can execute more instructions per second than one with a lower clock frequency.

Hardcore gamers try to squeeze extra performance from their computers by 'overclocking' – running the CPU clock faster than the manufacturer's specifications. One extremely likely side-effect of overclocking a CPU is to destroy it! An overclocked CPU generates more heat than the designer of the system intended. If this heat isn't removed, the chip overheats and parts of it will become hot enough to melt. There are websites that share experiences of how fast a family of chips can be overclocked and the most efficient cooling mechanisms needed to achieve long-term stable performance. There are also websites that show videos of people deliberately allowing their CPUs to overheat, and the subsequent damage this causes.

Activity 24 (self-assessment)

What is the purpose of a processor clock, and how does it differ from an everyday clock?

4.3   Control, address and data buses, and hardware interfaces

The wiring that connects the various components in the CPU to form a single unit is known as a *bus*. Modern CPU designs use a number of different buses, which connect circuitry inside the CPU and also extend outside the CPU to the other components in the system, such as memory and input/output ports.

At least three categories of bus are needed to ensure that the CPU can operate effectively:

* The *control bus* is used by the control unit to send and receive signals that coordinate the various parts of the CPU and peripherals.
* The *address bus* is used to carry the binary addresses of memory locations to be accessed.
* The *data bus* transfers binary data from place to place; the external data bus transmits data between the cache, registers and memory, while the internal data bus transmits data between the cache and different registers within the processor.

Computers also have a number of external ports (or hardware interfaces). These are connection points to the internal buses with additional control circuitry, which allow devices to exchange control signals and data with the processor. The most widely used interface sockets for peripherals conform to the USB standard, which allows peripherals (such as flash drives, printers, keyboards and mice) to be connected without the need to restart the computer.

Some technologies, such as audio and video processing, require large amounts of data to be transferred between the CPU, memory and peripherals. Specialised high-speed buses have been developed that connect performance-critical devices such as video devices and networking cards. Peripheral component interconnect (PCI) is one such technology. Devices attached to a PCI bus can transfer data to main memory without the CPU being directly involved. This permits very fast data transfers (30 MB per second) relative to CPU-controlled memory transfers (around 10 MB per second).

4.4 Multi-core processors

Some modern processors are *multi-core*. What this means is that the core components in the CPU are replicated multiple times on a single processor chip. 'Core' in this case is taken to mean the control unit, ALU, FPU, registers and cache.

A multi-core processor is capable of having each core perform different tasks – a form of parallel processing. However, the cores will still share access to the same external buses, main memory and external peripherals, so there will be some additional management needed to stop them interfering with each other.

Figure 32 shows the repetition of the cores in the Intel Nehalem processor. The cores are the areas in the upper middle part of the image, two on the left and two on the right of the centre line. The replicated grid-like area in the lower part of the image is the cache shared by the four cores, and the areas on the left, right and top edges of the image are circuits handling input, output and memory access management.

Most computer gaming platforms use multi-core processors. Games software is written to make very efficient use of the parallel execution this allows.

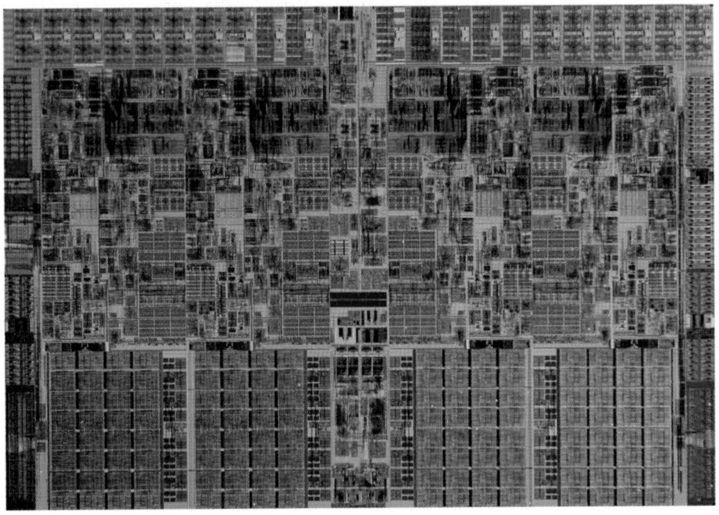

Figure 32   Intel Nehalem processor, a quad-core processor with four replicated cores

4.5 Memory

A computer has a number of different types of memory (or data storage). As a computer user you are probably most familiar with *main memory*, often referred to as RAM, and file-storage memory, such as that provided by a hard disk.

- Main memory is used to store the instructions of a program, and the data needed by the program, while it is running. Its contents are volatile, i.e. they are lost when the computer is switched off.

- File-storage memory is used to store large amounts of data for use at some later date. Unlike main memory, it is non-volatile or persistent – the data is not lost when the computer is turned off.

Some different types of memory are discussed in more detail below.

Main memory

Main memory can be thought of as ordered storage locations, each of which is big enough to hold a single binary value. The number of bits that can be stored in a single location in memory (i.e. the length of each binary value) is known as the word size of the computer.

Locations in main memory are sequentially numbered, so that each one has a unique *memory address* by which it can be directly accessed. That's why this type of memory is sometimes referred to as *random-access memory (RAM)*. For simplicity you can think of the storage locations as starting at address 0 and being represented by a long sequence of increasing addresses: 1, 2, 3, etc. If you want to see what is stored at address 32 you don't need to go to location 0, then location 1, then location 2 and so on until you reach location 32; you can go directly to location 32 and read its content. Accessing any location in RAM takes the same amount of time, regardless of its address.

Most forms of memory, such as disk storage, are random-access. However, the acronym RAM is usually reserved for main memory.

The size of the memory (the available number of storage locations) in a computer is measured in multiples of bytes. Modern computers can address incredibly large memories (in the terabytes range, one million million bytes), and in 2009 most desktop computers were sold with 2 gigabytes or more of main memory.

Activity 25 (self-assessment)

(a) List two characteristics of main memory.

(b) Is data stored on a CD-ROM persistent or volatile?

(c) How many bits are needed in a binary representation of a memory address capable of accessing 2 gigabytes (2 GB) of memory locations?

Read-only memory (ROM) and bootstrapping

You have just learned that RAM is volatile – when the power is turned off, the contents of the memory are lost. So how does the computer get the first instructions to execute immediately after it is turned on? There is another type of main memory inside the computer called *read-only memory (ROM)*. The data in ROM does not disappear when power is lost to the computer – it is non-volatile. ROM has fixed, permanent data built into the memory chips during manufacture.

An important function of ROM is to store a program, called a *boot program*, that is automatically executed when the computer is first switched on. This small program will typically do some hardware housekeeping, such as running a test of memory. It will then load larger programs such as the operating system into main memory. Using a short program to load a larger program is known as *bootstrapping*, which comes from the idea of someone 'pulling themselves up by their own bootstraps'.

ROM is the main type of memory in systems where there are no hard disk drives, such as a computer controlling a washing machine. In this case all the instructions for the control algorithm must be stored in ROM.

Secondary memory

Secondary memory is the term given to the storage devices such as hard disks that we can think of as external storage; that is, they are treated as peripherals with their own access protocols. These are non-volatile and typically many times slower than main memory. They are used to store program code and data files that are not immediately needed by the computer system, so they are sometimes referred to as *file-storage memory*. Secondary memory devices usually make up the bulk of the memory in desktop and mainframe computers, but may be completely absent in embedded computer systems.

Balancing performance and cost

You have seen that different kinds of memory have different characteristics, one of which is the speed of access to data. In general it costs more to build high-speed memory than it does to build low-speed devices, as shown in Figure 33.

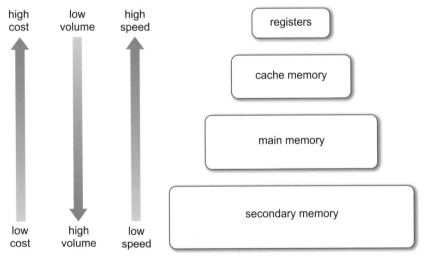

Figure 33   Hierarchies of memory

The fastest memory access takes place when accessing registers, but register memory is very expensive and built directly into the processor microchip. There is usually a fixed number of registers, typically less than 50, and it is not possible to add to them. At the other end of the scale, the slowest access is to external storage devices – roughly 10 000 times slower than for the registers – but the secondary memory these provide is much cheaper and expansion is usually possible by adding more disk drives.

Computer systems designed for intensive data-processing tasks – such as video processing, gaming and scientific numerical calculation – usually have large amounts of cache and main memory.

4.6 Operating system

I have briefly examined the important hardware components of a computer: the processor, the memory and their interconnecting buses. Managing these resources and coordinating all the computer's components is the job of a collection of programs known as the *operating system (OS)*.

In early computers, before the advent of operating systems, all the direct interaction between devices, users and executing programs was coded into each program. This made programs difficult to write, requiring specialist knowledge of the protocols for every peripheral the program would need to access. Programmers also needed specific knowledge of the components of the processor on which the program would execute. An operating system hides this complexity.

The operating system's component programs are each responsible for a specific part of the computer: memory management, device drivers, file storage, etc. They support application programs by offering standard services to those programs and accessing the hardware on their behalf. This enables the user to carry out a variety of complex tasks on the computer, without needing to know all the details of what goes on 'inside the box'. The interface that the programmer (and user) sees is a standard interface for the operating system; it isn't dependent on the type of processor or the specifics of the devices connected to the computer. This makes it possible to talk generally about, say, using a Windows computer or programming for the Windows operating system. It also allows a programmer to use standard instructions when writing to a printer, or saving a file to a disk, so that they don't need to know the specifics of how the hardware performs these tasks.

Some of the functions the operating system performs include:

You will meet user interfaces in a later part.

- *Provision of a user interface.* This enables us to communicate with our computers. It provides us with a means of inputting data and instructions, and displaying output in a form that we can understand.

- *Management of multiple programs.* When using a computer there is usually a lot of activity taking place at the same time – for instance, I'm currently editing this document, listening to a CD, downloading updates to my virus checker and watching for an email message. All of this is happening on a desktop computer with a single CPU. The operating system supports hardware designed to enable the processor to switch between different executing programs in order to multitask.

- *Management of memory.* During the processing of a program, data and instructions are stored in the computer's main memory. It is the job of the operating system to allocate appropriately sized areas of memory to each executing program, and to ensure that program instructions and data do not interfere with each other or with the data and instructions of other programs.

- *Coordination and control of peripheral devices.* In order to carry out its tasks, a computer will need to communicate with one or more peripheral devices. For example, it may wish to receive data from the keyboard or mouse, read from a file on a disk, send output to the monitor or printer, connect to a network and so on. The specific protocol required for each device will be encoded in a device driver. The operating system selects the appropriate drivers for the physical devices connected to the computer system. It also coordinates all these operations, ensuring that data is moved safely and efficiently between the components of the system.

- *Inclusion of other applications.* Additionally, it is becoming common for some application programs that were originally outside the operating system (such as web browsers) to be offered as standard parts of modern operating systems.

4.7 Conclusion

In this session I considered the core components of the modern computer – the CPU, the memory and the data, address and control buses. I briefly identified and explained the role of each component, and gave an overview of how these components relate to one another. You also saw how the ability to directly alter the value in the CPU's program counter allows a program's execution sequence to be controlled by values inside the program.

Finally you learned that the operating system, a collection of computer programs, helps to hide the complexity of the computer system from users and programmers. It does this by presenting them with a standard way of interacting with the system that avoids the need to be aware of the detailed interior of the computer system or CPU.

This session should have helped you with the following learning outcomes.

- Describe the purpose of each of the major components of a computer system, and use common terminology to describe these components.

- Describe the internal features of a simple central processing unit (CPU).

- Show, in outline form, how a computer program is executed on a computer with the von Neumann architecture, and explain the importance of the program counter in controlling the flow of the program.

5 Programming

Early computer programmers wrote instructions in a form that could be directly understood by their computer's family of processors, i.e. in some dialect of machine language. These instructions consisted of binary patterns that were entered directly into the hardware of the machine using plug boards or panel switches. Figure 34 shows an example of how this was done (this was, of course, in the days before von Neumann architecture).

Figure 34   ENIAC, the first general-purpose computer: the two women are wiring one side of the computer with a new program

An algorithm would be designed on paper and then hand-coded into binary representations of the machine instructions. The binary code was entered directly into memory, one instruction, address or data item at a time.

In Part 2 of Block 1 you saw binary to decimal and decimal to binary conversion.

For example, in the machine language of one processor family, the instruction to move data from the accumulator into memory address 53281 is:

    10001101   11010000   00100001

The first byte (the operator, 10001101) of the instruction is interpreted as 'store the contents of the accumulator in memory'; the second and third bytes (the *operand*), 11010000 00100001, represent the address of the memory location (53281) into which the value in the accumulator will be stored. As you can imagine, setting switches in this way for a full program is both tedious and error-prone.

Today we can use a wider range of *programming languages* that hide the complexity of the underlying machine instructions and simplify the task for the programmer. Modern languages use text representations of algorithms that are relatively easy to use, and some use graphical representations; a good example of such a programming environment is the Sense programming language used for TU100. However, what the processor executes is still binary representations of machine-language instructions.

In this session I will give an overview of how the high-level, modern programming languages of today relate to the underlying, low-level, machine-language instructions that are executed by the CPU.

5.1   Low-level languages

Any programming language in which a single instruction written by the programmer is translated into a single instruction in the machine language of the processor is known as a *low-level programming language*.

Machine language

The 'lowest' of the low-level languages is machine language, as this represents the native language of the processor that will execute the program instructions. The programmer is literally writing in the symbolic language that the processor executes, with nothing between them and the underlying machine. A programmer working in machine language can exploit the full capabilities of the processor – this can be important in some application development areas, such as programming interactive games or other time-critical applications.

Activity 26 (self-assessment)

Write down the distinguishing characteristic of a low-level language.

There are many disadvantages to reading and writing programs in machine language:

* Machine-language programs are difficult for humans to read and write. In particular, it is hard to memorise instruction codes that consist of binary sequences such as 10001101. It is also hard to understand machine-language programs without a great deal of annotation. Consequently they can be difficult to modify.

* Memory references are given as actual location addresses. So the programmer needs to maintain a 'memory map' in order to keep track of what values have been stored where in memory.

* One instruction on the CPU requires one instruction in the machine language, so written programs are very long.

- Each family of processors understands only its own machine language. A processor cannot correctly execute a program that has been written for another family of processors.

For these reasons, modern programs are rarely written directly in machine language. However, since machine languages are the native languages of the processors, all programs – regardless of what language they were originally written in – must be translated into a machine language before they can be executed.

Executing a low-level program: the fetch–decode–execute cycle

In Session 4 you saw that the instructions in a computer program are processed by the CPU, that data and instructions are stored in main memory but moved to registers in the CPU as required, and that operations such as addition and logical comparisons are carried out by the ALU.

Activity 27 (self-assessment)

(a) Which component of the CPU coordinates the movement of instructions and data?

(b) What does the acronym ALU stand for? What does it do?

(c) How is the sequence of execution of a program's instructions controlled inside the CPU?

In Session 3 you saw that executing an instruction really means recognising the bit pattern that represents that instruction and activating the right circuit to perform it. Performing the instruction usually involves two steps: the first step moves the necessary data (the instruction's operands) into the appropriate registers, while in the second step the instruction is executed.

The process of locating, transferring and carrying out a single instruction during execution of a program is referred to as the *fetch–decode–execute cycle* (or sometimes simply the *fetch–execute cycle*). The name indicates that for an instruction to be evaluated, it first needs to be fetched into the instruction register; then it needs to be recognised or decoded, and only then can it be executed.

During each cycle, the CPU uses the value stored in the program counter to load the next instruction's operator from memory into the instruction register. The specific instruction is then decoded. This identifies what type of instruction it is and what type of additional values it processes (numbers, memory addresses, register names, etc.). If the instruction requires additional values, say from the content of a named memory address, then those values are fetched into the appropriate registers for that instruction. The instruction then executes. Executing the instruction causes any registers, such as the status register, to be updated. At the end of the cycle the program counter is updated, before the cycle starts all over again. The control unit oversees this cycle and the processor clock ensures that the various circuits in the components involved remain synchronised.

I can summarise the steps carried out by the CPU when executing a computer program as follows.

*   Step 1: **fetch** the next instruction into the instruction registers.
*   Step 2: **decode** the instruction, identify and fetch any additional values it requires and place them in the appropriate registers.
*   Step 3: **execute** the instruction.
*   Step 4: update the program counter.
*   Step 5: go back to Step 1.

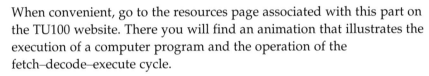

Activity 28 (exploratory)

When convenient, go to the resources page associated with this part on the TU100 website. There you will find an animation that illustrates the execution of a computer program and the operation of the fetch–decode–execute cycle.

Note that there is a second animation associated with this session, which you will be directed to in the next activity, so you may wish to keep the website open or wait until Activity 29 to watch both animations.

Assembly language

An *assembly language* is a low-level language that uses human-readable symbolic instructions and addresses that translate into machine-language instructions on a one-to-one basis. A low-level assembly-language program has the ability to access directly all the features and instructions available on the processor it is designed for.

Whenever a program is written in a language other than machine language, the instructions in the original program (called the source code) need to be converted into equivalent machine-language instructions. This task is carried out by special programs called *translators*. When the source language is an assembly language, the program that does this translation is called an *assembler*. An assembler takes an assembly-language program and generates an equivalent program in machine language. This machine-language program can then be loaded into memory and executed. Since each processor family has a different machine language and therefore a different assembly language, they each require a different assembler.

'Branch' is another word for 'jump'.

Assembly-language programs have a number of advantages over machine-language programs:

- Instructions are more memorable because they have *mnemonic* names (names such as STA for **st**ore **a**ccumulator, JMP for **j**u**mp**, BNE for **b**ranch if **n**ot **e**qual to zero).

- Assembly languages use symbolic names for memory location addresses. The assembler relates the names to real memory addresses, thus avoiding the need for the programmer to deal directly with memory addressing issues.

- Programmers can provide data in forms other than binary – ordinary decimal numbers or characters, for example. The assembler translates them into binary values.

- The programmer can include comments to help someone who tries to read their code. Comments are ignored by the assembler.

- Assemblers can carry out simple error checking before the program is executed, warning the programmer about the presence of some kinds of error.

The 6502 processor was one of the earliest processors used in a home/office computer. It could be found in, among others, the Commodore PET and the BBC Micro.

Figure 35 shows an example of a small program written using the 6502 assembly language. The textual description on the right of the thick line is not part of the code. I've simplified the code slightly to make it more easily readable and the program doesn't test to see if the result is too big for the available data representation – but you should be able to grasp the idea of the assembly-language representation of the instructions and data. Any line starting with a semicolon (;) is not part of the assembly-language program, but is a comment and will be ignored by the assembler.

You can treat this program very much like the algorithm in Section 2.2. Execution of the 6502 assembly-language code starts with the instruction in the memory location called start and follows through the code one instruction at time until eventually reaching the RTS instruction.

When the assembler program converts the program shown in this animation into machine language, it needs to know the actual address of the memory location that the first instruction is to be loaded into; from that it can work out the address of each memory location referenced in the code. References to :n, :m, :result, start and startsum would be replaced with actual memory addresses (using two bytes for each address). In addition the decimal values #3, #9 and #0 would be replaced with their binary representations (each using two bytes), each instruction mnemonic (name) would be replaced with its binary representation (each using a single byte), and the comment line would be ignored. This conversion would produce 19 bytes of machine-language code that would be copied into memory locations starting from the first instruction's actual address.

Memory location	Instruction		Description (not part of the code)
Symbolic name	Operator (instruction)	Operand (data)	
start	JMP	startsum	Go to (JuMP to) the instruction labelled startsum
n	#3		The memory location called n has the value 3 (decimal) placed in it at the beginning
m	#9		The memory location called m has the value 9 (decimal) in it at the beginning
result	#0		The memory location called result has the value 0 (decimal) in it at the beginning
; add together the values in the memory locations with the names n and m and put the total in the memory location called result. The values in n and m are preserved unchanged – there is no check for overflow.			A human-readable comment, not part of the program, here to help someone reading the program understand what it does
startsum	LDA	:n	LoaD the Accumulator with the value currently in the memory location called n
	ADC	:m	ADD to the accumulator (with Carry bit) the value currently in the memory location called m
	STA	:result	STore the value currently in the Accumulator in the memory location called result
	RTS		End routine

Figure 35   A small program using the 6502 assembly language

Activity 29 (exploratory)

When convenient, go to the resources page associated with this part on the TU100 website. There you will find an animation that illustrates the execution of the code shown in Figure 35.

Assembly languages have many of the disadvantages of machine languages:

- An assembly-language program can execute on only one family of processors.
- Although easier to read than machine language, assembly language is still difficult to understand and so is difficult to modify or update.
- Programs written in assembly language tend to be very long.

Activity 30 (self-assessment)

Explain in your own words what the author is saying in the following quotation from Tennent (1981):

> A programming language is a system of notation for describing computations. A useful programming language must therefore be suited for both description (i.e. for human writers and readers of programs) and for computation (i.e. for efficient implementation on computers). But human beings and computers are so different that it is difficult to find notational devices that are well suited to the capabilities of both.

5.2 Using computer programs to translate computer programs

Modern programming harnesses the power of the computer and its ability to execute complex programs to allow programmers to avoid low-level programming. Remember the von Neumann architecture in which both program instructions and data are held in the same areas of memory. This permits the symbolic instructions of a program to be treated as data by another program. In other words, we can use a computer program to process a symbolic representation of the statements in another computer program and generate the appropriate machine-language instructions.

The assembler program that converts assembly-language instructions into machine-language instructions is a simple example of such a program. The assembler program processes symbolic instructions in a form that a human can read, translates them into machine language and outputs this symbolic code. The code that is output by the assembler – the data the assembler produces – is a machine-language program that can be executed by a CPU.

5.3 High-level languages

It would be exceptionally tedious (not to mention error-prone) to have to deal with computer programs by writing in low-level languages and writing code specifically for each family of processors. Modern programming is not usually done this way. We use *high-level programming languages* in which each instruction in the high-level language is translated into many instructions in the machine language of the processor on which it is to execute. High-level programming languages include JavaScript, Java, C++, Smalltalk, Sense and a whole range of application-specific languages that attempt to make the process of writing programs easier for the humans involved.

Activity 31 (self-assessment)

Write down the way in which high-level programming languages differ from low-level programming languages.

When we write programs in a high-level language, we need the same kind of translation process that the assembler provides for assembly programs. There are two different mechanisms by which a program written in a high-level language is translated into machine language: compilation and interpretation.

Compilation

In compilation the program written in the high-level language, called the *source code* or *source program*, is used as the input to a translator program called a *compiler*. The compiler translates the entire source program into the machine language understood by the processor; this translation is referred to as the *object code* or *object program*. We say that the source code is *compiled* into the object code. The object code is then saved, and it is this machine-language program that is loaded into memory and executed when the program is executed. It's a bit like someone translating an essay into a foreign language – they do the whole essay and then save the result for later use. Languages such as C, C++, Visual Basic.Net and Java are designed to be compiled.

Compilers can be written that translate a common high-level language but that output object code for a specific family of processors. For a particular programming language, several different compilers will be available to take into account the fact that different families of processors have different versions of machine language, and that different operating systems interact with the processors in different ways. This allows the programmer to write a program in a high-level language and use a different version of a compiler to produce object code specific to a processor and operating system. For example, you can buy a C++ compiler that has been written for a PC executing Windows on an Intel processor, or a C++ compiler for a computer executing Linux on an Amdahl processor.

When you buy computer software, you are usually buying the right to run the object code that has already been compiled from the source code.

Compilers have the disadvantage that every change to the source code requires the code to be recompiled in order to generate a new machine-language representation. For this reason, detecting and fixing errors and updating software with new features can be a time-consuming activity.

Interpretation

An *interpreter* is also a program that translates a single high-level language instruction into several low-level machine instructions. However, while the compiler translates all the source code in one go, an interpreter translates each instruction in the source code only when it is required for that instruction to be executed. There is never a complete translation of the whole of the source code into machine language, and so no object code program is generated. (Think of a sign-language interpreter who does a live translation during a speech – if the speech is given again, the interpreter has to do the interpretation all over again as well.)

The advantage of an interpreted language is that the potentially lengthy process of compilation does not need to be gone through for each small change in the source code. Interpreted languages lend themselves to situations in which small incremental changes to a program are being made and need to be tested as quickly as possible. The main disadvantage is that the translation process must take place every time a program is executed, resulting in a slower execution of the program. Languages such as JavaScript, Perl and Basic are designed to be interpreted.

Activity 32 (self-assessment)

Briefly explain the similarities and differences between an assembler, a compiler and an interpreter.

There have been several thousand high-level languages developed for programmers, emphasising different ways of thinking about how to express algorithms and different approaches to representing and processing data. Different people find different styles of programming language easier to read and write. Some languages are designed to be more 'mathematical' in the way they represent their instructions, while others are more 'business' oriented. In addition, some languages are optimised for specific purposes – for example, engineers require provably correct programs, while games programs require speed and the ability to manipulate complex sounds and images.

5.4   Conclusion

Almost all modern programmers write in high-level languages because these languages are easier to use. They hide the complexity of the underlying computer system and the underlying machine language. The programmer can better concentrate on expressing the steps of the algorithm without having to be concerned with the low-level detail of the processor on which it will execute.

However, programmers writing code for time-critical applications may use low-level languages in order to make use of the full power of the processor available to them.

Whatever language a programmer chooses, what is ultimately executed on the CPU is machine-language instructions for that particular processor family. These machine-language instructions are executed by transistor-based logic gates in the CPU.

This session should have helped you with the following learning outcomes.

- Explain what a computer program is, and how low-level and high-level programming languages relate to the internal operations of the CPU.

- Show, in outline form, how a computer program is executed on a computer with the von Neumann architecture, and explain the importance of the program counter in controlling the flow of the program.

Summary

In this part of TU100 you've looked inwards, from the collection of peripherals making up a computer system and the symbolic communication between them, down into the CPU and at the transistors that form the computational heart of the computer. I have looked at specific examples of a desktop PC and given examples of processors such as the 6502, and talked briefly about specific operating systems, communications protocols and data standards – but it has not been my intention to focus on these specific components of specific computer systems. Rather, the aim was to treat the computer as a symbolic processor, capable of following symbolic instructions to process symbolic representations of algorithms and data.

As you study the rest of TU100 you will hear about some strange computing devices, and some complex computer applications processing complex collections of data. All of these devices can be modelled using the processor, memory and communication model presented in the videos, and at their heart they will be built around a transistor-based CPU. Furthermore, all of the computer application code will consist of algorithms in some appropriate symbolic representation that are translated into low-level processor instructions that execute one after another on a CPU. And all that complex data must ultimately have some representation as binary data if it is to be processed by a modern computer device.

If you didn't get a chance to look at the animations associated with Session 5 earlier then please do so as soon as you can. You should also ensure that you have investigated the other resources related to Block 2 Part 1 that are provided on the TU100 website. Otherwise, you're ready to start Part 2, which directly follows this part in the book.

Answers to self-assessment activities

Activity 3

(a) The word 'Keith' itself might be misheard in a noisy room, but the phonetic alphabet is unlikely to be misheard since it was designed for this purpose. Clearly any non-verbal form of the message would not be useful for a telephone conversation, and using an audible version of Morse code is likely to be error-prone for casual users. So I would spell out the name using the phonetic alphabet.

(b) The standard written form would be best for this.

Notice that if I wanted to keep the name secret I could use a ROT-13 cipher at the same time as using any of the other conventions.

Activity 8

(a) In step 2 the text 'the suit of the card' is the description of the distinguishing characteristic. The suit distinguishes which category the card belongs to.

(b) The algorithm finishes when there are no cards left in the pile in your hand. This is described in step 5, which states that 'you are finished' once there are no cards left. Note, however, that the decision that determines whether you have finished is actually located at step 4 – if you have cards left then you haven't finished.

(c) The algorithm would in fact work for any number of playing cards. The stated pre-conditions just require that you have 'some cards' at the start, and the algorithm itself doesn't depend on the number of cards you start with. The stated post-condition is restricted to apply to the case where there are 52 playing cards (four suits of 13 cards per suit). So you would need a different post-condition if you started with a different number of cards – for example, the post-condition could be that there are no cards unsorted, and each pile of cards contains cards from a single suit, and no two piles are of the same suit.

(d) One way would be to apply the algorithm repeatedly: apply it once to sort the letters so that there is a pile for each town, and then apply it again to each town's pile to make a new pile for each street. An alternative approach would be to apply the algorithm once, making a pile for each street in each town. The end result would be the same in both cases.

Activity 9

In the first approach each letter is examined once to sort it according to town, and then again to sort it according to street – so twice for each letter.

In the second approach each letter is examined only once.

If it takes the same amount of time to check the distinguishing characteristic in each of the algorithms then the second approach will take only half as long as the first approach. This means the second approach would be more efficient.

Activity 21

(a) The answer to this question is shown in Figure 36. I have also provided an animation that shows the steps involved in completing this table, which you can find in the resources page associated with this part on the TU100 website.

(b) There is probably an error. The instruction to write out the value of the accumulator (at memory address 5) is never executed, because the instruction at memory address 3 sends the program execution to the halt instruction at address 6. To correct the error, change the value placed in the program counter in the instruction at memory address 3 to 5, not 6.

Address of instruction executed	Accumulator contains	Program counter contains
1	5	2
2	6	3
3	6	4
4	6	2
2	7	3
3	7	6
6	7	undefined

Figure 36   Completed trace table for Activity 19

Activity 22

A jump (or conditional jump) is where the program counter is loaded with a memory address that is not the next in sequence. A jump instruction appears at address 4, where the program counter is always set to 2 causing the program execution to jump back to the instruction at address 2. A conditional jump instruction appears at address 3, where the value 6 is placed in the program counter only if the accumulator has the value 7 in it.

Activity 23

All data and instructions are stored as binary symbols within the computer.

The computer processor manipulates binary representations of data, using instructions that are themselves stored in binary format.

Activity 24

A processor clock keeps the flow of data, instructions and control signals synchronised. It does not tell the time; rather it sends out a pulse at regular, precise intervals. (Most personal computer systems also have a real-time clock, which keeps track of the time of day.)

Activity 25

(a) It is randomly accessible (or addressable). It is also volatile.

(b) It is persistent; it remains on the CD-ROM when the computer is turned off.

(c) You need 31 bits in a memory address to access 2 GB: 1 GB of memory (2^{30} bytes) requires 30 bits in the memory address, so 2 GB (which is 2×2^{30} bytes) requires 31 bits in the memory address.

Activity 26

The distinguishing characteristic is that a single low-level language instruction represents a single machine-language instruction. The programmer must instruct the machine directly in the language the processor can interpret.

Activity 27

(a) The control unit produces control signals that coordinate the flow of data and instructions.

(b) ALU stands for arithmetic and logic unit. It is the place where all arithmetic and logic operations are carried out.

(c) The program counter contains the address of the next instruction to be executed and so determines the sequence of execution of instructions. A program itself can update the program counter to cause the instruction sequence to change.

Activity 30

In a nutshell, the author is saying that a programming language must be readable by humans and computers, but that the needs of these two groups are so diverse that it is difficult to conceive of a language that could be effectively used by both.

Activity 31

A low-level programming language has instructions that each represent a single instruction in the machine language of the underlying hardware. In a high-level programming language, each instruction represents many instructions in the machine language of the underlying machine.

Activity 32

An assembler, a compiler and an interpreter are all pieces of software that translate source code into machine language. The main differences between them are as follows.

- An assembler is used to translate assembly language into machine language. In contrast, a compiler and an interpreter are both used to translate programs in high-level programming languages into machine language.

- A compiler and an assembler each translate the whole source program and create and save a whole new machine-language version, which can then be executed. In contrast, an interpreter translates each instruction only when that instruction is to be executed.

Glossary

accumulator   A register within a CPU that is used to store and manipulate data.

address bus   An electrical pathway that carries a symbolic representation of a memory address between the memory and the processor.

algorithm   A detailed list of instructions for solving a problem.

arithmetic and logic unit (ALU)   The part of a CPU that contains the circuits where the basic operations of arithmetic and logic manipulations are performed.

assembler   A program that translates assembly-language instructions into machine language. Sometimes used to refer to the assembly language rather than the program, as in 'assembler code'.

assembly language   A low-level computer language consisting of symbolic instructions and addresses that translate directly, symbol for symbol, into machine language.

Boolean algebra   A mathematical representation that is used to manipulate TRUE and FALSE values according to the operators AND, OR and NOT. It allows logic expressions to be manipulated in a similar way to arithmetic expressions.

bootstrapping   Using an initialisation program first to configure a computer immediately after it is switched on, and then to load a larger program (usually an operating system).

cache memory   High-speed memory that acts as a buffer between high-speed and low-speed parts of a computer system. For example, CPU cache memory enables the fast CPU to access data faster than it can access the slower main memory.

calculus   The branch of mathematics that deals with limits, functions, derivatives and infinite series. Calculus is typified by a form of repetitive calculation, and methods of handling approximations for calculations that are too complex to perform directly.

clock cycle   The interval between regular electrical pulses that synchronises events within a computer. The CPU clock cycle determines the speed at which instructions are executed.

compiler   A computer program that takes as input one or more files containing the text of another computer program, checks the text for errors, then translates it into another programming language before the program is executed. Usually a compiler translates a high-level language into a low-level language.

computation A term that is used generally as a synonym for information processing and can be applied to human or machine processing of data. More specifically, computation is the application of a well-defined process specified by an algorithm or protocol.

control bus An electrical pathway that carries symbolic data representing control instructions and control signals between parts of a computer system.

control unit The part of a CPU that is responsible for the overall control of the CPU and connected parts of the computer system.

data bus An electrical pathway that carries symbolic representations of data between parts of a computer system, usually between the CPU, memory and input/output ports.

device driver A program that controls hardware. Typically, a device driver contains code to implement the protocols and standards for specific hardware. These allow high-level programs to control the hardware by using the functionality offered by the device driver.

electrical A term that refers to the flow of electrons through metal conductors, such as copper wires.

electronic A term that relates to the branch of science concerned with the behaviour of the electron. It refers to the flow of electrons through non-metal conductors, also known as semiconductors. A transistor is an electronic device.

fetch–decode–execute cycle The algorithm followed by a CPU in order to process an instruction. It is central to the operation of all computers: first get the next instruction, then decide what type of instruction it is and thus what data it needs to have available, then execute the instruction.

floating-point number A representation that can be thought of as a number containing a decimal point, such as 3.3, 2.111 191 919, 0.000 0001, etc.

floating-point unit (FPU) The part of a CPU that performs arithmetic and logic operations on floating-point numbers.

format A predetermined arrangement of symbols or data, usually for a specific purpose or community of users. Computer files and communication messages have formats so that their content can be interpreted and processed. Useful formats are commonly standardised, although some companies treat their formats as proprietary information.

hardware The physical components of a computer system. These include the large components such as the screen, the small component parts such as circuit boards, and all the connecting cables.

hardware interface A physical connection, possibly implementing a protocol for symbolic exchange, between two or more components of a computer system.

high-level programming language A programming language in which the programmer writes statements that are translated into a complex series of machine-language instructions. The statements are usually thought of as being closer to a human language, or the language of the problem being solved, than to the language of the machine.

information Data that has been interpreted and placed in context so that it carries meaning.

instruction set The set of instructions that a family of central processing units can execute.

interpreter A computer program that takes as input one or more files containing the text of another computer program (known as the source code), then translates the program statements into another programming language only when required during the execution of the program.

low-level programming language A programming language that uses symbolic representations of instructions, data and addresses that are close to the machine language of the processor on which it will execute.

machine language A very low-level, symbolic representation of instructions at the level of the instruction set of a CPU, usually using a binary numeric representation. Also known as *machine code*.

main memory The internal memory of a computer system – temporary storage areas for programs and data. Usually takes the form of semiconductor memory chips commonly known as **random-access memory (RAM)**.

memory address The numeric value that signifies a specific location in memory at which data can be stored and retrieved.

mnemonic An easily remembered alternative to a complex phrase or list (e.g. the initial letters of 'Richard Of York Gave Battle In Vain' as a reminder of the colours of the rainbow in order). In assembly language, a mnemonic is an easily remembered name that stands for the binary value of an instruction (e.g. ADD, SUB, MUL, MOV for add, subtract, multiply, move).

object code Output from a compiler, usually in machine language, that is ultimately executed by a CPU. Also known as an *object program*.

operand A value to which an operation is applied (e.g. in 3 + 2, + is the operator and 3 and 2 are the operands).

operating system (OS)   A collection of programs that manages a computer's resources, provides an interface between the user and the computer, and organises the running of other programs. Examples include Windows, Mac OS and Linux.

parallel processing   The use of more than one CPU (or more than one CPU core in multi-core processors) to simultaneously execute parts of a computer program. It is usually more difficult to write a computer program to take advantage of parallel processing, as it is necessary to protect the execution of the parallel parts from interfering with each other.

post-condition   The conditions that are true after an algorithm has finished execution that indicate the algorithm performed correctly.

pre-condition   The conditions that should hold before an algorithm is executed to ensure that the algorithm will be able to operate correctly.

processor clock   A circuit inside a CPU that produces regular electrical pulses that are used to synchronise bus and control-unit activities within the computer system.

program counter   A register in a CPU in which the memory address of the next instruction to be executed is placed. Changing the value in the program counter allows the flow of execution of a program to be altered by the program itself; this allows conditional jumping (branching) during the program's execution.

programming language   An artificial language in which precise instructions can be stated and that can be processed by a computer system – either directly in the case of low-level programming languages, or after translation by a computer program (compiler or interpreter) for high-level programming languages.

protocol   A set of rules and formats that specify how to exchange messages between communicating systems.

random-access memory (RAM)   Memory that holds data only while it receives power; when power is removed the content of the memory is lost. The term 'random-access' signifies that direct access to any location in memory is possible, as opposed to serially addressable memory – that is, it takes the same amount of time to access data held in any location in memory.

read-only memory (ROM)   Memory that permanently holds data even when it is not receiving power (persistent memory). The data contained in ROM cannot be updated or deleted; it is only readable. Like RAM, ROM is also directly accessible.

register A small amount of very fast memory within a CPU, used for a special purpose or as storage during instruction execution. Traditionally the registers found in many CPUs include the accumulator and program counter, but modern CPU designs incorporate a collection of general-purpose registers that remove the need for such specialised registers.

secondary memory The part of a computer system in which programs and data are stored when not being executed/processed. Traditionally hard disk drives would have taken this role, but they are now frequently being replaced by network storage devices and other storage devices such as memory sticks.

sign Something perceived that suggests the existence of some fact or quality or condition; an action or gesture conveying information; an instruction or command. Compare to **symbol**.

software The programs that control the functioning of a computer system.

software interface Program code that connects two or more parts of a computer system. A software interface may convert formats and implement communications protocols to allow the connection of two or more pieces of hardware or software.

source code Text representing a program that is usually input into a compiler or interpreter. Source code is usually written in a high-level language, but can be written in low-level and assembler languages. Also known as a *source program*.

symbol A distinguishable notation or figure conventionally or arbitrarily accepted as representing some quantity, process, instruction, value, relationship or operation. Compare to **sign**.

trace table A table in which a programmer can note the effects of each instruction as a program is executing, so as to understand changes to the data.

translator A computer program that converts a program from one representation into another – for example, from a high-level to a low-level programming language.

universal serial bus (USB) A standard for connecting computers and peripherals, allowing them to communicate.

References

Grier, D.A. (2005) *When Computers Were Human*, Princeton, NJ, Princeton University Press.

Tennent, R.D. (1981) *Principles of Programming Languages*, Upper Saddle River, NJ, Prentice Hall.

Acknowledgements

Grateful acknowledgement is made to the following sources.

Figures

Figure 4: Based on an image taken from http://visite.artsetmetiers.free.fr

Figure 6(a) and (b): Taken from Google Inc.

Figure 7: © IKEA

Figure 32: © Intel Corporation (UK) Ltd

Figure 34: © "U.S. Army Photo" Archives of the ARL Technical Library

Part 2

The vanishing computer

Authors: Mike Richards and Nick Dalton

Introduction

So far in TU100 you have learned a great deal about how computers and networks function and how data is stored and processed. You can now start thinking of each new concept in terms of what you have already learned:

- Where is the computer?
- What is the data being processed?
- How is that data obtained, stored and dispatched to its destination?

And so on …

You have already heard a little about the revolutionary field of ubiquitous computing, and in this part you will continue your exploration of this area. Ubiquitous computing is often seen as something of an upstart in the discipline of computer science; yet, as you will see, its origins are more than forty years old. Radical thinking in the late 1960s directly influenced the computers we use today and will use in the future, but it is only now that the necessary technologies are sufficiently cheap and abundant to make ubiquitous computing possible. So, before you see what the future is going to be like, it is necessary to learn a little history in the form of the technological and societal changes that made ubiquitous computing not only possible, but inevitable. This builds upon the introduction to the development of computers that was given in Block 1.

Once you have learned more about what ubiquitous computing is and where it came from, it will be time to build your first ubiquitous computing application using Sense and the SenseBoard.

Learning outcomes

Your study of this part will help you to do the following.

Knowledge and understanding

- Describe the development of the modern computer and the origin of the personal computer.
- Explain the purpose of scientific papers, and identify key parts of a scientific paper.
- Define an embedded computer and give some examples.
- Define ubiquitous computing and give some examples.
- Explain the use of sensors in embedded and ubiquitous computing.
- Explain the concept of 'persuasive computing'.
- Explain what is meant by tagging and give some examples of printed tags.
- Explain the principles of radio frequency identification (RFID) and how it can be used to tag objects.
- Define ambient computing and give some examples.
- List some concerns over the deployment of ubiquitous computing.

Cognitive skills

- Evaluate evidence relating to social, economic, political and personal issues raised by the development of modern computers.
- Analyse a simple problem and identify the operations required for a solution.
- Discuss some of the legal and ethical issues raised by the processing, storage and communication of information produced by ubiquitous computers, and make reasoned arguments about these issues.

Key skills

- Write summaries, explanations and descriptions in your own words using an effective structure.
- Carry out calculations using scientific notation.

Practical and professional skills

- Use the Open University Library facilities to locate articles published in a journal.
- Use Sense and the SenseBoard to build a small digital system.

The computer of the future as seen from 1968

1

The second half of the 1960s saw two men grappling with their visions of the future. One was Stanley Kubrick, the world-famous director of *Spartacus* and *Doctor Strangelove*, backed by millions of dollars and almost unlimited access to some of the world's leading engineering companies and universities; the second was an unknown PhD student called Alan Kay, who saw the potential of some of the technologies taking shape in the USA's research laboratories. Incredibly, it was the precocious Alan Kay who most accurately predicted the modern computer.

In 1965 Stanley Kubrick began work on an ambitious science fiction film based on a short story by Arthur C. Clarke. Unlike almost all previous films from the science fiction genre, bug-eyed monsters and laser guns would be notable only for their absence. *2001: A Space Odyssey* was going to be a sober imagining of the then-distant twenty-first century. To reflect the futuristic setting, one of the key characters would be a supercomputer by the name of HAL 9000. Kubrick was determined that his vision would be grounded in reality, so just as he consulted NASA engineers for their ideas of the future of spaceflight, he turned to leading computer scientists at the Massachusetts Institute of Technology (MIT) and to the giant IBM corporation for their predictions of how a real HAL 9000 would look and function.

The 1960s were a time of almost unlimited technological ambition. There seemed to be no problem that could not be solved by science and engineering. It was the decade when humans first flew in space, reached the deepest point on the ocean floor, built a supersonic airliner, began the war against polio and developed the communication satellite. It was also a time when computer technologies made enormous steps forward, encompassing everything from the humble computer mouse to the lofty ambition of replicating human intelligence.

Although the computers of the 1960s were unreliable and almost impossibly hard to use, Kubrick's assembled experts were confident that the computer of the twenty-first century would be radically different. Rather than being used by trained experts, HAL would be able to understand the spoken word, and would talk, read and even interpret gestures. HAL would be clever enough to replace people in critical areas such as spaceflight and caring for humans who would spend months in deep-freeze as they raced across the solar system in giant nuclear-powered spacecraft. HAL would play chess, recognise faces, enjoy chatting to its human colleagues; it would even be able to make complex ethical decisions. Kubrick's advisers were confident that these possibilities would be real by the time the year 2001 dawned. There was only one thing they did not predict: that computers would become smaller. HAL was huge – so big in fact that an astronaut could scramble around inside its memory, as you can see in Figure 1.

Figure 1   HAL 9000, the twenty-first century computer as imagined in 1968

1.1 The age of the mainframe

The unusual combination of artists and hard-headed engineers designing HAL found their inspiration in the *mainframe* computer that not only dominated the computing industry, but also was very much everyone's idea of what a computer should look like. Mainframes were room-sized monsters housed in clinically clean environments and attended round the clock by teams of specialist staff.

What distinguished these early computers was that they were so few in number. Although individual components were manufactured by machine, final assembly was performed by hand. Consequently, computers were so expensive that even very large organisations could only afford a single computer. The US company IBM had been building computers since 1952, but even so the number of machines built was extremely small. The IBM 650 was the most popular computer of the 1950s, and yet only 2000 machines were sold! Box 1 contains some further information about the first computer designed for business.

Demand for computing power increased throughout the 1950s and 1960s, and a few computer companies grew into giants – the biggest of all being IBM. In 1964 it introduced the most important mainframe computer ever built: the IBM System/360. The 360 was a family of computers all capable of running the same applications, but with a huge range of processing abilities. IBM System/360 customers would not have to change their software as their processing demands increased; they'd just need to buy (or, more usually, rent) a bigger computer.

Box 1 The first business computer

The first computers were almost entirely given over to scientific and military calculations. The first computer designed for business, LEO, only appeared in 1951 – and it was British. LEO did not come from a well-established electronics company, or even a university: it was designed and built by the J Lyons and Co. bakery company. Lyons was an enormous business that manufactured a huge range of products, not only for shops but for other companies, and it also supplied a chain of high-street tea shops.

Lyons was a highly progressive company, employing the best business practices of the day. It saw the potential for automating routine payroll, costings and delivery calculations. The company set up its own electronics division and sought advice and expertise from researchers in the UK and the USA. LEO proved to be a huge success for Lyons – it was even put to work by the British government calculating tax tables for employers, and by the British Transport Commission calculating freight charges for the railways.

Lyons spun off a separate computer manufacturing company, LEO Computers, and had some success producing commercial mainframes for the UK and international markets. Despite being a profitable business, LEO Computers fell victim to government policies. It was repeatedly merged with rival and incompatible businesses in an attempt to build a British computer manufacturer that could compete with IBM. The industry was eventually nationalised in 1968 to form International Computers Limited (ICL), which ironically made much of its money from building US-designed computers. The very last LEO III mainframe computers were used by General Post Office telecommunications (the forerunner of BT) and were only decommissioned in 1981.

The 360 was one of the largest financial investments ever made by a company – IBM spent over US$5 billion (equivalent to about US$24 billion in 2009) on developing it – but the gamble paid off. Even before the first 360 rolled off the production line more than 1000 machines had been sold, and by 1966 IBM was building 1000 of its 360 mainframes every month. This might not sound a lot when modern PCs sell in the millions, but in 1965 an IBM 360/75 could be rented for between US$50 000 and US$80 000 *per month* (equivalent to about US$337 000 and US$539 000 in 2009) or bought outright for between US$2.2 million and US$3.5 million (equivalent to about US$14.8 million and US$23.6 million in 2009) depending on the specification.

It was hardly surprising that HAL's designers were influenced by the immense power implied by the ranks of gleaming cabinets and whirling tape drives of the mainframes; they reasoned that while individual components might become smaller and more powerful, computers would remain physically the same size. Even in the future, big organisations would have one mainframe computer that everyone was expected to share. And indeed, as Box 2 explains, mainframe computers are still used to carry out some tasks.

Box 2 Mainframes and supercomputers

Almost all early computers were mainframe machines. These days, however, mainframes account for only a tiny share of the computer market and are manufactured by very few companies. Despite this, they are a lucrative business with individual machines costing many millions of pounds.

Modern mainframes are used to process enormous amounts of data such as financial transactions, statistical breakdowns of censuses and scientific simulations. Yet they are not the only option for this kind of processing. Much of this type of work is now performed by computer 'clusters', comprising hundreds or even thousands of relatively modest computers working together to achieve very high performance.

The most powerful computers, whether they are mainframes or clusters, are known as *supercomputers* and are used in specialised applications such as genetics research, weather forecasting and scientific simulations including aerodynamics and climate change.

1.2 Using early computers

Compared to even the most basic modern PC, the mainframes of the 1960s would seem incredibly primitive. Familiar applications such as word processors, drawing programs and music players lay far in the future. Instead mainframes spent most of their time *batch processing* huge amounts of data, performing tasks such as calculating tax returns, producing statistical breakdowns of census information or calculating the stresses experienced by aircraft. Users did not constantly interact with the computer; instead, the computer program and the data would be transcribed onto punch cards or paper tape and laboriously loaded into the computer's memory. Once loaded, the program would run, sometimes for hours or even days. During this time the computer could not be used for any other purpose, and if an error occurred it was not uncommon for the whole task to be redone from the very beginning.

Figure 2 shows a late 1960s mainframe computer from the IBM 360 family. It shows a fairly typical mainframe layout with the operator working at a terminal in the middle of the scene. Data is processed in the large cabinet to the left of the picture and is stored on the reels of magnetic tape that are being loaded in the background. As you can see, there are no video displays; instead the output was constantly printed onto long reels of paper or written to even more tape.

Figure 2   A late 1960s IBM 360 mainframe computer

By the mid-1960s an alternative way of interacting with computers had been developed. *Time-sharing* allowed more than one person to work with a computer at the same time. Even in the 1960s, computers processed data much faster than humans could enter it; thus a central powerful computer could divide its attention between a number of users, each sitting at a terminal resembling an old-fashioned typewriter. The central computer polled each terminal in turn. If a terminal's user had finished typing in a command, that data would be collected by the mainframe and processed; if the user was idle or had not finished typing, the mainframe switched its attention to the next terminal. So long as the mainframe could scan the terminals rapidly enough, each user felt they had exclusive use of the computer's time and gained some interactivity with it; in reality, the computer's time was being shared between tens if not hundreds of individual users. Time-sharing made the use of a computer much more efficient. The immediate feedback resulting from time-sharing computers allowed users to write documents using the ancestors of modern word processors, to rapidly write and debug computer programs, and even to play the very first true computer games.

However, so long as computer hardware remained expensive, users were forced to share – in effect, each computer user of the 1960s owned a tiny fraction of a large, expensive computer.

1.3 The idea of a computer for everyone

The idea of a *personal computer* – one so cheap and reliable that it is possible for each of us to own one – is, in retrospect, completely obvious. After all, no one is surprised that an individual can own a car or a book, so why should a computer be any different?

Yet the words 'cheap' and 'reliable' hardly applied to the computers of the 1960s, which were built from hundreds of thousands of individual transistors all of which had to be hand-soldered into position. The construction and wiring of individual transistors made computers expensive. Adding more computer power required a colossal amount of redesign and rewiring. Even the most expensive mainframe computers contained pitifully small amounts of memory and were extremely limited in the range of tasks they could perform. Consequently, computer programmers spent much of their time and effort improving the performance of their programs. A 'good' computer programmer was one whose programs ran correctly, as quickly as possible, using the smallest possible amount of memory.

The time-consuming and error-prone process of wiring computers from transistors was made obsolete by the development of the *integrated circuit (IC)*. The British scientist Geoffrey Dummer believed that it was possible to replace individual components, wire and solder with complete circuits etched onto a semiconducting material such as silicon. There would be no joints to fail, components would be more robust, and because there was no need for people to assemble the circuit from individual components, the whole circuit could be made much smaller. Dummer was never able to realise his design, but his ideas influenced other engineers, including a pair of US scientists, Jack Kilby at Texas Instruments and Robert Noyce at Fairchild Semiconductor. Kilby's first integrated circuit, consisting of a single transistor and its supporting components, was demonstrated in September 1958. The microchip had been born.

Activity 1 (self-assessment)

What are the two main advantages of integrated circuits over circuits built from individual transistors?

As Dummer realised, the integrated circuit offers many advantages over a traditional wired circuit, just one benefit being the size of components. An individual, modern transistor, packaged and ready to be soldered into place in a circuit, is about 2 mm square; those in a modern microprocessor are commonly between 25 and 45 *nanometres* across.

Activity 2 (self-assessment)

Write out 1 metre in nanometres, first in full with the appropriate number of zeros and then using scientific notation.

The price of individual transistors dropped steadily throughout the 1960s, falling from about US$35 per transistor at the beginning of the decade to only a few cents apiece a few years later. Transistors revolutionised consumer electronics and changed our culture; millions of people suddenly had access to entertainment and information through portable transistor radios and cheap, reliable television sets. The price of making a transistor continues to fall; a single transistor on a modern microprocessor costs less than 1 millionth of a cent! A modern microprocessor contains several hundred million transistors, making the transistor quite possibly the most common manufactured item in history.

Integrated circuits also helped to create Silicon Valley. Just south of San Francisco, close to Stanford University, this was once a rural fruit-farming area – yet during the 1960s, it was gradually buried under futuristic factories that were devoted to making microchips. Much of the demand for these devices came from the US government; the integrated circuit is a product of the Cold War, as the USA and USSR battled for military and scientific supremacy. The first computers containing integrated circuits were used in US Minuteman II intercontinental ballistic missiles carrying nuclear warheads, but they found a more peaceful home in the Apollo Guidance Computer (AGC) designed at MIT to fly the NASA Apollo program spacecraft to the Moon and back. The AGC (shown in Figure 3a) was the first computer to be built solely from integrated circuits; it weighed almost 30 kg and had the same processing power as a modern-day cheap electronic calculator that squeezes its computing power onto a single microchip.

The AGC was dedicated to an individual user and offered immediate feedback to their instructions, but its operation was completely different from any modern computer you may have used. Most commands were entered as pairs of two-digit numbers called the Verb and the Noun. The Verb told the computer what action was to be performed; the Noun contained the value that was to be processed. As an example, the command '16 36' would display the time of the computer's clock. A list of some of the Verb and Noun combinations was printed on a panel inside the Apollo capsule, which can be seen in Figure 3(b).

Although the AGC did not have a great deal of computing power, it is a mistake to think that calculating the flight path to the Moon is a trivial task. Much of the work involved in planning the Apollo flights was performed by mainframe computers back on Earth.

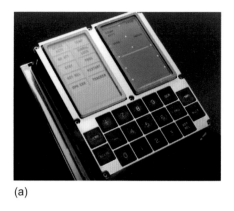

(a)

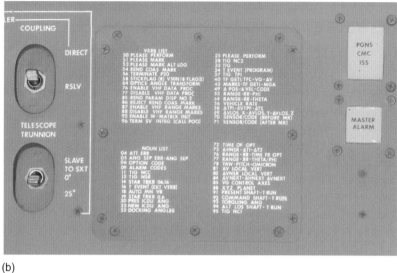

(b)

Figure 3 **(a) The control panel of the Apollo Guidance Computer, known as the Display and Keyboard (DSKY); (b) some Verb and Noun combinations**

Activity 3 (exploratory)

What do the following pairs of commands to the Apollo Guidance Computer mean? (Don't spend too long on this.)

05 09

25 36

16 36

Comment

You probably have no idea what they mean – although the third one is the command mentioned earlier that gives the time of the computer's clock. Don't worry, even trained engineers would need to refer to the computer's manual before programming the AGC.

The command '05 09' displayed the computer's alarm messages, while '25 36' began the process of setting the computer's time.

To complicate matters, codes allocated to the Verb Noun commands actually changed between missions. Some astronauts who flew more than one Apollo mission had to learn completely new commands for their second mission.

Activity 4 (exploratory)

Do you think this extremely limited control method caused problems for the astronauts? What if the Apollo Guidance Computer had been sold to the public?

Comment

The commands were hard to learn because they are just numbers with no relationship to the operations being attempted. However, the astronauts were highly experienced pilots who not only received a great deal of training in the computer's operation, but also had a very large team of support staff back on Earth. It's hard to imagine the same computer being popular with everyday users, who would not have the time to learn the multitude of operation codes.

Meanwhile, back on Earth:

If she can only cook as well as Honeywell can compute

Her soufflés are supreme, her meal planning a challenge? She's what the Honeywell people had in mind when they devised our Kitchen Computer. She'll learn to program it with a cross-reference to her favorite recipes by N-M's own Helen Corbitt. Then by simply pushing a few buttons obtain a complete menu organized around the entrée. And if she pales at reckoning her lunch tabs, she can program it to balance the family checkbook.

From the Neiman-Marcus catalogue, 1969

The US department store chain Neiman-Marcus is well known for some of the lavish items found in its catalogue, but even so the 1969 edition must have raised a few eyebrows. It contained an advertisement for the first computer ever targeted at consumers, shown in Figure 4. The Kitchen Computer was a Honeywell machine originally designed for controlling factory production lines, set inside a swooping streamlined pedestal with an integrated chopping board! Despite the catalogue's hyperbole, the computer could only be controlled by toggling a row of switches, with the results displayed in patterns of red lights. Even Neiman-Marcus admitted the machine's shortcomings: the housewife of 1970 would need to attend a *two-week* training class before she could use any of Helen Corbitt's recipes. At US$10 000 (equivalent to almost US$60 000 in 2009) it is hardly surprising that no Kitchen Computers were ever sold.

Fortunately, however, things were about to change.

Alan Kay's doctoral studies at the University of Utah in the late 1960s included working on the FLEX machine, a computer that is recognisably the ancestor of the modern desktop computer. FLEX's design was strongly influenced by previous research at the University of Utah that had created the field of computer graphics and the computer mouse. In 1968 Kay began to look beyond FLEX when he saw one of the world's first flat plasma displays. Kay was well aware of Gordon Moore's predictions and, in a 'back of an envelope' calculation, worked out that it would be about ten years before a computer as powerful as FLEX could be squeezed onto

The flat-panel display was invented at the University of Illinois in 1964 and used the same technology found in modern plasma televisions, although the first displays could only produce monochromatic orange light.

Figure 4   Advertisement for the very first home computer in the 1969 Neiman-Marcus catalogue

the rear surface of a one million pixel flat-panel display a little larger than a paperback book.

Activity 5 (self-assessment)

Try to express Moore's law in your own words without referring back to Block 1 Part 2.

Following Moore's law, Kay altered his view on how his computer's processing power would be used. As improved technology allowed for smaller transistors to be etched onto silicon, the number of transistors in an integrated circuit could continue to grow without increasing the cost of the computer. In a few years the 'average' computer might have more processing power and memory than would be required for everyday tasks such as entering text or performing arithmetic calculations. Kay began to consider how to put this spare power to work. Possibilities included drawing the high-resolution display complete with attractive fonts and animated graphics, controlling a pointing device and perhaps generating sound and music. Although Kay's peers might have been horrified at his profligate use of computer power, Kay was actually designing the modern computer interface.

At the time Kay was having his epiphany the 'average' computer user would have been a white, well-educated man with a background in mathematics or engineering, but this was beginning to change. Time-sharing computers had been networked across university campuses, high schools and government buildings, attracting a wide range of users including college students, school children and secretaries. A computer that could be owned by an individual would appeal to even more people. Kay believed that children would be the machine's natural audience, not only because it could revolutionise education and entertainment but also because it could satisfy their natural curiosity. He called his machine the *Dynabook*; Figure 5 shows a sketch of children using it.

Figure 5   A 1968 sketch by Alan Kay showing children using their Dynabooks: this drawing went on to influence the design of physical models built at Xerox PARC

Activity 6 (exploratory)

If computers were to be attractive to a more diverse audience, what non-technological issues would their designers have to consider? Think about the users of mainframe computers and compare them to the audience Kay had in mind for the Dynabook, and to current computer users.

Comment

The designers of computers would have to remember that they were no longer designing products for people who had technological or mathematical backgrounds.

In the 1950s and 1960s, the average computer user would have been white, male, middle-aged and with extensive qualifications – usually in mathematics, science or engineering. The new computer users might well be less educated than before, or educated in different specialised areas – they might even be children. They would be less willing to invest time and effort in learning to use a computer, and would expect it to behave in a more understandable manner. Computers would have to become user friendly.

In Figure 6 you can see one mock-up of the Dynabook. A number of possible designs were created: some used a sliding screen covering the keyboard (similar to that found on some mobile phones), others predicted the laptop's folding screen, whilst some even predicted a touch-screen tablet. Not only would the Dynabook use the intuitive graphical user interface to make it a more approachable machine, it would come complete with a large number of applications designed to help educate and entertain its users.

Figure 6   One of a number of mock-ups of Alan Kay's 1968 Dynabook concept

After receiving his doctorate, Kay applied for a job as a researcher at the prestigious Xerox PARC in California (more information about which is given in Box 3). According to Michael Hiltzik (2000, pp. 95–6), during his job interview Kay was asked what his greatest achievement at PARC would be. He replied: 'It'll be a personal computer.'

His interviewer had no idea what that meant. Kay explained with the aid of a small student notebook. He held the cover upright and said: 'This will be a flat-panel display. There'll be a keyboard here on the bottom and enough power to store your mail, files, music, artwork and books. All in a package about this size and weighing a couple of pounds. That's what I'm talking about.'

Despite his interviewer's scepticism, Kay got the job. The most astonishing part of the interview is not the scale of Alan Kay's ambition, but his insight into the digital future. At the very beginning of the 1970s, when eight-track represented the very height of audio technology and people were still committing memories to celluloid film, Kay was thinking about an age when all information would be not only digitised but also portable.

Activity 7 (self-assessment)

What sort of modern computing device does the Dynabook remind you of?

Box 3 PARC (The Palo Alto Research Center)

PARC is a company based in Palo Alto, California on the edge of Silicon Valley. It was founded in 1970 as a wholly owned subsidiary of the Xerox Corporation. At the time it was widely believed that computers would make printed materials obsolete, so Xerox was looking for new business opportunities offered by computer technologies.

PARC was set up to attract the very best engineers and computer scientists and provide them with the necessary environment and funding to develop Xerox's future technologies. Among its many accomplishments, PARC produced the Ethernet networking system found in many homes and offices, the laser printer, the first 'what you see is what you get' (WYSIWYG) document editor, bitmapped computer graphics, the graphical interface, the Alto (the first computer to use a virtual desktop like those found on modern PCs) and the Star (the first commercial computer to use the desktop), as well as technologies as diverse as electronic paper, computer worms and live music broadcasting over the internet.

Xerox's worries that computers would herald the end of printing were misplaced. The combination of PARC's easy-to-use computers, intuitive interfaces, document-editing software and the laser printer means that we now print more material than ever before.

Source: based on information from http://www.parc.com/

Although the Dynabook was not realised as a consumer product, its influence is clear; as well as inspiring the idea of a personal computer, it lives on in the design of the modern laptop computer, and especially the ultra-small netbook design computers that have become extremely popular in Europe following their introduction in late 2007.

During his time at PARC, Alan Kay was part of the team that developed Smalltalk, a programming language designed for children that was used to develop the first graphical interfaces. He later went to work for Apple, where he worked on the Dynabook-inspired computers Newton and eMate before moving to Disney and developing the powerful multimedia Squeak programming language – used, among other things, to write Sense.

Activity 8 (exploratory)

In the summer of 2010, I was able to meet Alan Kay at MIT and he agreed to be interviewed about his work. I have broken the interview into several parts: in the first Kay talks about his life before joining Xerox PARC, in the second he talks about PARC itself and in the third he talks about the development of the Dynabook. These videos can all be found in the resources page associated with this part on the TU100 website and you should go online to watch them when convenient.

More recently, Kay helped to design the One Laptop Per Child (OLPC) XO-1, a small, ultra-cheap computer designed for the developing world and education markets. Rather than being adapted from an existing design, the XO-1 is an entirely new computer whose rugged shell contains an extremely low-energy CPU and novel display screen that can be swivelled so that it can be shared with other users. The screen also folds flat over the keyboard to convert the XO-1 into an ebook reader. The two green 'horns' are wireless networking antennas (see Figure 7).

In order to improve its reliability in remote areas and extreme climates, the XO-1 contains no moving parts and instead relies on solid-state memory for storage. An entirely new operating system, called Sugar, was developed for the XO-1. In contrast to Windows and other familiar operating systems, whose design reflects the workings of a Western office and so organises data using a desktop and folders, Sugar is geared to supporting learning. Data is organised in a searchable journal, and is created, used and modified with a large number of free pre-installed applications including word processors, paint packages, web browsers and media players.

The XO-1 was originally intended to cost as little as US$100; it actually cost almost twice as much. Despite its laudable intentions, the project has been criticised – even a cheap laptop is much more expensive than a book and is comparable to the salary of a teacher in many countries. By late 2009, almost 1.3 million XO-1s were in use in 39 countries, purchased either as part of government initiatives or through a novel 'buy one, get

Figure 7   **The OLPC XO-1 laptop**

one free' scheme in which Western customers could buy an XO-1 for themselves and donate an identical machine to the developing world.

The specifications of the Dynabook, a typical netbook and the XO-1 are given in Table 1.

Table 1   Comparison of computer specifications

	Dynabook (1968–1972)	**Acer Aspire One (2008)**	**OLPC XO-1 (2007)**
Display	c. 1 million pixel plasma flat screen	1024 × 600 (614 400) pixel LCD flat screen	1200 × 900 (1 080 000) pixel LCD flat screen
Processor	Intel 4004 Clock speed 740 kHz	Intel Atom Clock speed 1.6 GHz	AMD Geode Clock speed 433 MHz
Memory (RAM)	8 kilobytes	Up to 1.5 gigabytes	256 megabytes
Storage	c. 1 megabyte magnetic tape or floppy disk	8 or 16 gigabytes of solid-state memory, or 120 or 160 gigabyte hard disk	1 gigabyte of solid-state memory
Network	Ethernet 300 kilobits per second	Ethernet 10/100 megabits per second, and 802.11b/g wireless 54 megabits per second	802.11b/g wireless 54 megabits per second
Price	US$294 (1972), equivalent to about £1000 in 2009	£240 (2009)	£135 (2009)

Activity 9 (exploratory)

Do you think Alan Kay's concept of the Dynabook has been realised in the modern netbook computer and in the XO-1? Can you see any particular advantages and disadvantages to each design? In particular, think back to Alan Kay's original vision of how a Dynabook could be used.

Comment

Clearly the physical specifications of the modern netbook are very similar to, if not greatly in advance of, Alan Kay's ideas. Processor speeds, memory and storage capacities are far ahead of what Kay could have predicted. The biggest difference between the netbook and the Dynabook is that the modern computer still lacks the ease of use envisaged for the Dynabook and the necessary educational software. The XO-1 might have a superior specification to the original Dynabook, but the way it has been designed to support learning means that it should be considered to be the first real Dynabook.

Alan Kay's lasting monument is the colossal personal computer industry, whose sales have grown from just 48 000 machines in 1977 to 288 million units worldwide in 2008 and which continues to expand by approximately 12% per year. It has produced incredible wealth: one of the biggest manufacturers, Dell, was founded in 1984 with just US$1000, yet in 2008 alone it had sales of more than US$61 billion in computers and software.

Activity 10 (self-assessment)

If the PC industry had continued to expand by 12% every year, how many units would have been sold worldwide in 2009? You will probably need to use a calculator for this activity.

The personal computer industry is not just made up of hardware manufacturers; there is an enormous commercial software business employing many millions of people, from manufacturers of computer peripherals, computer consultants, educators and training companies all the way through to corner shops and high-street retailers who sell and repair personal computers.

Alan Kay and *2001*

There's a fascinating link between the ideas of Alan Kay and those of *2001: A Space Odyssey*. As the idea of the Dynabook was forming in Kay's mind, Arthur C. Clarke was writing the novel (drawing on his earlier short story) that would accompany the film and that would help the prop and set designers. One of the technologies mentioned in the novel is the Newspad – you might find it familiar.

When he tired of official reports and memoranda and minutes, he would plug his foolscap-sized Newspad into the ship's information circuit and scan the latest reports from Earth. One by one he would conjure up the world's major electronic papers; he knew the codes of the more important ones by heart, and had no need to consult the list on the back of his pad. Switching to the display unit's short-term memory, he would hold the front page while he quickly searched the headlines and noted the items that interested him.

Each had its own two-digit reference; when he punched that, the postage-stamp-sized rectangle would expand until it neatly filled the screen and he could read it with comfort. When he had finished, he would flash back to the complete page and select a new subject for detailed examination.

(a)

Floyd sometimes wondered if the Newspad, and the fantastic technology behind it, was the last word in man's quest for perfect communications. Here he was, far out in space, speeding away from Earth at thousands of miles an hour, yet in a few milliseconds he could see the headlines of any newspaper he pleased. (That very word 'newspaper', of course, was an anachronistic hangover into the age of electronics.) The text was updated automatically on every hour; even if one read only the English versions, one could spend an entire lifetime doing nothing but absorbing the ever-changing flow of information from the news satellites.

Clarke, 2001 [1968], p. 53–4

The Newspad sounds very much like not only a Dynabook but also modern tablet computers such as Apple's iPad (Figure 8a), which blur the line between mobile phones and computers and are marketed as a way of accessing books, news, reference materials and web pages over wireless internet connections. Clarke was less accurate in suggesting how we might interact with such a handheld device – thinking of numerical codes rather than touch-screen interfaces or buttons – but his onscreen representations of newspaper pages sound very much like the icons we use in most modern computer interfaces, another development from Xerox PARC. The Newspad appears in the film of *2001* as an IBM-branded device that is used as a portable flatscreen television receiving text and television programmes via satellite broadcasting (Figure 8b).

(b)

Figure 8 **(a) The Apple iPad; (b)** *2001: A Space Odyssey***'s realisation of a portable information reader called the Newspad**

1.4 Conclusion

This session provided a short history of the modern computer, from the period when mainframe computers dominated the industry through to the advent of the modern PC. The development of the computer was driven by developments in semiconductor technologies, most importantly that of the transistor. The speed of these developments became known as Moore's law.

Related to this, there has been a constant decline in the price of individual computer components. As components became cheaper it was possible to provide greater amounts of computing power to individuals; while each computer of the 1950s was shared among hundreds of people, the same or greater amount of computing power could be owned by an individual of the 1970s.

The general specification of a personal computer was predicted by the researcher Alan Kay. He foresaw the need for computers to become more user friendly and to run a rich suite of compelling applications, including those for entertainment, if they were to attract large numbers of users.

This session should have helped you with the following learning outcomes.

- Describe the development of the modern computer and the origin of the personal computer.
- Evaluate evidence relating to social, economic, political and personal issues raised by the development of modern computers.

The disappearing computer

2

Alan Kay's idea of a computer that was exclusively your own was realised almost ten years after he first began work on the Dynabook. In 1977 the Apple II became the world's first mass-produced personal computer and went on to spawn a colossal new industry. Since 1977 onwards, more and more of us have acquired our own computer – some of us have several.

But is that the end of the story? The answer, as you may have guessed, is no. Almost every home contains a number of objects that use computer technologies. For every conventional PC sitting on our desks or in our laps, there are hundreds of other devices containing a computer that allows them to perform their tasks.

2.1 The embedded computer

Donald Norman's book *The Invisible Computer* (1998) draws an analogy between computers and the electric motor: the electric motor has come to play a major part in our lives, and yet at the same time it has become almost invisible. A motor by itself is not much use to the average person; it is an enabling technology like the wheel or the printing press, a technology that makes modern life possible. In 1918 it was possible for a household to buy a 'home electric motor', a large and expensive device (see Figure 9). Having acquired your motor you could then buy, from catalogues, a whole range of attachments allowing you to use the motor for many household tasks, including a mixer, a fan, a sewing machine, a vacuum cleaner, a grinder and a drill. As time passed, the cost of building electric motors fell dramatically and they became cheap, mass-produced, standardised objects small enough to be incorporated into other devices.

The analogy between motors and computers becomes even more interesting when you consider how electric motor technology developed in terms of cost, size, reliability and power requirements. A modern household contains dozens of electric motors. The list seems almost endless: from electric shavers and hairdryers, through fan-heated ovens and refrigerators, to coffee grinders, food mixers and power tools. Yet the average householder probably gives little or no thought to the fact that there are motors embedded in any of these appliances, and certainly does not need to know how they work or to interact with them directly.

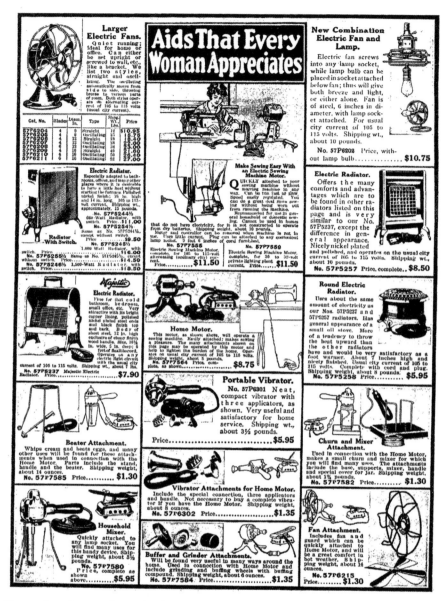

Figure 9   A page from the Sears Roebuck catalogue of 1918 demonstrating the many (occasionally eye-opening) uses for a standalone electric motor

Activity 11 (exploratory)

Write down two electric motor-based devices that you use on a regular basis, but that wouldn't have been available in the early part of the twentieth century. For each of them, give reasons whether you think they are, on balance, beneficial uses of the technology.

Comment

I chose my electric toothbrush and my DVD player. My electric toothbrush actually lies unused in my bathroom: I'm not really convinced that it does a better job than the ordinary one. As for my DVD player, it means I can watch my favourite films even when they're not playing in the cinema; this helps me relax, which I find beneficial.

Following Norman's analogy, in the same way that electric motors have disappeared from our immediate awareness, computers – in the form of microprocessors and their associated sensors (similar to those for measuring temperature and movement on your SenseBoard), motors and displays – are increasingly *embedded* into appliances. As with motors, the cost of individual computers has dramatically reduced until they have become a relatively minor proportion of the total cost of the item. They are in dishwashers, bread makers, watches, cameras, mobile phones and DVD players. Moving away from the domestic scene, they are in photocopiers, cash machines and CCTV surveillance cameras. Unlike electric motors, however, these *embedded computers* accept instructions from us, or acquire information from their environment and deliver appropriate actions and results. We do not need to know anything about their complex internal processing, nor do we interact with them directly, yet they provide us with efficient task-specific appliances.

Activity 12 (exploratory)

Write down two examples of devices incorporating computers that you use on a regular basis, but that wouldn't have been available (perhaps in their current form) to your parents or grandparents. For each of them, give reasons whether you think they are, on balance, beneficial uses of the technology.

Comment

I wrote down my bread-making machine and my car. My bread-making machine allows me to time my production so that there is a fresh loaf of bread when I get up in the morning. That's a real pleasure! As for my car, I think this is definitely a beneficial use of computer technology; cars are much safer now than they ever have been, as you will see below.

A car is a very good example of something that contains embedded computers. It might surprise you that even quite basic cars may contain fifty *different* computers. Some of them are dedicated to improving the efficiency of the car's engine, calculating fuel/air mixtures and ignition timing or power distribution; others drive the instrumentation panels and lighting, or the increasingly complicated entertainment and navigation systems. In more sophisticated cars, embedded computers control the internal climate and the suspension, and even memorise individual user preferences; the future trend will be to include even more computer power. The effect of incorporating computers into cars has been a general improvement in vehicle reliability and efficiency, but a decrease in user serviceability. Most modern cars require dedicated servicing, and there is very little the average driver can do apart from fill up with fuel, water and oil and check the tyre pressure!

2.2   Embedded computers and car safety

One of the most important computer technologies found in modern cars is, if you are lucky, one you will never need: the airbag. An airbag is a fabric envelope that is normally stowed in a deflated state behind the front fascia or steering wheel of a car. In the event of a collision, a small explosive charge fills the bag with gas, forming a soft cushion to protect the occupant from injury. In order to offer full protection, an airbag must reach its full size less than 1/25th of a second after the collision takes place, and for this to happen, the decision to deploy the airbag must be made in less than 1/30th of a second. A dedicated computer, the unimaginatively titled airbag control unit (ACU), controls the airbags in a car. The ACU uses sensors throughout the car to constantly monitor the state of the vehicle. The most important sensors are called *accelerometers* and measure changes in the car's velocity. Accelerometers are found in many consumer goods; for instance, they are used to measure hand movements in video game controllers such as the Nintendo Wii and Sony SixAxis. They also detect hand shake in still and video cameras and help to control motors that adjust the lens or mirror to stabilise the image. Many mobile phones use accelerometers to rotate their screen as the user turns the phone, while iPod users can shuffle their music by shaking the player – again an accelerometer does the hard work.

Since the airbags must only be deployed in an emergency, it is vital that the ACU receives correct information from the sensors. This demands that the accelerometers are *accurate* (giving the correct values), *reliable* (they should not fail within the normal lifetime of a car) and, perhaps most importantly, *robust* (they should continue working despite the enormous forces of a crash). Rather than being laboriously assembled from individual components, the accelerometers are *microelectromechanical systems (MEMS)*, etched from single pieces of silicon less than 3 mm square using technology similar to that used to make microprocessors. And just like silicon chips, mass production means that each accelerometer costs only a few pence. Further information about MEMS is given in Box 4.

The accelerometer shown in Figure 10 is the small black square at the centre of the circuit. Most of the space on the circuit board is given over to wiring that is sufficiently large that it can be handled by humans. However, in many consumer devices the accelerometer circuit can be made much smaller since the product will be assembled by robots.

Box 4 MEMS

MEMS are found in many household electronics, including the printing heads of inkjet printers where they control the size of individual drops of ink. Accelerometers and solid-state gyroscopes are used to detect movement of mobile phones and video game controllers, while microscopic moveable mirrors lie at the heart of digital projectors used in homes and cinemas.

Figure 10   A MEMS accelerometer similar to that found in an airbag

In the unfortunate event of a collision, the tiny accelerometers measure the deceleration of the vehicle. When the deceleration exceeds a critical value (usually about thirty times the force of gravity), the ACU detonates pyrotechnic charges in the airbags, filling them with gas. More sophisticated ACUs can measure the direction of the collision and use that to deploy airbags at different times, to fire more airbags on the side of the vehicle worst affected by the collision, to control the amount of gas let into the airbags and to pre-tension the seatbelts to help restrain the occupants of the car. Since their widespread introduction in 1990, it is estimated that airbags have been used more than 3 million times in the USA alone and have been directly responsible for saving more than 6000 lives.

The ACU is a good example of an embedded computer – the car occupants are almost certainly unaware of the presence of a computer constantly monitoring their safety through a network of sensors. Of course, the ACU is an unusual computer in that it offers very little interaction with its users. If all is well with the car, the ACU apparently does nothing. This raises the question of how users can be sure the ACU is working (without crashing the car).

2.3   Intelligent structures

Many researchers hope that embedded systems can be deployed in other environments. One proposed application is in so-called 'intelligent structures': buildings and bridges that harness computer power either to monitor their own health or to actively respond to their environment. Many existing buildings are equipped with sensors to detect fire or intruders, and environmental sensors that adjust heating or cooling to keep their inhabitants comfortable. However, it is possible to incorporate a much wider range of sensors into a building's structure.

The economic boom around Asia's Pacific Rim has been marked by the construction of some of the world's tallest skyscrapers. The region is regularly shaken by devastating earthquakes and lashed by ferocious typhoon winds. Conventional buildings such as those in New York and London are unsuitable for these conditions; while many could physically survive an earthquake or storm, the vibrations would cause the structures to sway uncontrollably – a deeply unpleasant experience for their occupants. Rather than using more pillars and thicker window surrounds to make buildings more rigid (but also darker and less welcoming), architects have mounted accelerometers throughout their structures. These measure the motion of the building and relay the results to hydraulic cylinders that move to compensate for any shaking. Currently the tallest building using this 'active damping' technology is the prestigious 52-storey (233 m) Shinjuku Park Tower in central Tokyo, but it is likely to become popular with the designers of slender ultra-tall skyscrapers since active damping prevents the unsettling swaying found in many tall buildings even on the calmest of days.

2.4   Online intelligent structures

The Forth Road Bridge, shown in Figure 11, was completed in 1964 and is a vital transport link between Edinburgh and Fife. Originally designed to carry approximately 30 000 vehicles every day, it routinely carries more than twice that number. This increased load may have not only reduced the bridge's original 120-year predicted lifespan, but also caused structural damage that makes the bridge less safe.

Growing concern over the bridge's health led the Forth Estuary Transport Authority to commission a detailed survey of the structure. Engineers concentrated their attention on the thousands of steel wires that make up the giant suspension cables from which the road hangs. Inspections that took place between 2003 and 2005 showed that the majority of the wires had been corroded by the Forth Estuary's damp salty air, and that some had actually cracked. This damage had reduced the strength of the bridge by almost a tenth; although it was still safe for the time being, if the

Figure 11   The elegant Forth Road Bridge in Scotland

damage were left unchecked, the bridge would become too weak for heavy traffic by 2013 and would have to be closed entirely by 2020. The bridge would have lasted a little less than half of its intended lifespan.

Engineers were able to resolve the corrosion problem by pumping dehumidified air into the interior of the suspension cables, but this method can't prevent cracking caused by heavy loads and age. The bridge's engineers wanted to know the number of cracks and the rate at which they were occurring, but they couldn't access the whole of the interior of the cables without closing the bridge.

In 2006, fifteen tiny microphones were placed inside each cable to listen for the distinctive sound of a wire cracking. The data is collated by a computer and immediately sent over the internet to Canadian experts, who use specialist software to locate the cracks and advise the bridge's operators of their severity. Continuous monitoring of the bridge has shown that cables continue to crack at the rate of about one a month. Fortunately for the bridge's users and owners, the cracks are randomly scattered between wires and along the length of the bridge. If this pattern were to change – for instance, if the rate of cracking greatly increased or became concentrated in a particular area – it would be possible to close the bridge almost immediately and not risk lives.

Activity 13 (exploratory)

To help you understand this section, I have included a ten-minute excerpt from the BBC television series *Coast* featuring the Forth Road Bridge in the resources page associated with this part on the TU100 website. You should watch this video when convenient.

2.5 Conclusion

This session follows on directly from the development of the personal computer. The same manufacturing processes that spawned the microprocessor meant that it was possible to include relatively cheap computers inside other manufactured objects. Embedded computers improved the performance of many everyday items, but remain inaccessible to end users. A more recent development has been to incorporate network technologies alongside these computers, allowing them to communicate with the outside world. You were given the example of the Forth Road Bridge, which is now constantly monitored for weakness from Canada.

Perhaps the most important thing you can learn from this session is that even as the computer becomes more powerful and more common than ever before, it is starting to disappear from view. Right now, if you were to ask a person in the street what a computer looks like, they would almost certainly describe a desktop or laptop computer; yet in just a few years' time, those designs will look even more archaic than the computers of the 1960s appear to us now.

This session should have helped you with the following learning outcomes.

- Define an embedded computer and give some examples.
- Explain the use of sensors in embedded and ubiquitous computing.
- Evaluate evidence relating to social, economic, political and personal issues raised by the development of modern computers.

The ubiquitous computer

3

Computers will die. They're dying in their present form. They're just about dead as distinct units. A box, a screen, a keyboard. They're melting into the texture of everyday life … even the word 'computer' sounds backward and dumb.

Extract from the 2003 novel *Cosmopolis* by Don DeLillo

The Forth Road Bridge contains one of the most recent visions of the future of computing, one that also began at PARC. It is a world where computers have disappeared from view but remain contactable using wired or wireless networks. This vision is called *ubiquitous computing* (commonly contracted to *ubicomp*), *pervasive computing* or sometimes *everyware*.

Ubiquitous is a relatively modern word, dating from the middle of the nineteenth century, and it simply means 'present or appearing everywhere'. We might talk of famous people or popular brands being ubiquitous – no matter where you go or what you do, you can't escape from their presence. Ubicomp is a world straight out of science fiction, where computers can be found at every location and in every object, and where computer services can be accessed at any time and in any place.

3.1   The invention of ubiquitous computing

Science fiction authors had used the idea of a ubiquitous computing presence as scenery dressing for much of the twentieth century. However, little practical work had been done in the area before the PARC researcher Mark Weiser wrote his 1991 *Scientific American* article 'The Computer for the 21st Century'. In this section you will find and read the full article in order to learn more about Weiser's thinking and the predictions he made for the field. The paper is quite approachable and I hope you will find it an enjoyable read.

Activity 14 (exploratory)

This activity shows you how to obtain a copy of 'The Computer for the 21st Century' using The Open University's Library search service and then guides you through reading the paper. You will find the instructions for it in the resources page associated with this part on the TU100 website. The activity should take you about 2 hours; when you have finished, return to this text.

3.2 Ubiquitous computing in the real world

Since 1991, Weiser's vision of ubiquitous computing technologies has been taking shape in corporate research laboratories and universities around the world. Actual or planned ubicomp environments cover almost every possible scale from the very small to the very large.

Intelligent cities

Perhaps the most ambitious are intelligent cities that are constantly monitored for pollution, criminal activity and travel patterns. These ideas have proved especially popular in the fast-growing, rapidly industrialising countries of Asia's Pacific Rim, but were considered less acceptable in the West where the idea of constant surveillance has been coloured by George Orwell's classic novel *1984*. However, following the 2001 terrorist attacks on New York, Western governments have begun to explore whether ubiquitous computing could mitigate or even prevent future attacks.

Existing surveillance systems such as CCTV networks could be linked together to constantly monitor every part of a city. Cameras equipped with suitable software can recognise vehicle licence plates, and some are capable of distinguishing individual faces. Others have been demonstrated that recognise people's gaits or 'suspicious' actions. Cameras would be joined by sophisticated sensors monitoring the air and water for chemical, biological and radiation threats. In 2010 the US Department of Homeland Security began its Cell-All program, which encouraged mobile phone manufacturers to place chemical sensors into mobile telephones. Suitably equipped phones would alert authorities with their position if their sensors detected a hazardous substance.

Of course, one of the risks in any system using sensors is that they can make mistakes – more often than not by claiming a hazard is present when there is no threat. Any system using such sensors must cope with these 'false positives'. This is usually achieved by relying on reports from multiple sensors; only when a certain number of warnings had been received would an alarm be raised. If only a single sensor reported a threat whilst nearby ones remained silent, the system would consider the warning to be down to faulty hardware.

As yet, there have been no deployments of the technologies discussed above, but certain facilities – such as airports, railway stations and certain secure government buildings – have been fitted with sensors. Billions of dollars are being invested in researching applications for ubiquitous crime prevention technologies.

Intelligent buildings

On a smaller scale are ubiquitous networks covering individual structures. As you saw earlier, the Forth Road Bridge is an existing structure that has been retrofitted with sensors and computers to become a ubiquitous network.

Activity 15 (self-assessment)

I said earlier that the Forth Road Bridge is an example of ubiquitous computing. Use Weiser's definition of ubiquitous computing to explain why this is the case.

Sensors and networks can be included in buildings during their construction. Sensors can be placed inside girders or buried in freshly poured concrete, allowing engineers to monitor the health of parts of a structure even after they are no longer accessible. On a day-to-day basis, similar sensors could be used to monitor energy usage and air quality within the building as well as the comings and goings of individual users.

Interactive art

One of the more appealing uses of ubicomp is in the creation of new forms of public art. *Cloud* (shown in Figure 12) is a three-storey-high kinetic sculpture located in the central atrium of The Open University's Jennie Lee Building. The sculpture consists of 24 hollow fibreglass balls, half of which are grey and half of which are orange. The balls are suspended from extremely thin nylon cables connected to a gantry near the ceiling of the building. During the day the balls move up and down in response to the behaviour of the building's inhabitants, forming differently shaped clouds.

When first installed, *Cloud* was programmed to respond to how people use the building's stairs and lifts. The building has two entrances, one on the east side of the building and the other on the west. Next to each entrance is a flight of stairs leading to the upper floors, as well as a lift. A third staircase is located in the atrium itself. *Cloud*'s designers located pressure sensors at the foot of each staircase and at the ground-floor entrances to the lifts. The sensors are activated by the weight of a person. Each sensor is wired to an Arduino microcontroller that is in turn connected to a central server using network cabling.

The central server collects information from all the Arduinos over a half-hour period, totalling up how many times the stairs and lifts are used. After thirty minutes, the server uses Ethernet to send the totals to

The Arduino is a standalone computer widely used in ubiquitous computing. Your SenseBoard is controlled using Arduino chips.

Figure 12   *Cloud*, **a kinetic sculpture at The Open University that changes its appearance depending on the behaviour of the building's inhabitants**

Kinetic, or dynamic, sculptures are those that change their shape as opposed to more traditional static sculptures.

a second computer located on the top floor. This computer uses yet another Arduino to drive the motors that raise or lower the balls on their cables. Orange balls show the number of people using the stairs, while grey balls represent lift usage. The more a method is used, the higher the relevant balls are raised above the floor.

Activity 16 (self-assessment)

Identify the parts of *Cloud* that make it a ubiquitous computer according to Weiser's definition.

Cloud's designers wanted to use the installation as a way of persuading people to use the stairs, thus increasing their activity levels and reducing the building's energy consumption. *Cloud* can be called a *persuasive computer* – rather than lecturing people about their habits, it makes people unconsciously change their behaviours.

Activity 17 (self-assessment)

In your own words, define a persuasive computer. Why can *Cloud* be considered a persuasive computer?

Cloud is also proving to be a useful way of finding out how people use the Jennie Lee Building. Traditionally, the only way to see how people respond to new environments is to monitor their movements and make them complete intensive questionnaires or interviews – which obviously is intrusive, expensive and time-consuming. In contrast, *Cloud*'s sensors are recording people's movements without ever interfering in their work; nor does it intrude on their privacy, as it is unable to identify individual workers. *Cloud* has already revealed that people entering the building on the east (the side closest to the centre of campus) are significantly more likely to use the lift than those entering the building from the west. The reasons for this are unclear; it might be that many people using the east entrance are unfamiliar with the building's layout, do not see the stairway and so use the lift, which is located directly in front of them.

Cloud could easily be reprogrammed to respond to other data sources. Its designers have suggested that it could be used to monitor total energy usage inside the building, or even to record student reservation numbers or their assessment scores.

A similar (though much more expensive) sculpture called *The Source* is located in the atrium of the London Stock Exchange. *The Source* is made from 729 balls laid out as a $9 \times 9 \times 9$ grid suspended from vertical wires. Each ball contains lights and electric motors that allows it to move independently of the others in response to commands from a central computer. At the beginning of the day the balls form a cube, which gradually dissolves into a series of patterns relating to fluctuations in the stock market. At the end of the day, the balls reform into a cube and display an animated arrow indicating the performance of the market during the previous trading session.

Intelligent rooms

Many office buildings already use credit-card-sized swipe cards to unlock doors. When a card is inserted into or brought close to a reader, the information on the card is read and checked against a central list of authorised users. If the holder of the card is allowed into the building, the door is unlocked and they can enter.

Enterprising companies are already finding new uses for this technology. In 2005, Brittan Elementary School in Sutter, California made each pupil wear a badge containing a radio tag that communicated with receivers mounted above every classroom door as children passed underneath. This InClass system was developed by two local teachers and aimed to reduce teacher workload and monitor truancy. When children entered class, their tags would send a unique identification number to the reader and from there to a central computer. The list of attendees could immediately be compared with the list of children who should be in the class. The teacher would not need to take the register and the principal's office would know if any students skipped class.

Activity 18 (exploratory)

Can you foresee any problems with the InClass scheme? Without using any online searches, try to think of reasons why this scheme might be less effective than its makers thought and of any personal reasons why you might object to its use in school.

Comment
Possible reasons you might have thought of include the following.

- The radio tag in the badge does not actually identify a child, only the badge itself. There is no reason why children couldn't swap badges, or why one child couldn't carry a collection of badges belonging to others who were playing truant.

- You may have been worried about the storage of the data and whether it could be used to track children's movements – this is a privacy issue that is especially serious when children are involved, as they might not be able to make a considered decision about using such technology.

- You may have been concerned about compulsion to use the technology; refusal to wear the badges might affect the child's school records. It is not uncommon for the individual rights of children to be ignored when technologies are introduced that affect them. Many proponents of such schemes believe that the approval of parents is sufficient and that the child does not need to be consulted.

A number of parents, furious at not being consulted about the deployment of the new technology, managed to bring a great deal of unwelcome media attention to the school and the InClass trial was ended after less than a month. At the time of writing (2010), the InClass system was still being offered for sale as well as a similar system designed for university campuses, although there was no evidence that any systems were up and running.

Intelligent devices
Even smaller again are personal networks – computers in and around individual people. These very small-scale networked computers have attracted a great deal of attention from researchers and the first consumer products have been launched. Most of these products are aimed at the lucrative US health and fitness market.

One such example is the SenseWear BodyMedia armband (see Figure 13), which is designed for people who are attempting to lose weight and increase their levels of physical activity. The BodyMedia armband records the wearer's activity using skin sensors to measure temperature, water levels, motion and heat output. Each day, the armband is plugged into a computer and the recorded data is transmitted to the patient's doctor for analysis. At the same time, the patient is informed of their progress towards meeting certain goals agreed with their physician, as the results are broadcast to the wristwatch. BodyMedia's designers feel that patients who receive immediate, detailed, easy-to-understand feedback on their progress are more likely to respond to exercise regimes than those who only receive feedback at widely spaced intervals.

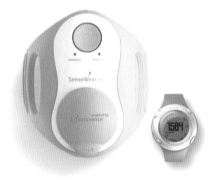

Figure 13   The SenseWear BodyMedia armband (left) and wristwatch

BodyMedia is the first of many such devices that could be used to address the endemic illnesses of Western society. Similar systems are under development to monitor activity levels in diabetes patients. One experimental system developed by Intel's Seattle research laboratory uses motion sensors to monitor activity levels. The sensors use a Bluetooth link to send activity reports to the patient's mobile phone, which in turn sends the data to the doctor's computer using the mobile phone network. The user can get an up-to-the-minute report on their activity levels from the mobile phone's display, as well as helpful advice on staying active. Meanwhile, their doctor receives a more detailed daily report on the patient's progress from their PC.

Smart Dust

How small can we make a computer using existing technology? From 2001 onwards, the Smart Dust project (a collaboration between the University of California, Berkeley and the Defense Advanced Research Projects Agency (DARPA)) attempted to answer this question.

The aim of the Smart Dust project was to cram a useful amount of computing power, sensors, power supply and network connectivity into a 1 mm cube. A single Smart Dust computer was so radically different from our perception of a computer that its originators came up with a completely new name for it: the *mote*.

The Smart Dust project ended without a true mote being created, although it did make enormous advances towards this aim in the fields of low power consumption, energy storage and the software needed to operate a mote. Figure 14 shows a 'Golem Dust' mote sitting on a US one-cent coin, which is about 19 mm in diameter. The mote is solar powered and contains a light sensor as well as an accelerometer; it uses a tiny radio antenna to communicate with other motes and nearby computers.

Figure 14   A prototype 'Golem Dust' mote developed at the Berkeley Sensor & Actuator Center at the University of California, Berkeley

Even without any real Smart Dust to play with, innovators have imagined a dazzling range of uses for motes, including:

- dropping clouds of it over enemy territory to act as an unimaginably large number of eavesdropping devices
- relay stations for radio networks in remote, sparsely populated areas
- miniaturised space probes
- tiny environmental monitors tracking seismic or volcanic activity
- tracking the spread of pollution or water quality in remote areas
- intelligent food packaging monitoring the conditions in which food is stored.

Perhaps straying further into the realm of science fiction, there is also the possibility of Smart Dust nail varnish, which when painted onto the fingernails would communicate the movement of the user's fingers – turning them into mouse pointers or even the ultimate air guitar!

Activity 19 (exploratory)

Kris Pister was one of the original Smart Dust team. Since leaving Berkeley he has set up Dust Networks, a company that has commercialised some of the Smart Dust research into actual products. Near the beginning of the Smart Dust project he wrote an article about some uses for Smart Dust in 2010 and 2020 (Pister, 2001), which you will find in the resources page associated with this part on the TU100 website. Read the article as far as the heading 'Rough Limits'. Have any of the predictions come true?

Comment

I was unable to find any Smart Dust-inspired products that are available in 2010 (2020 is still somewhat in the future at the time of writing). Some of the functions imagined in the article – such as smart rooms – are available, although they are being controlled by devices such as mobile phones. My belief is that no one could have anticipated in 2000 just how attached we would become to our mobile phones and how we would start to use them for more than just talking and sending text messages.

3.3   The universal remote control

A modern hotel may offer internet access to guests who can connect their computer to the hotel network. The hotel's network is a resource that can be used by any guest for (almost) any purpose. Some more modern hotels also provide flat-screen televisions that double up as computer monitors. Once again, all the guest has to do is plug their laptop into the television and then they can use a large display.

Imagine if this could happen automatically: that when you walked into your hotel room your computer would establish connections to the hotel's network, to the television, to printers and so on. You'd never have to worry about finding connections and configuring your computer – only about paying the bill. A computer that can be taken from place to place, seamlessly establishing links with the local infrastructure, is sometimes called a universal remote control.

In this view of the future, data can be accessed from anywhere through a range of wired or (more usually) wireless connections. Large amounts of data need not be stored on your computer's disk or in its memory; instead, data is held on distant computers and accessed over the internet whenever it is needed. A copy of the data is stored on your computer just as long as it is needed by an application; when you save the file or close the application, the revised file is sent back to the remote server for safe storage. Under this setup you would never need to know precisely where your data was held, it would always *appear* to be stored on your machine. This scenario, as you saw in Block 1, is called the *cloud*. Storing data in the cloud is already a reality, with companies such as Google, Microsoft and Amazon offering gigabytes of online storage to their users. So far most cloud users have accessed their data through PCs, but many smart phones now incorporate some support for the cloud (see Figure 15).

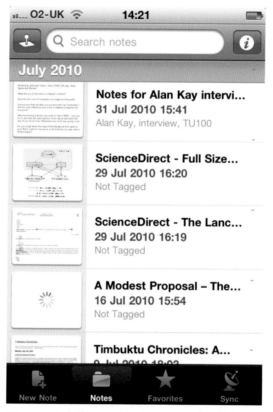

Figure 15   The Evernote application, which stores data in the cloud, being run on an iPhone (taken from personal iPhone)

Cloud computing takes the idea of remote computer resources even further. A user might not require a powerful computer of their own to perform computationally intensive tasks such as database searches, computer graphics rendering and mathematical simulations. Instead, their relatively slow personal computer would send requests to extraordinarily powerful servers located elsewhere on the internet. The results would be calculated much more quickly than is possible with a personal computer and transmitted back over the internet.

If cloud computing becomes commonplace then it will change the type of computers we own. With no need for powerful processors or large amounts of data storage, devices can become much smaller. Taken to the extreme, a universal remote control computer might be little more than a screen with a network connection and some way of identifying you to the network – all of the complexities of storing and processing data would be handled by the cloud. The computer of the future might resemble a mobile phone more than a PC. We can glimpse this future in the form of the smart phone: a type of mobile telephone containing enough processing power and memory to run complex applications such as web browsers, productivity packages (word processors and spreadsheets), media players and games. This might all sound strangely familiar: in many ways cloud computing is very similar to the way people interacted with the mainframe computers of the 1950s and 1960s before Alan Kay had his epiphany! You will be able to learn more about cloud computing in a later part.

The number of mobile phones already exceeds that of PCs, and the rate at which sales are growing is higher than that for PCs. Smart phones accounted for only about 13% of the 269 million handsets sold in 2008, but they represented the fastest-growing segment of the mobile phone market. In time, all mobile phones will be smart phones and the majority of devices people use to connect to the internet will be mobile phones.

Activity 20 (exploratory)

Why do you think smart phones are proving so popular with consumers?

Comment

There are many reasons, but here are three that I thought of.

- Part of the attraction must lie with the ability to access information almost anywhere – people like being able to send and receive email, send instant messages and update their friends on social networking sites.
- Another aspect might be that smart phones come with attractive features such as music players and games.
- Finally, many handsets are relatively cheap because they are subsidised by mobile networks or even offered free in exchange for lengthy contracts. They are a much more affordable way of getting online.

Activity 21 (self-assessment)

Can a smart phone be thought of as an example of Weiser's *tab* computers?

Activity 22 (exploratory)

In a previous activity you were asked what designers of early PCs had to bear in mind when considering their users. What assumptions do you think the designers of ubiquitous computers can make about their users?

Comment

You might have realised that the designers of the ubiquitous computers of tomorrow will not be able to make any assumptions about their users. If computers are going to be everywhere then they might be interacting with people of all ages, cultures, nationalities, intelligences, disabilities, religions and social backgrounds. This poses a huge challenge for designers, and you should not be surprised to learn that there are no simple solutions. I will explore some of these issues in greater detail at the end of this part.

Activity 23 (exploratory)

In the resources page associated with this part on the TU100 website, I have listed a number of examples of ubiquitous computing applications that have been developed in the laboratory. Choose two examples from the list and perform a small amount of research into them using the Web. For each example, write one or two paragraphs in your own words explaining the purpose of the device; then explain why it is a ubiquitous computer according to Weiser's definition that you explored earlier. Finally, in no more than a paragraph, say whether you would find these devices useful in your life or the lives of friends and relatives.

3.4 Conclusion

This session introduced you to a new concept in computing technology called ubiquitous computing. The term was coined by Mark Weiser in a 1991 *Scientific American* paper, laying out many of the concepts used by ubicomp researchers today. Weiser's paper defined a number of types of ubiquitous computer, most of which have not yet been realised. It also laid out a near-future scenario showing how ubicomp might be used in everyday life.

A key part of this session was an extended activity where you searched for information (in this case Weiser's paper) using a number of sources. You learned that the same piece of information was available in a number of forms, some of which were more satisfactory than others. Finally you used the Open University Library to locate the definitive version of the paper.

After reading Weiser's paper you were in a position to define a ubiquitous computer and explored a few examples of actual ubicomp applications, ranging from extremely large to extremely small-scale devices.

Finally, this session introduced the concept of the cloud as a mechanism for providing ubiquitous services to users. Cloud computing could result in a dramatically different type of computer; one that relies on remote computers and high-speed networks to store, process and move data, reducing the personal computer to little more than a networked display device with some form of input.

This session should have helped you with the following learning outcomes.

- Use the Open University Library facilities to locate articles published in a journal.
- Explain the purpose of scientific papers, and identify key parts of a scientific paper.
- Define ubiquitous computing and give some examples.
- Explain the concept of 'persuasive computing'.
- Evaluate evidence relating to social, economic, political and personal issues raised by the development of modern computers.
- Write summaries, explanations and descriptions in your own words using an effective structure.

4

It's more than just computers

So far I have considered the ubiquitous computing world in terms of computers – devices, which even after generations of Moore's law still cost a considerable amount of money. Even if we accept that Moore's law and economies of scale will continue to drive down the manufacturing cost of a computer, it will never reach zero. A ubicomp computer will always be more expensive than the much larger number of other manufactured objects whose cost ranges from a few pounds to infinitesimal fractions of a penny. We use many of these objects every day without thinking about their individual cost – after all, how much does a single paper clip cost, or an individual sheet of paper? Most of these 'dumb objects' are simple, disposable artefacts that we casually use and dispose of when no longer needed; however, dumb objects often carry useful amounts of information.

Activity 24 (exploratory)

Food packaging is a good example of a 'dumb object' that has no computer power but that holds a lot of information. Choose an item of food packaging in your household. List the types of information on the packaging and give a reason why you think they might be there.

Comment

I chose a soft drink can, shown in Figure 16.

I noticed the following types of information on it (not all of which are visible in the image).

- Branding – to identify it on the shelves and distinguish it from rival brands.
- Volume – how much of the product is in the can.
- Serving suggestion – how best to enjoy the product.
- Link to the manufacturer's website – additional marketing.
- Ingredients – what is used in the product's manufacture, useful for people seeking to avoid certain ingredients (e.g. sugar) for dietary or medical reasons.
- Nutritional information – useful for people monitoring their calorie intake.
- Recycling information – what the can is made from (aluminium) and how to dispose of it when no longer needed.

Figure 16   A soft drink can

- Expiry date – health information, giving the date after which the product should no longer be used.
- Manufacturer's address and phone number – contact details for customer complaints, etc.

If we are to live in a truly ubicomp world then dumb objects such as soft drink cans will need to interact with computers and computerised systems. Dumb objects need to be identifiable – either as one of a kind of object (*a soft drink can*) or, ideally, as an individual (*soft drink can number 5936 927 710*). Such identifiers are known as *tags* and the process of applying a tag to an object is called *tagging*.

4.1   Smart labels

Look again at the soft drink can in Figure 16. You can see that the surface of the can is already crammed with information, but there is plenty more information that could be included. The can is only labelled in English, posing problems for non-English speakers, especially those with medical, dietary or religious restrictions on their diet. It might be possible to cram additional languages onto the can, but which ones? Canada has two official languages, South Africa has eleven and the European Union has 23! Either the can would have to be made much larger to accommodate all this, or the print would have to shrink to an unusably small size.

If there were enough room, there is plenty of other information that could be included on the can. It could contain information about the working conditions of the people who raise the crops used in the drink, who work in the canneries and who distribute the product. It could explain the environmental stance of the company – such as what herbicides and pesticides are used, the source of the metal in the can, the purity of the water and the amount of energy needed to make the can and its contents and deliver it to shops – the health benefits or otherwise of the ingredients, and so on and on.

In fact, that humble drink can already has ways of providing more information than can fit on the physical container: there are telephone, postal and web links where customers can ask for more information about the drink and the company. When I type in the URL on the can, I'm taken to a site advertising this and other brands. The site also gives detailed health information, careers information and information about the manufacturer's ethical stance. However, printing a web link is a slightly clumsy way of creating a smarter object. Rather than making the can smart, a web link relies on a smart user keying in the URL. It would be better to label the can in such a way that it can be read by computers.

Barcodes

Perhaps the most familiar kind of machine-readable information is the *barcode*. This was developed as long ago as 1949, but only standardised in 1973 around the IBM *universal product code (UPC)*. A UPC barcode represents twelve decimal digits using lines of varying thickness; two of the digits are reserved for special purposes and the other ten serve to uniquely identify the type of item. When an item is scanned at a supermarket checkout, the number associated with the barcode is sent to the store's main computer or transmitted over the internet, where it is used to retrieve the corresponding price in the store's database. The price is returned to the checkout computer, which calculates the final bill.

The very first sale made using barcodes and a reader was of a pack of Wrigley's chewing gum at 08:01 on 26 June 1974 in Marsh Supermarket in Troy, Ohio. You will be delighted to learn that this great moment has been preserved; the gum was rescued from being consumed and is now in the Smithsonian Institution in Washington, DC.

In fact, the greatest benefit of barcodes has not been making transactions easier for shoppers and cashiers; it has been in the field of stock control. Because every barcode transaction is immediately recorded, it provides up-to-the-minute records of every product in stock and the rate at which they are being consumed. Stores and warehouses can therefore order just-in-time replacements rather than having to keep items in stock for prolonged periods or run out. Likewise, bestselling items can be promoted more heavily and underperforming stock removed from sale, or discounted much more readily than before.

With room for only ten digits, the original UPC does not contain very much information. Indeed, there are so many products being sold these days that longer barcodes are now commonplace. However, it is possible to make barcodes that contain even more information. A UPC is read as a single line of text:

00169 01240

More information could be stored if the barcode was two-dimensional, consisting of line after line of digits:

00169 01240

33895 32008

88888 05040

The biggest restriction of the tags mentioned so far is that they only store numbers. Digits might have been useful for identifying product lines, but we use far more textual information than numeric – names, addresses, URLs and so on. And we don't just use alphabetical information; a large proportion of the world's population uses pictographic languages (such as Chinese and Japanese). Tags would be even more useful if they could hold any type of information encoded in a computer-readable format such as binary.

QR codes and other 2D codes

One of the most widespread two-dimensional barcodes is the 'Quick Response' (QR) code from the Denso Corporation of Japan. A QR code is a square block of black and white pixels that can be printed alongside text on paper or plastic. These codes have become extremely popular in Japan, where they are regularly used on consumer packaging and in magazines. They have proved attractive because they can be read by any digital camera (including those on mobile phones) equipped with the necessary decoding software, which is often pre-installed on Japanese mobile phones. Figure 17 shows the QR code for the URL of the TU100 public website.

Computers can recognise the code in an image because of its high contrast against the background and because of the three position recognition markers set into the top left, top right and bottom left of the code. These markers not only show the corners of the code, but also allow the computer to correct for the code being held at an angle or being printed on a surface that is not entirely flat. An additional position marker can be located near the bottom right and is used on large codes where there is more likelihood of distortion or damage to the underlying surface. Once the computer has recognised the code's presence, the information held in the code can be reconstructed from the pattern of the black and white pixels.

Figure 17   QR code for the URL of the TU100 public website (http://tu100.open.ac.uk)

QR codes can contain varying amounts of data. The largest can contain up to 7089 decimal digits or 4296 alphanumeric characters. QR codes are not restricted to familiar Western characters; instead, thanks to a system known as Unicode (see Box 5), they can represent almost any writing system in the world.

Box 5 Unicode

Computers were invented in the West and were originally restricted to the small number of characters used in Western languages. However, as computers have become ever more widespread they have needed to display an ever greater range of symbols. Unicode is an attempt to produce a single, standardised set of symbols that can be used by any computer system. The project is far from complete, but so far characters from more than 90 languages – as well as numbers, punctuation and musical and mathematical notation – have been stored in more than 107 000 Unicode characters. Unicode is supported by all major operating systems and applications.

Activity 25 (self-assessment)

A standard UPC barcode contains twelve decimal digits. How many times this amount of numeric information can be stored in the largest QR code? You may wish to use a calculator for this activity.

QR codes have spread from these relatively conventional domains and are becoming popular with designers and planners alike. Tokyo's fashionable Ginza district has incorporated them into street signs, allowing confused

Westerners to access local information without having to learn Japanese. Free online QR code generators mean that anyone can design their own personal code and use it without paying for a licence. The codes have even been adopted by graffiti artists, who incorporate personal codes into their work. Passers-by can scan the code using their phone and are linked to a web page containing a message from the artist.

Other 2D barcode standards are also being developed. ColorCode, developed by South Korea's Yonsei University, stores information in square tiles containing patterns of red, blue, green and either black or white. Although originally laid out in blocky tiles, inspired designers have begun to produce ColorCodes incorporating corporate logos, flowers and even small pictures. A 5 by 5 four-colour square can hold one of more than 17 billion unique identifiers, and larger patterns are possible. Perhaps for nationalistic reasons, ColorCode has proved incredibly popular within South Korea and is making inroads into the lucrative Japanese market. In Figure 18, a conventional four-colour square code made up from a 5 by 5 pattern of square tiles is shown on the left. The ColorCode for the Japanese Apamanshop Network property rental company in the middle obviously uses a 5 by 5 grid, but the right-hand tile for the Shonan Koshigoe beach resort in Japan hides the pattern in an attractive artwork.

Figure 18   A range of ColorCode symbols

Even more ambitiously, the Fujitsu group developed Fine Picture (FP) code, a pattern of fine yellow lines that can be printed over any picture without obscuring the image. Normally invisible to the human eye, the lines can be reconstructed by a suitably equipped mobile phone, although this does raise the intriguing question of how people will know if pictures contain FP codes or not!

The future of smart labelling

Machine-readable tags can be applied to almost any item using conventional printing technology. As such, once incorporated into a design, label or advertisement they are remarkably cheap – costing a tiny fraction of a penny apiece.

Printing technology already exists that allows for unique tags to be placed on each item as it comes off the production line. Technologies such as QR codes can store very large serial numbers in a relatively small amount of space. These numbers can be tracked throughout an object's lifetime with delivery teams, warehouse employees, customers and disposal companies

You will have used machine-readable tags if you have printed an airline boarding pass or train ticket on your own printer.

scanning tags when the object enters and leaves their care, with the resulting information being stored in a database. Once an object can be individually labelled it becomes much easier to calculate the total cost of projects, determine the origin of components, order replacements when they fail and dispose of objects safely.

When tags appear on products, other companies and individuals find uses for them – ones that could not have been envisioned by their originators or the manufacturers. Barcodes might originally have been designed as a way of accurately tracking and pricing goods, but they have spawned businesses as diverse as Barcode Battler, a phenomenally popular Japanese game from the 1990s in which players scanned everyday barcodes to 'power-up' their game characters and unlock treasures, through to RedLaser, an application for mobile phones that allows users to perform comparisons between in-shop prices and those available on the internet. We can be sure that new tagging technologies will spawn new companies, hobbies and interests – we simply can't predict what they will be.

Even if we don't know exactly what form these tags will take, it's reasonable to predict that many of them will contain an internet address. IPv6, introduced in Block 1, is easily capable of giving a unique identity to every manufactured object ever made (and all of those that are likely to be made into the foreseeable future). So even as humble an object as the soft drink can of the future might have its own internet address. Even if the can itself is not connected to the internet, its printed tag could be scanned by a suitably equipped computer or phone.

Activity 26 (self-assessment)

Can you think of any health and safety benefits to consumers and manufacturers of putting individual tags on products?

4.2   Tagging and tangible computing

The type of tagging I have discussed so far allows dumb objects to have some form of presence on, or connection to, the internet. Similar technology has also been used to create novel methods of interacting with computers. The Music Technology Group at the Universitat Pompeu Fabra in Barcelona researches innovative ways of creating and playing music. One of its most popular projects is the Reactable, which emulates the earliest electronic synthesisers that created extraordinarily complex unique sounds by physically wiring electronic components together.

The Reactable is a circular translucent table set over a compact video projector and a video camera, both of which are connected to a personal computer (see Figure 19). The display is used in a darkened room, where the table surface appears as a luminous space onto which graphics are projected.

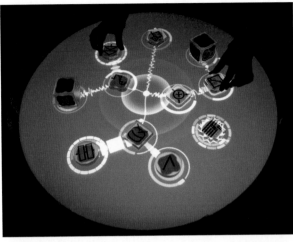

(a)

(b)

Figure 19   (a) The Barcelona Reactable; (b) close-up of pucks

Rather than relying on a keyboard or a mouse, the Reactable is an example of a *tangible device* – that is, one that users are expected to touch. Musicians place a range of small plastic pucks on the table surface. Each puck is responsible for a simple musical component such as sound generators, samplers, loops and filters. Placing a puck on the table adds a musical effect to the composition; bringing one puck close to another combines their effect, while rotating the pucks changes their volume.

At first it might be assumed that the pucks contain electronics that communicate with a PC under the table; however, the pucks are in fact nothing more than translucent plastic. The underside of each puck contains a printed tag called a reacTIVision marker (see Figure 20). These markers are examples of what are known as *fiduciary markers* (sometimes called *fiducials*).

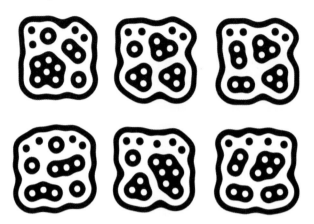

Figure 20   A set of reacTIVision fiduciary markers

Activity 27 (exploratory)

To help you understand how people use the Reactable, I have included a short video from its creators in the resources page associated with this part on the TU100 website. You should watch this video when convenient.

The fiduciary markers are points of reference for specialised computer software. With the room in darkness, the camera beneath the table only 'sees' the black and white markers. Images from the camera are processed by the computer in real time; the colour image is converted to black and white and the fiducials isolated.

Each fiducial corresponds to a particular function of the Reactable. So when a 'sound generator' puck is placed on the table, the computer not only recognises the fiducial associated with that puck but also begins to run the necessary software to play that sound. Each marker both uniquely identifies the puck it is attached to and allows the computer to locate it on the table's surface, so when two pucks are brought together the table's software can link them to create a more complex effect. The camera is also able to track a fiducial's rotation; as the user twists the puck on the table, the volume of the associated effect can be changed by the software just as if the user were turning a physical knob.

Some other applications for fiducials are given in Box 6.

Box 6 Fiducials

Outside the field of ubiquitous computing, fiducials are used as markers to identify parts of the body during motion capture. Computers monitor the changes in position of the fiducials and reconstruct a person's movement. This process is widely used in the generation of computer graphics for games and films, as well as in analysing the motion of athletes.

Fiducials made from gold or stainless steel are also used in cancer therapy. Radiation treatment can be very effective against cancer, but may damage healthy cells. The metal fiducials are placed around tumours to show their precise position on X-ray images. Radiation can then be precisely targeted at the tumours, minimising the risk to the patient's healthy cells.

Activity 28 (exploratory)

I have developed a simple fiducial application that could be useful to tourists planning a trip to an attraction. Follow the instructions in the resources page associated with this part on the TU100 website to download the application to your computer and have some fun with the materials. When you have finished, return to this text.

4.3 Tangible computing without tags

Microsoft Research Laboratories have developed their own tangible interface, code-named Milan, which has been sold commercially as *Surface*. The Surface table-top system appears to be superficially similar to Reactable. However, unlike Reactable, Surface does not need objects to carry tags; rather it uses image recognition software to detect and identify objects placed on the surface and to track the movements of people's fingers. When an object known to the system is placed on the table, the Surface software displays appropriate actions. If the object supports wireless networking, the table automatically creates a link allowing the table's user to browse the object's contents – so, for instance, if a suitably equipped mobile phone or media player is placed on the table then any photos held in its memory are displayed in a cloud around the device. Users can touch any of the photos and move them with their fingertips, dragging, rotating and resizing the images as they wish. Copying an image from one device to another is as simple as dragging the photo from its cloud to the cloud surrounding the destination object.

Surface can also recognise infrared tags, which behave like reacTIVision markers but are invisible to the human eye.

In 2008, Surface became the first commercially available *tangible computing* device when Microsoft began selling the tables to companies. So far it has been used by the US telecom giant AT&T as a point-of-sale information device, and by Sheraton Hotels where it is being placed in hotel lobbies to provide guests with local tourist information and act as a jukebox (see Figure 21).

Figure 21   Guests at Sheraton hotels across the USA can use Microsoft Surface computers installed in the lobby to learn about the surrounding area

4.4   Radio tagging

Obviously there are certain circumstances in which printed labels are not feasible – some objects are simply too small, or hidden inside other objects where they cannot be seen. One solution is to use a technology known as *radio frequency identification (RFID)*, which is similar to the electronic article surveillance tags used in stores to protect items such as DVDs and books.

The science fiction author, futurologist and technology writer Bruce Sterling has promoted the name 'arphid' for these tags.

RFID devices (generally called tags) consist of a small microchip and a radio antenna. The microchip contains a tiny amount of processing capacity and an equally small amount of memory – usually just enough to contain a unique identity number, as well as some specialised circuitry that can send and receive radio messages (see Figure 22).

The most common RFID tags are 'passive' (they contain no power source of their own). These work in conjunction with readers that can be incorporated into supermarket checkouts, ticket barriers or hand-held wands. The reader emits a low-powered radio signal that activates the chip in the tag. The chip then returns a very weak radio signal containing the data held in its memory, which is received by the reader; from there it

Figure 22   An enlarged image of an RFID device, which is about the size of a small postage stamp; the small black square near the centre of the image is the RFID chip, while the copper spiral is an antenna that sends and receives radio signals

can be processed like any other data. The alternative to this is 'active' RFID, in which the tag draws power from its own battery, but this is less common.

An example of passive RFID is the tag built into a London Underground Oyster card. When the card is brought near to the reader in the ticket barrier, the chip in the card broadcasts the unique account number of the ticket holder. The barrier receives this account number and requests the balance of the account from a central database. If the account number belongs to a valid account and there is enough money in the account, the barrier opens and the user can make their journey. The InClass system discussed earlier used RFID tags built into the frames of children's identity badges.

RFID tags can be made incredibly small, since they are manufactured using similar technologies to those used to build microchips and MEMS sensors. As an illustration, an experiment at Bristol University on the nesting behaviour of ants used RFID tags only 3 mm square glued to individual members of the colony (Figure 23).

Even this is far from the limit on the size of RFID tags. At the time of writing, the smallest tags are experimental devices produced by Hitachi that are only $150 \times 150 \times 7.5$ µm in size (100 µm is a common diameter for a single human hair). Further reductions in the size of RFID tags are possible, but reducing the size of the antenna means that the strength of

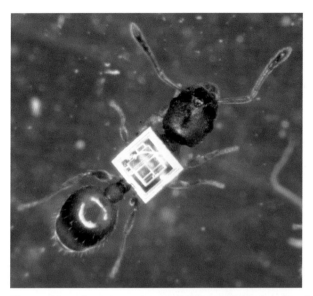

Figure 23   A rock worker ant with an RFID tag glued to its thorax as part of a scientific study of insect behaviour conducted by Bristol University

the radio signal also diminishes, requiring more sensitive (and more expensive) readers. Some experimental tags dispense with radio signals entirely and use light-detectors and tiny LEDs for communications. In theory these devices could be made much smaller than is possible for those relying on radio antennas.

RFID is a growing technology, driven in part by a rapid decline in the price of tags. As recently as 2007, a single basic tag cost approximately 50 cents; by mid-2009 the same tag cost less than 5 cents and prices have continued to fall. As tags have become cheaper, organisations have begun to incorporate them into products and packaging, allowing goods to be tracked through the supply chain. The Pentagon and Wal-Mart (the parent of Asda in the UK) were two of the first major users of RFID. In 2003, both organisations demanded that their leading suppliers begin to attach RFID to shipments. For the Pentagon this change in policy covered some 46 000 providers and cost over US$100 million. In both cases, RFID promised and delivered better inventory control and fewer lost or delayed consignments, with individual containers being tracked from the factory to the individual store or unit. The Pentagon is considering taking this process one step further by attaching RFID tags to individual items, allowing them to be tracked from manufacture to the end user.

RFID might even be able to help in another area where misplaced items cause problems: lost bags at airports, a problem that costs airlines around the world more than US$2.5 billion every year. At all but the very smallest airports, luggage handling has been automated. Paper luggage tags include 10-digit barcodes containing the flight number. A computer reads the barcode and directs the luggage into the appropriate container ready for transport to the plane. During luggage sorting, these paper tags can become dirty, torn or lost entirely, in which case the luggage cannot be directed to its destination. Up to 10% of all luggage must be hand-sorted, which is not only inconvenient for the passenger but also expensive for the airlines.

Activity 29 (self-assessment)

Why do you think RFID luggage tags might be a better solution than the existing paper tags?

Successful trials of RFID luggage tags have been conducted at Hong Kong International Airport, but no airline has yet replaced paper tags with the new technology. The introduction of RFID tags on luggage is likely to be gradual and involve an extended period where luggage will have to carry both types of tag; however, ever-increasing security demands and passenger dissatisfaction with lost luggage makes it likely that RFID will soon be widely deployed at major airports.

Activity 30 (self-assessment)

RFID tags on luggage appear to offer clear benefits to airlines. Why might they not have been adopted?

You will return to RFID tags in a later part.

4.5   Conclusion

This session covered the subject of tagging – adding computer-readable identifiers to objects that do not contain computer components. The session began with an explanation of why such identifiers could be useful on economic grounds and explored how the familiar barcode works. It then moved on to demonstrate other forms of tag that can store greater amounts of information about objects and be used to link to websites.

Another purpose of tags is to identify objects in time and space. They have been used to track objects moving in front of a camera to produce so-called tangible devices such as the Reactable musical synthesiser. You explored the potential of these tags in a couple of activities that showed how they could be used to supplement information on physical objects, such as tourism brochures, and to track hand motions.

Finally you learned about RFID tags, which can be read remotely using wireless technology. A more detailed explanation of RFID will follow later in the module.

Table 2 compares the different types of tagging systems covered in this session.

Table 2   Different types of tagging systems

Tag type	Scanned using	Characteristics	In commercial use?
UPC barcode	Laser or still camera	1D black and white	Yes
QR Code	Still camera	2D black and white	Yes
ColorCode	Still camera	2D colour printing	Yes (mostly in Asia)
FP Code	Still camera	2D colour printing	No (2010)
ReacTIVision	Video camera	2D black and white	Yes
RFID	Radio	Microchip	Yes

This session should have helped you with the following learning outcomes.

- Explain what is meant by tagging and give some examples of printed tags.
- Explain the principles of radio frequency identification (RFID) and how it can be used to tag objects.
- Carry out calculations using scientific notation.

Ambient computing

5

We live in an age where people are said to have increasingly short attention spans. More and more of us seem to prefer ever quicker ways of communicating, whether it be email, SMS or the 140-character limit of Twitter messages. At the same time as wanting shorter, more to-the-point methods of communicating, we are also sending and receiving more information. We are in danger of being overwhelmed by a flood of information from a multitude of sources. Figure 24 shows a typical computer screen.

This computer screen is fairly typical of my way of working. Although I am busy working in a word processor, a number of other applications are running and actively downloading new information. My email program downloads new mail every quarter of an hour; the main window

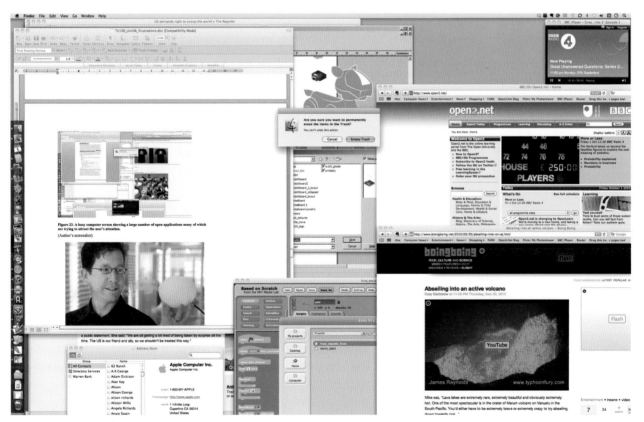

Figure 24　**A busy computer screen showing a large number of open applications, many of which are trying to attract the user's attention**

of the web browser is currently pointed at an RSS news feed which is refreshed every half hour, while the smaller window is playing the live BBC Radio 4 broadcast. As well as these obvious demands for my attention, the computer is also displaying a number of other information feeds – a clock dial in the top right of the window is next to a series of other icons showing the state of my wireless connections and the status of my online storage and backup disks. In addition to all this information, the computer is demanding I answer a question about whether I really want to empty the trash.

5.1 Your attention is the only limited resource

Although the range of available information sources has exploded in the last few decades and they are more up-to-date and comprehensive than ever before, one thing has not increased at nearly the same rate – our ability to assimilate information. All these sources of information must now compete for a limited amount of attention. Coming up with methods of attracting our attention is something that advertisers have a great deal of experience in achieving.

Activity 31 (exploratory)

Take a few minutes to consider a range of advertising from a variety of media (such as in print, on TV, online or on the radio). Try to identify some ways in which advertisers try to gain our attention.

Comment

Some of the ways I found were:

- bold use of colours, large text, clear images (easyJet, the AA, Apple)
- beautiful people (any fashion or perfume company)
- on television, changing the sound so it is perceived as being louder than surrounding programs
- similarly, shouting a message, or using memorable jingles or sounds
- slogans (*Vorsprung durch Technik* – Audi, *A Diamond is Forever* – De Beers)
- humour.

Imagine the unbearable cacophony of a world of ubiquitous computers, all of which tried to attract our attention using the methods developed by advertisers. It would be almost impossible to complete any tasks without being interrupted by one or another computer – and if the future is anything like the present, many of those interruptions would be advertising.

5.2   Calming down the computer

Clearly a new way of interacting with computers is needed; one where computers do not actively attract attention (unless requested by the user), but instead live quietly in the background. Such a computer could provide limited amounts of information – such as changes in temperature, household power consumption or the presence of certain people – by changing their colour, playing an unobtrusive sound or even changing their shape, size or texture. Creators of such devices have tried to design interfaces from which a useful amount of information can be gained just by glancing at them (or hearing a single musical tone, touching their surface and so on). Because this type of computer could only display a small amount of information before it became too intrusive, each of us (or our homes, offices, car, etc.) would have many such devices, each one dedicated to delivering a single service. This idea has been called *ambient computing* or, perhaps more poetically, *calm computing*.

One of the first demonstrations of ambient computing was the ambientROOM developed by the Tangible Media Group at MIT's Media Lab. First demonstrated in 1998, the ambientROOM was a freestanding area configured as an office space. Information could be conveyed using patterns of light and sound. Changes in information, such as the number of unread email messages or fluctuations in stocks and shares, were reflected in changes to the environment of the room. The creators of the room chose 'natural' phenomena such as imitations of sunlight, birdsong and rainfall to carry information. These patterns are familiar from everyday life and we are extremely good at 'tuning them out' so that they do not interfere with our concentration. However, we are equally good at noticing changes in these phenomena – when they begin, stop and fluctuate – and it is these changes that carry important messages in the ambientROOM.

5.3   Ambient computing is here already

Ambient computing became a consumer product in 2002 when Massachusetts-based Ambient Devices released the Ambient Orb, a US$150 device that looked like no previous computer (Figure 25). Rather than a familiar plastic box with a screen, keyboard and mouse, the Orb was a grapefruit-sized frosted glass sphere that glowed from within using a number of coloured LEDs. The Orb also contained a wireless receiver and tiny computer, and was configured to receive data from a number of wireless services and reflect changes in the value of this data by gradually varying its colour. One of the most popular services tracked fluctuations in the stock market; increases in prices made the device glow green, while declines were shown in red.

Figure 25   David Rose, president of Ambient Devices, holding an Ambient Orb

You may wonder why Ambient Devices chose to focus on the stock market when developing the Orb. In fact, the creators of many early ubiquitous computing projects thought that potential customers were interested in every movement of the stock market. This is probably a reflection of the 1990s economic boom and the fact that many of these systems originated in the USA. If the projects had been British they would probably have concentrated on the weather! In fact, you will be designing just such a device in a later activity.

Activity 32 (self-assessment)

The Ambient Orb allows you to track changes in data using changes in its colour. What can't it tell you about this data?

Ambient Device's business plan was to make money not only by selling Orbs, but also by charging users a monthly subscription service for certain data feeds such as personal stock portfolios. Users could also opt for a premium service and have their Orbs report the status of personal information.

The Orb was only the first of Ambient's products. The Energy Joule (Figure 26) is a smart energy meter that not only provides useful information about household energy consumption, but also supplies weather forecasts (allowing users to plan their heating or air conditioning needs). The background of the Energy Joule changes colour from green (when power is cheapest) through yellow to red (when energy is most expensive), reflecting the changing price of electricity throughout the day.

Figure 26   Three views of Ambient Device's Energy Joule smart meter: as well as providing detailed information about the energy usage of the home, it can display the local weather and tell users about energy-saving plans offered by their power company

Activity 33 (self-assessment)

Do you think the Energy Joule is a true ambient computing device? Is it a ubiquitous computing device?

Perhaps Ambient's most unusual device is the Ambient Umbrella, which responds to predictions of bad weather by changing the colour and brightness of lights in the handle. The umbrella uses a wireless internet connection to remain in constant contact with a weather forecasting service provided by AccuWeather.com to some 150 US cities. Of course, the age-old problem of forgetting to take your umbrella with you is now replaced by the problem of remembering to charge your umbrella's power supply!

Microsoft's Cambridge Research Laboratory has developed a semi-ambient device whose inspiration comes from the *Harry Potter* novels. The Microsoft Whereabouts Clock (Figure 27) is designed for homes and shows, at a glance, where members of the family are. A circular screen is divided into segments – one for each location, such as home, work and school. The Whereabouts Clock displays a picture of each person in the appropriate segment of the screen. The clock receives location information from users' mobile phones; as they move between locations, their image on the clock moves from segment to segment. You can see that the clock resembles a domestic appliance much more than a computer.

(a)

(b)

Figure 27 **(a) Laboratory prototype of the Microsoft Whereabouts Clock; (b) close-up of the screen of the clock with the flap removed**

Activity 34 (exploratory)

Now that you have learned about ambient devices, it is time to use the Sense programming environment to build one for yourself. This activity comprises a number of short sections, some of which will help you to revise what you have already learned. You will find the instructions for it in the Sense activities section of the 'Study resources' page on the TU100 website.

This activity will take you between 2 and 3 hours, so make sure you leave enough time to complete it.

5.4 Conclusion

In this session you learned about ambient computing, an attempt to overcome the possibility that people will be overwhelmed by the amount of information they receive. Ambient computing aims to make computers less intrusive while still providing useful amounts of information.

You then spent some time developing your programming skills with Sense by building an application that uses ambient principles to display live information, first from a sensor connected directly to the SenseBoard and then using the internet to read information from a remote location.

This session should have helped you with the following learning outcomes.

- Define ambient computing and give some examples.
- Evaluate evidence relating to social, economic, political and personal issues raised by the development of modern computers.
- Analyse a simple problem and identify the operations required for a solution.
- Discuss some of the legal and ethical issues raised by the processing, storage and communication of information produced by ubiquitous computers, and make reasoned arguments about these issues.
- Use Sense and the SenseBoard to build a small digital system.

6

Living in a ubiquitous world

Even before we move into a world of ubiquitous and pervasive computing, researchers are becoming increasingly concerned with the possible unintended consequences of deploying computer systems on such an incredible scale. To conclude this part, I will look at just a few of the problems that as yet have no clear solution.

6.1 Artificial intelligence

One of the most popular futuristic ubicomp devices is a mobile phone that behaves in different ways depending on what you're doing and where you are. It might ring most of the time, but automatically switch to voicemail when you are in a meeting or at the cinema, switch to hands-free operation when you are driving, and turn off entirely when you board an airliner. This is quite an appealing prospect; there can't be many people who haven't been annoyed by a phone (sometimes their own) ringing at an inappropriate moment, and superficially it appears simpler to build a smarter phone than a more considerate user. However, it is much harder to realise such a device than to describe it on the page. The problem can be described as one of *context awareness*: how does a telephone know that you are in a cinema and should remain silent, or that you are a passenger in a car who can take calls rather than a driver who should not be distracted, or that your flight has landed safely and has been delayed waiting for an available gate rather than being late but still in flight?

Many of the ubiquitous computing systems that have been proposed require what is known as *artificial intelligence (AI)* to make them work. AI is a long-standing field of computer research that is concerned with simulating intelligent activities seen in animals and people such as machine learning, image recognition, planning and understanding language. Although a staple of science fiction writers and filmmakers, AI has proved to be extremely hard to achieve. While AI has proved hugely successful in certain limited areas, it has so far failed to demonstrate that it can replicate human intelligence or even perform apparently simple tasks such as understanding a simple conversation. As you saw at the start of this part, the incredibly influential film *2001: A Space Odyssey* was written with the assistance of leading computer scientists, all of whom were confident that an intelligent computer could be realised by the turn of the twenty-first century. Perhaps fortunately, realisation of the film's homicidal HAL 9000 supercomputer lies decades in the future, if it is possible at all.

Ubiquitous computing scenarios that suggest we will interact with computers using speech, or those that predict the development of intelligent buildings that can interpret their users' moods, rely on as-yet undeveloped AI techniques. Often the requirement for AI is omitted from the description entirely, giving the misleading impression that the ubicomp device can be built using existing technology.

6.2   The law of unintended consequences

All good designers must take time to work out the consequences of using their products. Obviously a great deal of time is spent exploring the benefits of any new product – does it save you time? Make you happier? Clean up the environment? Increasingly, product designers are also confronting the negative implications of using their products: all new electrical appliances come with energy ratings informing you how much power they consume, cars list their fuel consumption and carbon dioxide emissions, and even soft drinks tell you not to overindulge. Generally we are very good at working out the direct consequences of using a novel technology, but much less capable of working out the indirect consequences– especially when technologies are combined with one another, leading to unpredictable interactions.

The world of ubiquitous computing promises (or threatens) to produce any number of unexpected consequences. That is because it will be possible to monitor, and act on, a huge number of data sources. The designers of these technologies will be tempted to combine data sources to produce entirely new applications and products.

Example 1: Medical information

The Japanese company Toto already makes an 'intelligence toilet' containing a number of sensors that can measure blood sugar, blood pressure, body fat and weight. The toilet makes the necessary measurements and sends the results to a home PC in less than a minute, where they can be viewed as a spreadsheet or as time charts along with relevant health advice.

There is no technological reason why this data could not be sent outside the household – to doctors or medical insurance companies, say. For someone in seemingly good health, this might be beneficial; they would be more likely to receive early diagnosis of degenerative conditions such as diabetes, they might receive personalised exercise regimes, and if they have private medical insurance then their premiums could be lower.

Activity 35 (exploratory)

There are some drawbacks to allowing personal medical information to be transmitted to a remote location. Using the example of the hypothetical toilet above, try to think of some problems that might be encountered by users.

Comment

I thought of the following potential problems:

- Users might be reluctant to use the technology if they felt that personal information was being seen by people they did not necessarily know or indeed trust.

- There is a security risk in sending any personal information to a remote location. It might be lost or copied in transit, or at its final destination.

- Users might not like being told about their unhealthy habits by a piece of technology.

- Unhealthy people might have problems obtaining healthcare or insurance if they had one of these toilets and it reported adverse information about them.

- People might be compelled to buy this technology in order to qualify for medical cover.

You may have thought of more.

Example 2: Databases and sensors

US law requires information about individual political donations to be made available on public websites – today, if you want to know about political donors then you just have to go online and do a little bit of searching. And smart CCTV systems can identify individuals from their faces or even their walk patterns. A little into the future, it will be relatively simple to combine these two apparently disparate sources of information to do something useful: identify people in a public area and know something about their personal political affiliations. Data could also be obtained from police records, border controls, even our shopping patterns.

In themselves neither the databases nor the sensors are malign, but it is arguable that combining the two is not in our best interests. How can we guarantee that these possibilities will not be misused, either by companies who want to target us for advertising or by governments? How will we even know if such systems exist and are in operation?

Activity 36 (exploratory)

California state law requires that anyone convicted of child sex offences remains on parole for the remainder of their life after serving their sentence. A common condition of their parole is that they must not come within a set distance of their victims, schools or children's play areas. Failure to comply with the terms of the parole results in the offender being returned to prison.

In recent years, parolees have been constantly monitored using electronic ankle tags that must be worn at all times. Each tag contains a GPS receiver and a mobile phone transmitter that regularly sends the parolee's geographic coordinates to their case worker. An automatic alert is sounded if the parolee breaks the conditions of their parole. The parolee commits an offence if their tag is removed or disabled in any way. If the tag does not make regular contact with the parole officer's computer then another alert sounds. The parole officer must take some form of action if they receive any alerts from the tags.

(a) Is the ankle tag system a ubiquitous computer system?

(b) Can you think of some unforeseen consequences of using this technology?

Comment

(a) It is most definitely a ubiquitous computer system. The tag contains a small computer and a network connection and runs a ubiquitous application (storing and transmitting time and position information).

(b) There are a number of issues raised by the tag system. These include – but are not limited to – the following.

- The parolee might simply be passing close to a forbidden area to get to somewhere else. They may be using a bus, the route of which they have no control over, or they may be unaware of a new school or play area.

- Tags break and batteries fail without warning, or the parolee might simply forget to charge their tag.

- GPS is not a completely reliable technology. There are large numbers of black spots, such as valleys or areas with thick vegetation where it is not possible to pick up satellite transmissions. It does not work indoors or in some vehicles. And finally, GPS receivers can 'drift' with time, reporting incorrect geographic coordinates.

Tag technology promised a solution to many problems, but it has also seen an increase in the workload of parole officers who must deal with false alarms as well as handling genuine breaches of parole. A significant drawback to the tags is that parole officers now spend less time working in the community and with parolees, and more time with computers. Unexpectedly, the system has also resulted in greater public expenditure; because parole officers have less time for their cases, more officers must be recruited and trained to cover all of the workload.

This research was conducted by a team from the University of California Davis, led by Irina Shklovski, and presented in a paper at the UbiComp 2009 conference in Orlando, Florida (Shklovski et al., 2009). If you wish to know more about this study then you can find a link to the paper on the resources page associated with this part on the TU100 website.

6.3   Identifying and fixing problems

The next problem is one that is all too familiar to existing computer users. Upgrading computers, plugging in new peripherals or installing new software can result in complete failure, intermittent problems, or an existing piece of hardware or software suddenly stopping altogether. Despite the best attempts of manufacturers, devices often don't work as advertised or contain undocumented bugs that prevent them from behaving correctly. The worst of these problems arise when different manufacturers or software programmers interpret standards in slightly different ways – devices that *should* be compatible, and are advertised as such, *might* not be.

In the current world of computing, where it is relatively easy to identify computing devices or pieces of software, many of these problems can be resolved by the relatively simple task of either rebooting the computer or updating the relevant software. But imagine how complicated this task might be when each of us is surrounded by an ever-changing cloud of hundreds, if not thousands, of computers. In such an environment it might simply be impossible to locate, let alone identify, all the computers we are interacting with – and there is a very high probability we won't own most of them.

Faced with such problems, we might be forced to switch off all the ubiquitous computers and then gradually turn them back on again one by one until the fault can be isolated, or to disconnect our own devices from the wider network. But is this really possible when ubiquitous devices might be responsible for maintaining our health, controlling the flow of traffic in a city or even keeping a building standing in the middle of a storm or earthquake?

6.4   Am I being watched?

The future of computing is one in which users may be completely unaware that they are interacting with a computer at all. As we use these machines, they will inevitably gather information about us – not just information we choose to enter, but also information about how, when and where we use computers.

Even in liberal Western democracies the use of the internet is closely monitored by law-enforcement bodies. Internet service providers already collect large amounts of information about users including the time they log on, how long they connect, the telephone number being used and so on. In some countries, ISPs might also collect the URLs of visited websites and the destination addresses of email messages.

When a mobile phone connects to a network, it sends its unique identity to nearby transmitters so that they can route calls to and from the phone. As the user carries the phone from place to place, the phone's identity is recorded by a series of towers along with the time and date it enters and leaves their domain. It is quite easy for telephone operators (and increasingly third parties) to use this information to reconstruct the movement of phones – and presumably the movements of their owners.

As I mentioned in a previous section, RFID tags can be scanned at a distance. There is no requirement that the person carrying the tag need know that this has been done. A common ubicomp scenario that you may find thrilling, or deeply depressing, is for advertising boards and shops to incorporate RFID readers scanning for tags on passers-by. Shoppers would then receive targeted advertisements, perhaps encouraging them to buy more of their favourite brands or to switch to a competitor.

Many of the concerns over privacy and ubicomp are unique to Western democracies and have been coloured by popular culture. Aldous Huxley's novel *Brave New World*, Philip K. Dick's short story *Minority Report* and Terry Gilliam's film *Brazil* all feature powerful corporations or governments using technology to intrude on private lives.

Conversely, many Asian societies regard the state as having a beneficial guiding role in an individual's development. One (quite extreme) example of this relationship is Singapore's Social Development Unit – Social Development Service (SDU–SDS). Founded in 1984, it is a state-run dating service aimed at increasing the number of Singaporean graduates who marry one another, in the belief that they are more likely to raise highly educated children. All graduates from Singapore's leading universities are automatically enrolled in the system (there is an opt-out), as well as employees of major businesses. SDU–SDS maintains a database containing personal information about all its members, which is made available to accredited dating agencies. The service also arranges events at which graduates can meet one another, ranging from dance classes to wine appreciation and foreign travel.

Finally, we must consider the rights of those who may not be in a position to make informed choices about their privacy. Earlier, you learned about the deployment of the InClass registration system in a Californian school where neither children nor their parents were given an opportunity to express their opinions. In the UK there has been some controversy over children being fingerprinted to gain access to school libraries or receive school dinners – again, children are frequently not asked their opinions on whether they wish to engage with a computer system. A world where ubiquitous computing is commonplace will undoubtedly produce many more situations where our privacy can be affected.

6.5 Who's in charge?

At the moment, that's an easy question to answer – the person pressing buttons on the keyboard, or holding the phone, or putting their bank card into an ATM is the 'user' of a computer. The computer handles their interactions to the exclusion of almost everything else. Yet problems arise when we have to share computing resources. The situation quickly becomes similar to two children fighting over a toy – who should the computer obey?

Imagine the smart house of the future, equipped with sensors that allow it to know who is in the house at any given time. Perhaps you like the living room cool; your partner prefers it much warmer. When just one of you is in the living room, the solution is simple: the computer chooses that person's preference. But what should happen when both of you decide to sit down together? Is one person considered more important than the other? Should the computer try to find a temperature between your two preferences? Should it enter into some form of negotiation between the two users, or should it give control back to the users and allow them to fight it out between themselves?

Obviously this example is a simplification; a smart home could be monitoring hundreds of factors and many people as members of the family, their friends and neighbours enter and leave its area of responsibility. Ideally, all these interactions will take place without the users ever noticing that a computer has intervened; any ubiquitous system that requires a lot of button-pressing before it can accommodate our needs will have failed Weiser's vision and will most likely end up unplugged and unloved.

6.6 How do I opt out?

I'd hope that you and your fellow students are enthusiastic about the potential of ubiquitous computing, but I have to recognise that many people will be horrified by the possibility of a world filled with computers mediating almost every human activity. Even those of us who think that ubicomp offers enormous benefits differ on the boundaries beyond which this technology might be considered intrusive.

A potentially huge question for society is how far ubiquitous technologies will become compulsory for citizens. Devices that monitor our health, our energy use, the environment, traffic flow, suspicious behaviour and a hundred other aspects of everyday life become useful only when they are widely deployed across countries and populations. Attempts by democratic governments to force computer technologies on people, such as the ill-fated British scheme for biometric identity cards, have generally met with resistance as they are seen to be infringing personal rights.

Technologists have recognised a condition in society known as 'the digital divide' for a long time. People can be excluded from the benefits of digital technologies because of relative or actual poverty, poor power or network infrastructure, lack of education or support for their language, and many other reasons.

Whether people choose to disengage from technologies or are excluded from their benefits, there is a risk that sizeable populations might become an underclass in their own society.

Activity 37 (exploratory)

Finally, a chance to relax. The science fiction author and technology correspondent Cory Doctorow wrote a short story called *The Penalty Kick* for The Open University. This story uses a number of concepts discussed in this part and should give you some ideas about the potential threats raised by ubiquitous computing.

You will find the story in the resources page associated with this part on the TU100 website. You should spend a few minutes reading it, making notes on the issues and technologies that you feel are significant.

6.7   Conclusion

This session gave you a brief introduction to some of the potential pitfalls awaiting ubiquitous computing, ranging from purely technological issues such as the shortcomings of current artificial intelligence techniques through to purely social concerns that can never be solved by technology. Many of these issues are not unique to ubicomp, and some of them have well-established histories in other technological developments; however, if ubiquitous computing is to become – as the name suggests – ubiquitous, these problems and concerns have the potential to affect far more people than any of their predecessors.

Hopefully by the end of this session you will have become aware that every technological development has consequences for its users. Some of these consequences are beneficial, some are not; some consequences are easy to predict, many are hard to forecast; however, as responsible developers, it is our task to consider as many outcomes as possible and to make plans for the future.

This session should have helped you with the following learning outcomes.

- List some concerns over the deployment of ubiquitous computing.
- Evaluate evidence relating to social, economic, political and personal issues raised by the development of modern computers.
- Discuss some of the legal and ethical issues raised by the processing, storage and communication of information produced by ubiquitous computers, and make reasoned arguments about these issues.

Summary

This part of the block has introduced you to the world of ubiquitous computing, a technological field that could become the largest market for computing technology.

You explored technological trends that began in the 1960s and how they served to relentlessly drive down the cost of both individual components and computer systems.

The personal computer, first imagined by Alan Kay, has been the dominant computer system for more than three decades, but the same technological changes that made it possible have continued to reduce the size and cost of computing components until it is possible to place computing power in a wide range of devices. Many consumer devices such as cookers, television sets and cars contain embedded computers that either extend their functionality by adding new features, or serve to improve their efficiency. Most households contain many more embedded computers than PCs. The embedded computer doesn't represent the endpoint in the evolution of the computer; instead, it shows the way towards the ubiquitous computer.

Ubiquitous computing or ubicomp is a field originally conceived by Mark Weiser and his team at Xerox PARC in California. It relies on a multitude of small, cheap computers running software, united by universal access to a computer network. You learned how to find Weiser's original, incredibly influential paper using the Open University Library and then learned how to extract the crucial information from the document. After exploring Weiser's vision of ubicomp you explored some real-life ubiquitous computing applications, some of which have diverged greatly from Weiser's vision.

Ubiquitous computing is concerned with more than just computers; it also researches how objects lacking any form of electronics can be recognised by computer technology. You were introduced to the idea of tagging objects, either with printed labels or with radio tags, and how these objects can then interact with computers.

You came to appreciate that the sheer number of ubicomp devices that might exist in the near future requires a different way of interacting with computers. Ambient computing is one way of making computers blend more seamlessly into our environment. You saw some real-life ambient devices, and then used Sense and the SenseBoard to build your own simple ambient device.

Finally, I raised questions about how we might live with ubiquitous computing. Some of these questions will be addressed later in the module.

Once you have completed your work on this part and investigated the other resources related to Block 2 Part 2 that are provided on the TU100 website, you're ready to start Part 3, which directly follows this part in the book.

Answers to self-assessment activities

Activity 1

First, transistors in the integrated circuit can be made much smaller. Smaller components do not just result in smaller computers; they are also less power hungry, and they run cooler and work faster.

Second, integrated circuits are more reliable. Because there are no joints to be connected, there is no risk of incorrect wiring or a faulty connection.

Activity 2

1 m = 1 000 000 000 nm = 1×10^9 nm.

Activity 5

Moore's law as originally formulated stated that the density of electronic components in an integrated circuit would double every year until at least 1975.

These days Moore's law is often said to predict a doubling of transistor counts every 18 months, although Moore himself eventually settled on a figure of two years. In some areas microprocessor technology has lagged behind Moore's predictions, while in others – such as graphics processors – the doubling has been much faster.

Activity 7

The Dynabook strongly resembles a modern laptop or netbook computer with a graphical user interface and a flat-screen display.

Activity 10

288 million can be written as 288×10^6.

$(12/100) \times 288 \times 10^6 = 34.56 \times 10^6$.

So the number of units sold in 2009 would be $(288 + 34.56) \times 10^6$ = 322.56×10^6 units, or 322 560 000 units.

Activity 15

Weiser believed that ubiquitous computing required three distinct technologies:

1   cheap, low-powered computers

2   networks

3   software running ubiquitous applications.

Let's see if the bridge example meets these requirements.

1   The bridge uses one or more cheap, low-power computers to collect the sounds from the microphones and convert them into a digital format.

2   The computers then send these recordings over the internet to another computer in Canada, which analyses the recordings.

3   The bridge's computers run software that processes sound information.

Therefore the Forth Road Bridge is an example of ubiquitous computing.

Activity 16

The *inexpensive, low-power Arduino microcontrollers* are running *simple application programs* that respond to pressure on their sensors. This data is relayed to a central server using a *network*. The network is used again to send the total figures to another computer. The results are displayed by the pattern of balls hanging from the ceiling.

Activity 17

A persuasive computer is one that has been designed to change or influence people's attitudes or behaviours. *Cloud* is a persuasive computer because it illustrates the number of people making lift journeys compared with those using the stairs.

Activity 21

The best way of answering this question is to see if smart phones meet the twin requirements of complying with Weiser's definition of a ubiquitous computer and matching the size profile of a tab. Clearly they contain a computer and have access to a network, and likewise they can run ubiquitous applications – so they are ubiquitous devices. Weiser was not entirely clear about the size of a tab; he mentions 'inch-scale computers' such as calculators and PDAs, which are of a similar size to a smart phone.

I am inclined to think of a smart phone as having the attributes of a tab; although some of the applications mentioned in Weiser's paper have not yet been realised.

Activity 25

$7089/12 = 590.75$ times as much information!

Activity 26

I immediately thought that the tags could be used to identify unsafe food. If a product was returned to a store because it had not been manufactured correctly or had deteriorated before its use-by date, it would be possible for the retailer and manufacturer to identify items in the same batch and remove them from sale before there was a risk to the public. Similarly, manufacturers could issue precisely targeted recalls on products containing faulty components. You might have thought of other examples.

Activity 29

From what you have learned so far, you should have realised that RFID tags are smaller and more robust than paper tags and are less likely to be damaged or lost in the sorting process. Since an RFID tag uses radio waves, it does not need to be visible to the reader; bags can be read no matter which way they are lying on the belt.

Activity 30

Even though they cost only a few cents each, RFID tags remain much more expensive than paper tags and the cost of re-equipping airports with readers is very high.

Activity 32

The Orb cannot give you a precise value, only the direction of any change (such as glowing red for falling stock prices) or the relative value of the data (such as glowing blue when the weather is very cold). Precise values would require more detail than a simple colour change could manage. Even displaying the temperature in Celsius would undermine the ambience of the device – it takes a measurable amount of time and effort to read a temperature, as well as some understanding of the meaning of that value. Likewise, is a stock market price of 500 good or bad? You can only know by referring to previous information.

Activity 33

The Energy Joule shows some features of an ambient device. The colour-changing background can provide useful information at a glance and is an ambient feature. However, the more detailed information it provides (such as the weather forecast, energy consumption rates and the like) is *not* ambient information.

According to Weiser's definition, the Energy Joule is a ubiquitous computing device. It contains a small, cheap computer; it uses a network connection to receive information about energy prices; and it runs a ubiquitous computing application to display information.

Glossary

accelerometer   A sensor that measures changes in the speed and direction of a moving body.

ambient computing   A form of ubiquitous computer interface designed to convey meaningful information without requiring a great deal of the user's time or effort. Rather than using text, digits or complicated graphics, ambient computing uses changes in colour, sound or other sensory outputs to reflect changes in data. Also known as *calm computing*.

artificial intelligence (AI)   An important field of computer science that aims to replicate aspects of intelligence found in animals and especially in humans. Amongst other topics, artificial intelligence is concerned with problem solving, machine learning, planning, perception and robotics.

barcode   A machine-readable representation of data. Barcodes are an early and extremely familiar form of tagging. Most barcodes consist of alternating black and white stripes, the most common form of which is called the **universal product code (UPC)**.

batch processing   A method of processing large amounts of data on a computer with little or no user interaction after the job has been started.

cloud   A digital resource offering storage and services universally and independent of location.

cloud computing   A method of using remote computers to process and store data and run applications.

context awareness   An area of ubiquitous computing concerned with developing devices that react to changes in their environment by altering their behaviour. An example would be a mobile phone that automatically muted its ringer when it was carried into a cinema.

Dynabook   The first recognisable design for a personal computer, developed by Alan Kay during his work at Xerox PARC. The Dynabook was never put into production, but it is acknowledged as the ancestor of all modern personal computers and laptops. Kay also referred to the machine as the KiddiComp.

embedded computer   A computer designed to perform one or more specialised tasks as part of another device that might contain electrical and mechanical components. Generally embedded computers do not allow new programs to be loaded and run, and they can be accessed only by interacting with the device they have been embedded into.

fiduciary marker   A physical object that is attached to another object or person acting as a point of reference, allowing a suitably equipped computer to track its motion and rotation. Such markers are used to easily distinguish objects of interest from their background and allow even relatively low-powered computers to perform image tracking. Also known as a *fiducial*.

integrated circuit (IC)   A miniaturised electronic circuit whose components have been etched using photographic techniques onto a sheet of semiconductor such as silicon. Also known as a *chip, microchip* or *silicon chip*.

mainframe   A very large, expensive computer designed to perform high-speed, reliable computation. The name 'mainframe' comes from the frame-like cabinets in which such computers were originally housed. Mainframes are usually installed in purpose-built rooms with specialised power and air-conditioning systems.

microelectromechanical systems (MEMS)   A group of technologies concerned with the construction of extremely small mechanisms, usually from silicon. MEMS are extremely cheap and robust, and are incorporated into a wide variety of devices. Also known as *micromachines*.

mote   An extremely small networked computer as envisioned by the University of California's Smart Dust project. To qualify as a mote, a computer and its sensors, antenna and power source would have to fit inside a 1 mm cube.

persuasive computer   A computer that has been designed to change or influence people's attitudes or behaviours, either to their benefit (e.g. smart meters in the home) or otherwise (e.g. surveillance technology).

radio frequency identification (RFID)   A form of tagging that uses radio waves for communications. RFID tags contain a simple integrated circuit and a radio antenna, and may be 'passive' (where the chips are energised by a low-power radio signal emitted by an RFID reader) or 'active' (where the tag draws power from a battery). RFID may also be written as *arphid*, which is how it is pronounced.

supercomputer   A type of mainframe distinguished by the highest processing speeds, often used for scientific work such as simulations of nuclear explosions, weather forecasting and aerospace development.

tab   A class of small, portable ubiquitous computers first described by Mark Weiser.

tag   A computer-readable identifier that is uniquely associated with an object or person.

tagging   The act of placing computer-readable identifiers on objects or people.

tangible computing   A method of interacting with a computer that relies on physically picking up or moving objects.

tangible device   A device that users are expected to touch. The reacTIVision software, which relies on fiduciary markers to identify objects, has been used to develop tangible devices such as the Reactable.

time-sharing   A way of sharing the processing power of a single central computer amongst multiple users each sitting at their own terminal. The central computer polled each terminal in turn: if the user had completed a command, their data was sent for processing; if not, the computer moved to the next terminal. Time-sharing allowed computers to be used almost continuously and gave users a great deal more interaction than the earlier batch-processing method. The Web, where many users share the resource of servers, is a form of time-sharing.

ubiquitous computing   An area of computer science that is interested in the development and implementation of computer technologies when they have been integrated into everyday objects and environments. Also known as *ubicomp*, *everyware* or *pervasive computing*.

universal product code (UPC)   The most common form of barcode, developed by IBM during the 1970s. UPC stores numeric information in alternating black and white stripes that can be printed on almost any surface.

References

Clarke, A.C. (2001 [1968]) *2001: A Space Odyssey* (Special Edition), Orbit.

Hiltzik, M.A. (2000) *Dealers of Lightning: Xerox PARC and the Dawn of the Computer Age*, Orion Business Books.

Norman, D. (1998) *The Invisible Computer*, Cambridge, MA, MIT Press.

Pister, K.S.J. (2001) *Sensor Networks in 2010* [online], Smart Dust Project, University of California, Berkeley, http://robotics.eecs.berkeley.edu/~pister/SmartDust/in2010 (accessed 1 October 2010).

Shklovski, I., Vertesi, J., Troshynski, E. and Dourish, P. (2009) 'The Commodification of Location: Dynamics of Power in Location-Based Systems', *Proceedings of the 11th International Conference on Ubiquitous Computing* (UbiComp 2009), Orlando, FL, pp. 11–20.

Weiser, M. (1991) 'The Computer for the 21st Century', *Scientific American*, vol. 265, no. 3, pp. 94–104.

Acknowledgements

Grateful acknowledgement is made to the following sources.

Figures

Figure 1: © Kobal Collection/The Picture Desk

Figure 2: © International Business Machines Corporation

Figure 3(a): Copyright © NASA

Figure 3(b): Brandrodungswanderfeldhackbau/Wikipedia

Figure 4: Taken from Neiman-Marcus catalogue, www.wikipedia.org

Figure 5: Copyright © Alan Kay/Viewpoints Research Institute

Figure 6: Taken from www.wikipedia.org

Figure 7: Copyright © Mike McGregor. Covered under Creative Commons licence 2.5, http://creativecommons.org/licenses/by/2.5/

Figure 8(a): © Apple Computer Inc.

Figure 8(b): From www.wired.com/gadgets/wireless/magazine/17-02

Figure 9: © Sears, Roebuck and Co.

Figure 10: Windell H Oskay, www.evilmadscientist.com

Figure 11: Copyright © Duncan Smith

Figure 13: © Image courtesy of BodyMedia, Inc.

Figure 14: Brett Warneke, Kris S. J. Pister and Joseph Kahn, Berkeley Sensor & Actuator Center, University of California, Berkeley

Figure 16: © Getty Images

Figure 18: © Colorzip. Reproduced by permission

Figure 19(a) and (b): Copyright © Reactable Systems

Figure 20: Taken from www.reactivision.sourceforge.net

Figure 21: Copyright © Microsoft

Figure 22: Copyright © Sagedata

Figure 23: Copyright © Nigel Franks

Figure 25: © ROBERT SPENCER/AP/Press Association Images

Figure 26: Copyright © Ambient

Figure 27(a) and (b): Copyright © Microsoft

Every effort has been made to contact copyright holders. If any have been inadvertently overlooked the publishers will be pleased to make the necessary arrangements at the first opportunity.

Part 3
Making faces

Authors: Mustafa Ali and Nick Dalton

Part 3 (pages 155–232) has been removed from TU100. You should continue directly on to Part 4, which begins on page 233.

Part 4

Information overload

Author: Paul Piwek

Introduction

Computers, especially networked computers, have led to an explosion in the amount of information that is readily available. In this part you will learn in what sense computers have led to information overload, and also how they can help us deal with it. The question that will be asked repeatedly throughout the part is 'What is information good for?' This question will prove useful for understanding what information overload is and how to overcome it. The part will provide you with practical advice on how to find information, how to determine whether the information you've found is any good, and how to organise information so that it remains useful both for yourself and for others.

In short, this part will help you to gain both a deeper understanding of the notion of information and a range of practical skills for handling information. It aims to:

- study how the digital age has led to an increase in the amount of information that is available
- explain two key concepts that relate information to choice: the economy of attention and the long tail
- explain the purpose of information as a resource that helps with making decisions
- show that finding and evaluating information is in many ways a balancing act; it involves weighing up, for example, the amount of time available against the required level of confidence in the information
- develop your practical skills in finding, evaluating and organising information
- demonstrate the capabilities of intelligent agents for dealing with information.

> Note: Session 3 of this part, 'Finding, evaluating and organising information', is an online study component that includes several quizzes and other interactive activities. You should allow about 3 hours for this online study, which can be accessed from the resources page associated with this part on the TU100 website.

Citing sources

Generally speaking, in an Open University Level 1 module such as the current one, authors try to minimise the number of references in order not to overwhelm you. However, since this part directly addresses the issue of how you should evaluate and present information, the use of citations mirrors more closely what would be expected when you are writing a report or essay, especially for a TMA.

Learning outcomes

Your study of this part will help you to do the following.

Knowledge and understanding

- Compare the two perspectives on information, i.e. construction and discovery.
- Explain the concept of the 'economy of attention'.
- Explain the concept of the 'long tail'.
- Explain the concept of 'wisdom of crowds'.
- Explain the basic principles on which search engines are based.
- Describe how intelligent agents can filter information and make information navigation more personal and natural.

Cognitive skills

- Evaluate evidence relating to social, economic, political and personal issues raised by the processing and communication of information.

Key skills

- Avoid plagiarism by quoting, summarising and/or paraphrasing other people's work.
- Use referencing appropriately.
- Carry out calculations involving multiplication, division and percentages.

Practical and professional skills

- Locate, evaluate and use information on the Web and in a digital library to support learning.
- Prioritise information sources according to various criteria.

Too much information?

1

In this session you will:

- study how the digital age has led to an increase in the amount of information that is available
- explain two key concepts that relate information to choice: the economy of attention and the long tail.

1.1 More information

Click? Pic? Look, Eye, Now, Flick, Here, There, Swift, Pace, Up, Down, In, Out, Why, How, What, Where, Eh? Uh! Bang! Smack! Wallop, Bing, Bong, Boom!

(Bradbury, 2008 [1953], p. 73)

Throughout human history, the amount of information that is being created and stored day by day (whether on paper, tape, disc or other media) has increased steadily. One simple cause of this may be that the world population has been increasing rapidly, resulting in an ever larger pool of information producers. Undoubtedly, another important contributor has been the development of new technologies that make it ever faster and easier to store and exchange information: think of the changes involved in moving from clay tablets to papyrus, the invention of the printing press and, more recently, the advent of devices such as the telephone, record player, tape recorder, CD player and mobile phone (Figure 1).

The degree to which we have been surrounded by an ever-increasing ocean of information, even before the era of the networked computer, is illustrated nicely by the rise of scientific journals between 1750 and 1950: during that span of time the number of journals multiplied roughly by ten every 50 years. Consequently, whereas in 1750 there were a mere ten journals in circulation, by 1950 the number had risen to about 100 000 (Martin, 1978, p. 116).

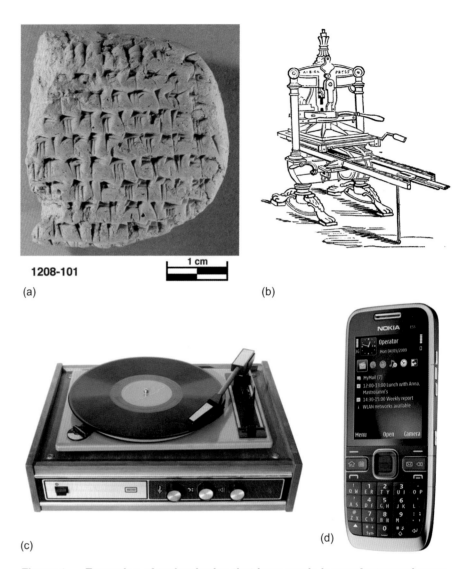

1208-101

1 cm

(a)　　　　　　　　　　　　　　　　　　　　　　(b)

(c)　　　　　　　　　　　　　　　　　　　　　　(d)

Figure 1　**Examples of technologies that have made it ever faster and more easy to store and exchange information: (a) a clay tablet; (b) a printing press; (c) a record player; (d) a mobile phone**

Activity 1 (self-assessment)

The 30 volumes of the 15th edition of the *Encyclopaedia Britannica* (Figure 2) contain 42 million words from over 4000 contributors (Preece, 1981). In contrast, the English version of Wikipedia contains over one billion words and has over 75 000 regular contributors (Wikipedia, 2009).

Suppose I want to read the entire English version of Wikipedia from beginning to end. I decide to dedicate no less than 12 hours a day to this task and read, on average, 200 words per minute. You may assume that

Figure 2 **The 30 volumes of the *Encyclopaedia Britannica***

Wikipedia has one billion words. If I started today, how many years would it take me to finish? You may ignore leap years and assume that a year has 365 days. Explain how you made your calculation. You will probably need to use a calculator for this activity.

The networked digital computer has taken this information explosion to the next level. Google (2010) claims that its search engine searches billions of web pages. Facebook (2010) states that 'More than 30 billion pieces of content (web links, news stories, blog posts, notes, photo albums, etc.) [are] shared each month', and Wikipedia's English version contained around three million articles at the time of writing. What is more, the internet has overtaken other media as a source of information: according to Estabrook et al. (2007, p. v), the internet is the most frequently used source for US Americans who are solving a problem – more frequent than sources such as professional advisers, friends, family members and books. In the UK, the Communications Consumer Panel (2009) found that 50% of their respondents 'agreed' and 34% 'tended to agree' that 'Having broadband at home makes it easier for people to access information, services and activities'. Of those already having broadband, 42% felt that it was 'essential' and 31% 'important'. Additionally, much of the information on the internet is not bound by national borders; for example, many UK-based online newspapers have most of their readers abroad (comScore, 2009).

What makes the internet special is not just the quantity of information that is available on it. Take the Library of Congress, which has about 745 miles of bookshelves stocking roughly 145 million items, including 33 million books (Library of Congress, 2010). To access those physical items I will have to travel to the library and its reading rooms. In contrast, any of the more than eight billion items indexed by Google can be displayed in an instant on my computer screen, or that of a mobile device with mobile internet capability. Thus, this information is at my disposal not just as a theoretical possibility but in practice.

Information or knowledge is generally viewed as a good thing to have. You have probably heard the phrase 'knowledge is power'. The internet has put a tremendous amount of information at our fingertips – and yet, you may have come across or personally experienced 'information glut', 'data smog', 'information overload' or the 'tsunami of data'. The idea that

From all this you may conclude that information has become completely free and accessible to everyone everywhere. However, in later parts you will learn about various efforts by both governments and companies to restrict the free flow of information on the internet.

too much information can be a problem is something we can all easily understand, and the examples are numerous. For instance, you may have searched for a friend with a fairly common name and seen Google throw up thousands or even millions of results; or you may have experienced the dread of opening your email inbox after a holiday for fear of a deluge of messages.

Herbert Simon, the 1978 Nobel prize winner in Economic Sciences, has suggested that the problem of information overload can be understood in terms of economics (Simon, 1969). He views information overload as a scarcity or resource allocation problem. The scarce resource in question is, of course, not information itself. So what is it? Simon proposes that the scarcity resides with whatever is consumed by information: the attention of the information recipient. Attention is a scarce resource because people are generally not able to attend to more than one thing at a time. Consequently, the information recipient is faced with the problem of allocating the limited amount of attention they have to only a fraction of all the information that is available – they need to allocate their attention in the way that best serves their goals. Simon coined the term *economy of attention* for this problem.

An information recipient benefits most from spending their attention in ways that further their goals and satisfy their constraints. But our attention is also important to others: it is the gateway for influencing our decisions and behaviour. By getting us to focus attention on specific information, others can influence our actions.

In the economy of attention, control of attention is an important issue. Two extremes can be identified: situations where the information recipient has total control over their attention, and situations where this power lies with others. Of course, there are many possibilities between these extremes. When control is entirely with the information recipient, we speak of *information pull*; the recipient 'pulls' information as and when it is required. When control is not with the recipient and information is 'pushed' towards the recipient by others whose interests may not be the same as those of the recipient, we speak of *information push*.

Activity 2 (self-assessment)

Give an example of both information push and information pull in your own life.

1.2 More choice

I've discussed the information explosion as exemplified by the number of pages indexed by search engines such as Google, and the tremendous amount of information created every month by users of social networking services such as Facebook. Another area in which the information explosion has left its mark is the entertainment and publishing industry, which has traditionally produced and distributed music, books, films, etc.

For a long time, entertainment media were not only stored on physical carriers – whether it be records, tapes or (more recently) CDs and DVDs – but also sold together with the physical carrier. This meant that in a traditional store, these items occupied shelf space. Even stores without retail overheads, such as mail-order companies, needed to stock their items in a warehouse from where they could be dispatched to the customers. The internet and the advent of high-capacity storage devices have radically changed this. Content (films, music tracks and other media) can now sit somewhere on a server and be provided to customers by simply copying bits over the internet to a storage device (e.g. a hard disk) in their home.

This new model is not only convenient for many consumers; it has also changed the economics on the sales side. Whereas shelf space was once a scarce commodity, limiting the choice that a single store could offer to its customers, now this factor has been all but eliminated. What an online retailer of music such as iTunes offers for sale is no longer constrained by the limitations of shelf space. Consequently, the biggest online stores have significantly more products on offer than any physical superstores can stack. For example, back in 2004, Apple announced that the iTunes store now had over one million tracks (Apple, 2004).

Even for media that still rely on physical carriers, online retail has had a significant impact. Take, for example, the book trade. In the UK, mainstream bricks-and-mortar bookshops carry from 5000–10 000 (WH Smith high-street stores) to 30 000–40 000 (Waterstones) titles (Competition Commission, 2006). In contrast, the online bookseller Amazon has an inventory of several million books. Because of the commercially sensitive nature of these figures and the fact that they are still changing rapidly, it is virtually impossible to provide up-to-date figures that are accurate, but the difference between the numbers of books available in online and physical stores is clearly large.

Activity 3 (exploratory)

The rise of digital media has drastically reduced the costs for retailers of storing and shipping their products. But even when the products are entirely digital (e.g. music tracks that can be downloaded from iTunes), there are still some costs – for instance, the cost of storing data. Search the Web to find some information that gives a rough idea of the cost of data centres in terms of energy and money.

Comment

I searched the websites of the *Guardian* and *Times* newspapers. By searching with `"data centre" cost energy` on the *Guardian* website, I found an article claiming that the energy consumption of Google's data centre in The Dalles is equivalent to more than 50% of the output of a British nuclear power station such as Sizewell B (Johnson, 2009). Using the same query, I found an article in *The Times* by Holly-Davis (2009), which states that 'Data centres typically account for 25% of total corporate IT budgets, but this is rising by as much as 20% a year – outpacing overall IT spending, which is growing by 6%'.

Activity 4 (self-assessment)

A company had an overall IT budget of £400 000 in 2009. Using the information about IT budgets and spending on data centres from the previous activity, calculate:

- how much the company spent on data centres in 2009
- the overall IT budget of the company in 2010
- how much the company spent on data centres in 2010
- what percentage of the overall IT budget of 2010 was spent on data centres.

You will probably need to use a calculator for this activity. You may assume that the 25% figure from the previous activity holds for 2009.

According to Chris Anderson, editor of the magazine *Wired*, digital media have made a massive demand visible that didn't register before. If we rank products such as music tracks by their demand, and plot this against sales, we obtain a curve as depicted in Figure 3. The most popular products are to the left of the horizontal axis.

At the head of the curve there is a concentration of bestselling tracks, the songs at the top of the music charts. These are the tracks that have traditionally been targeted by mainstream bricks-and-mortar stores. The

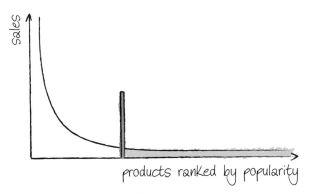

Figure 3   The long tail

limited amount of shelf space forces them to focus on the head of the curve where the highest sales numbers are found. Tracks beyond a certain point, indicated by the red vertical line, simply do not get stored. Thus, demand for these tracks is not visible – that is, until online stores came along. With the goods stored digitally and distributed via the internet, costs of storage and distribution to anyone anywhere with an internet connection are reduced significantly. When royalties only need to be paid on sold goods, there is virtually no penalty for offering the customer base as much choice as possible. Thus, the *long tail* of the demand curve can become visible. What is more, it makes economic sense to exploit this tail. Even though the sales of individual tracks in the tail might be low, the large number of tracks means they can still account for a substantial portion of overall sales. Anderson reports in his book *The Long Tail* (2006) that for online retailers Rhapsody (music), Netflix (DVDs) and Amazon (books) in the USA in 2006, a substantial part of the sales came from titles not available in traditional stores (40% for Rhapsody, 21% for Netflix and 25% for Amazon).

The move to digital has increased choice, but not only by bringing already existing products to the market. It has also stimulated new production of digital media, specifically by non-professionals. Take YouTube, which in May 2009 claimed that every minute 20 hours of video is uploaded (June, 2009).

Activity 5 (exploratory)

Go to the YouTube homepage at http://www.youtube.com/ or to another video broadcasting site, and have a look at the 'Most Popular' section. Who produces the content? Are they traditional content providers or others?

Comment

I had a look at YouTube. A lot of the content comes from partnerships of YouTube with the likes of CBS, the BBC, The Open University, Universal Music Group, Sony Music Group and The Sundance Channel (YouTube, n.d.), but much content also comes from non-professional users.

With the advent of digital media, there is no lack of information, shelf space or warehouse capacity. When these were scarce, it was important to identify the products that would be most successful on the market. This meant that products were filtered before even coming to the market by editors, marketers, record label scouts and others. The long tail economy operates differently: everything can be put on the marketplace, and filtering is performed by the consumers themselves. Recommendation services help by aggregating the reviews and opinions of many consumers (see Session 4). When products are filtered before coming to the market, we speak of *pre-filtering*; in contrast, *post-filtering* refers to filtering being applied to products that are already on the market. Whereas pre-filtering is carried out by information providers, post-filtering is done by the consumers themselves.

The market of abundance combined with post-filtering can have other beneficial side-effects for consumers. For example, Brown and Goolsbee (2002) found that price comparison sites for insurance products have contributed to a decrease in the price of these products.

Activity 6 (self-assessment)

Write three bullet points on why the advent of digital media revealed the long tail of demand.

- The first bullet point should describe pre-filtering and why it was common when media content was stored on physical carriers.
- The second bullet point should introduce post-filtering and how it was made possible.
- Finally, the third bullet point should describe the main consequence of the move from pre- to post-filtering.

1.3 Conclusion

This session described how technology has led to a continual increase in the amount of information that is being produced and stored. Several examples, such as Facebook, Wikipedia and YouTube, were given to illustrate the extent to which we have experienced an explosion of information, especially in the past decade or so. The abundance of information has led to a scarcity in attention (which consumes information). Information recipients are now faced with the problem of allocating their attention in a way that best serves their needs, a problem that is known as the economy of attention.

The session concluded by discussing how we're faced with not only more information but also more choice than ever. This is the central claim underlying the notion of the 'long tail'. The idea is that the advent of digital media has led to reductions in the production and distribution costs of content. As a result, products that previously did not make it to the market are now offered by mainstream sellers, giving consumers more choice.

This session should have helped you with the following learning outcomes.

- Explain the concept of the 'economy of attention'.
- Explain the concept of the 'long tail'.
- Evaluate evidence relating to social, economic, political and personal issues raised by the processing and communication of information.
- Carry out calculations involving multiplication, division and percentages.

2

The purpose of information

Having discussed information overload in Session 1, I will now take a step back and investigate the notion of information itself. This session aims to help you get to grips with the notion of information through the question 'What is information good for?'. It will explain the purpose of information as a resource that helps with making decisions. You will also learn about the differences between data, information and knowledge.

2.1 What kind of stuff is information?

Talking about information as some kind of 'stuff' should not be done carelessly. It can get us into a bit of trouble, because it leads to all sorts of questions that we normally ask about stuff, such as 'What is it made of?', 'What does it look like?' and 'Where can I find it?'. These questions are fine when we're talking about something natural, for instance water. We can answer that water is made of H_2O molecules, is transparent, can be found in lakes and seas, and occasionally (or quite often, depending on where you live) falls from the skies. However, the limits of such questions become readily apparent when we try them on another familiar object: the chair. What are chairs made of? Surely, you'll say, it depends on the chair. What do chairs look like and where do we find them? Again, the answer seems to be 'it depends'. None of these questions really help us understand what a chair is. For *artefacts* such as chairs, to get to the bottom of what they are, we need to ask what their purpose is – what they are good for. To understand what a chair is, it is most helpful to know that chairs are objects that are made for one person to sit on.

Activity 7 (exploratory)

Having read the comparison between water and chairs, do you think information is more like water or more like chairs? Briefly explain your answer.

Comment

To me it seems that information is more like chairs than like water. You saw that for water we can ask what it is made of, what it looks like and where it is found. In contrast, I can't make any sense of the questions 'What is information made of?' and 'What does it look like?', though I admit that it may make sense to ask where information can be found. Most importantly, however, I can see that it makes sense to ask about the *purpose* of information, just as it makes sense to ask about the purpose of chairs. We use information to guide our decisions and actions. For example, when I hear on the radio that all trains to Milton Keynes, my place of work, have been cancelled today, that information helps me to decide whether to work from home or in the office.

Information versus data

Before looking in more detail at the purpose of information, let's examine the difference between data and information. You have already come across *data* as the sets of numbers, letters or symbols that may be used for processing by a computer. In a computer, such data is represented as binary numbers and processed according to the rules of binary algebra. These rules, which you studied in Part 1 of this block, operate on 0s and 1s, with no reference to meaning.

For instance, take the sentence 'It is raining'. For me, it is meaningful because I have experienced rain. In particular, I can recognise rain when I come across it. For the computer, all this is irrelevant; as soon as 'It is raining' has been represented by a 0 or a 1, the rules of binary algebra can do their work without taking the meaning of the sentence into account. In short, a computer can store and manipulate data without having an inkling about its meaning. In contrast, *information* is the meaning that we, as human beings, can extract from a piece of data such as the letters that make up the sentence 'It is raining'.

The next activity will allow you to explore some of the implications of this view of information. For now, it is fine if you have an intuitive grasp of the notion of 'meaning' – I will try to pin down more precisely what I mean by this term later in this session.

Activity 8 (exploratory)

Consider the following two sentences:

1   This box is empty.
2   Deze doos is leeg.

The second sentence is written in Dutch; when translated into English it says 'this box is empty'. Suppose that we have two boxes, A and B: box A has sentence 1 printed on it, whereas box B has sentence 2 printed on it (Figure 4).

Now, consider Joan and Jan: Joan speaks only English and Jan speaks only Dutch. For each person, determine which box carries the information that it is empty. Briefly explain your answer.

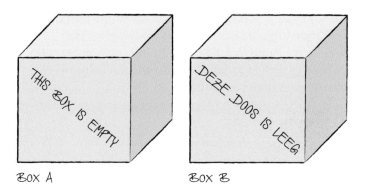

Box A   Box B

Figure 4   Two boxes, each with text printed on it

Comment

For Joan, only box A carries the information that it is empty, whereas for Jan only box B carries this information. Sentence 1 on box A conveys information to Joan because she, as a speaker of English, understands what it means. For Jan, sentence 1 is merely data (a sequence of characters) because he doesn't understand English. For sentence 2 on box B, we have the opposite situation: Jan, as a speaker of Dutch, can easily make sense of the sentence, whereas Joan, who doesn't speak Dutch, can't.

From this very simple activity you should take away three things:

- We can only speak of information in relation to the person who is supposed to have that information.
- What counts as information for one person can be merely data for another. For data to become information, abilities, skills and background information are required; in this case, the practical abilities and skills involved in reading a sentence and interpreting it. These rely partly on other information – for example, about the meaning of words such as 'box' and 'empty' (recall the discussion of conventions in Part 1 of this block).
- The *same* information can be conveyed by *different* data. In this particular activity, sentences in two different languages both convey the information that the box is empty.

Information from different points of view

The view this part takes of the difference between data and information is by no means the only one. There are many fields in which data and information are studied, ranging from mathematics to business studies, each with their own take on the difference. Figure 5 shows one way of looking at the differences between information, knowledge and wisdom.

Figure 5   Information, knowledge and wisdom

Information, misinformation and disinformation

In the previous activity, Joan understood from the sentence on box A that box A is empty. Now, perhaps the box really is empty; then again, maybe it contains a couple of delicious Belgian chocolates. We don't know, and neither does Joan. The point is that the information Joan gained by reading the sentence on box A doesn't necessarily need to be true. In some sense that doesn't matter: information remains information, even if it turns out to be false. False information is usually referred to as misinformation, or even disinformation (we speak of disinformation rather than misinformation in the event that the box was labelled incorrectly on purpose).

Information versus knowledge

You have seen that information is always information for someone, unlike data which can exist independently of human beings (for instance, in the memory of a computer). I have spoken rather vaguely about someone 'having' some information. In fact, the relationship between a person and the information they have or hold can be one of many: a person might *believe* that a certain box is empty, *doubt* it, *consider* it, *know* it, *suspect* it, etc.

I now want to examine briefly what it means for a person to know some piece of information, i.e. to have *knowledge*. Perhaps most importantly, for anyone to know a piece of information, that information must be true. I can't know that box A is empty if it contains chocolate. This view of knowledge goes back to the classical definition of knowledge as *true justified belief*. For example, I know that box A is empty if and only if:

1   I believe that box A is empty

2   box A is indeed empty, and

3   my belief is justified – in other words, I have a good reason for holding the belief. (For example, I may have peeked inside the box.)

The classical definition of knowledge is discussed by the Greek philosopher Plato (*c*.470–399 BC) in the *Theaetetus*. The *Theaetetus* is one of the dialogues Plato wrote to explore a wide range of philosophical questions.

The purpose of the next activity is to apply this definition to a new situation. Being able to apply definitions correctly is a skill that is useful throughout this module and beyond.

Activity 9 (self-assessment)

My local football team will be playing this Saturday. I'm an optimist and therefore believe that we will win. I stick to my belief, even though I know that the team we are playing have beaten us every time we have played them in the past. As it happens, we do indeed win the match. Is it correct to say that I knew my team would win? Explain your answer.

Hint: the classical definition of knowledge has three conditions. For information to be knowledge, it has to be (1) believed, (2) true and (3) justified. For each of these conditions, check whether it applies to the situation described above. If one of them doesn't apply, you can conclude that I did not know my team would win.

2.2   What is information good for?

Having clarified the distinction between data, information and knowledge, I will now return to the question about the purpose of information.

Activity 10 (exploratory)

Suppose you're planning a summer holiday. You will need to make quite a few decisions. Select one of them and make a list describing the information you'll need in order to make that decision. You can formulate each item on the list as a question that you need to answer in order to make your decision.

Comment

There are many decisions to make, including where to go, who is coming and how long to stay away. I will focus on where to go. Here is my list:

- What kind of weather would I like there to be at my destination?
- How much am I prepared to pay for my holiday?
- What places can I go to?
- Which of these places matches with my constraints and goals, e.g. regarding the cost and weather?

Probably your list for the previous activity was not exactly the same as mine. For one thing, you may have selected a different decision from the one I picked. I can, however, group the items of my list into three distinct kinds of information.

1   I need to be clear about my *constraints and goals*. This gives rise to questions such as 'What kind of weather would I like there to be at my destination?' and 'How much I am prepared to pay for my holiday?'.

2   I need to find out what the *options* are. This raises the question 'What places can I go to?'. Perhaps I have a couple of possible destinations in mind. I might have heard these mentioned by other people or visited them before.

3   I need information that *relates* the options I am considering to my goals and constraints. I'm interested in finding out which of the places I am considering matches with my constraints and goals. So, for each of the options I may want to ask questions such as 'What is the weather there likely to be at the time I will be on holiday?', 'How expensive is it to get there?' and 'How much will I have to pay for accommodation?'.

Activity 11 (exploratory)

Have another look at your own list and group your items according to the three kinds of information about (1) your goals and constraints, (2) your options, and (3) the relationships between your goals and constraints on the one hand and your options on the other.

Comment

If you did not have items for each of the three kinds of information, can you think of any items that you could add?

Having worked through these two activities, you should note that the reason for collecting information was to help you make a decision. This can be summarised by the plan in Box 1. I will return to this plan throughout this part because it provides a good reminder of how information fits in with real activities.

Activity 12 (self-assessment)

Imagine you are buying a new computer. Describe the information you require in terms of your goals and constraints, your options and the relationship between the two.

> **Box 1   Information gathering for decision making (IGD) plan**
>
> In order to make a decision you need to collect information on:
>
> 1   **What you want** – what are your goals and constraints?
>
> 2   **What your options are** – what are the alternatives that you can choose from?
>
> 3   **How the options relate to your goals and constraints** – is each option good or bad from the point of view of your goals and constraints? How does it fare when compared to other options?

2.3   Information gathering as decision making

Activity 13 (exploratory)

Let's return to the task of planning a holiday. Suppose you have identified a particular hotel on a website that contains travel information. You have also searched the Web for reviews of this hotel. Unfortunately you can find only two reviews: one that praises it and another that gives a damning verdict. The decision you need to make is whether to stay in this hotel. However, given the two reviews, there is another decision that must be made first: which source of information to rely on. Describe this decision problem in terms of the three components of the IGD plan (Box 1).

Comment

1   My goal is to find correct information regarding the hotel.

2   My options are to trust either the first or the second review.

3   In order to see how my goal of finding correct information relates to the options, I may want to investigate each of them in more detail. Questions that come to mind include 'Who wrote the review and why?' and 'When was it written?'.

In Session 3 you will study some criteria that can help with gathering information.

The aim of the previous activity was to show you that the IGD plan not only helps with understanding the role of information in decision making, but also can be applied to information gathering itself. This is possible because information gathering consists of making choices, in particular where to look for the information and which information to select. Box 2 illustrates the difficulty of making a decision when information is missing.

Box 2 Making decisions in a maze

The maze is a great way to visualise the difficulties of decision making when some information is missing. Consider the maze shown in Figure 6.

Figure 6   'American Maze' by Dale Wilkins

The person at the beginning of this maze – let's call him Bob – has a clear goal in mind: to obtain a green card for permanent residence in the USA. Once Bob has entered the maze, the options are laid out neatly: at each junction there is a limited number of ways to move on. The trouble for Bob is that he has no way of knowing which option at each stage brings him closer to his goal.

Considering this from the perspective of the IGD plan I introduced in Box 1, although the information regarding items 1 and 2 of the plan is available, information on item 3 is missing.

In this session I have emphasised that information plays an important role in behaviour that is directed at one or more goals. It can guide that behaviour by helping us to decide between alternatives. We should, however, not forget the excitement and fun that can accompany the discovery of something new. This in itself can be a reason for collecting information. Consider studying with the OU: you may do this to improve your career prospects, to find out how to accomplish a specific task, etc., but perhaps also because a particular topic fascinates you and you enjoy learning new things about it.

Activity 14 (self-assessment)

Can you relate Simon's 'economy of attention' (introduced in Section 1.1) to the IGD plan?

2.4 Information, meaning and truth

Earlier in this session you learned that *meaning* and information are closely linked: for data to become information, the data has to be meaningful to someone. I defined information in terms of meaning: the information some data conveys to a person is the meaning which that person extracts from the data.

Extracting meaning from data is non-trivial. The sentence 'Es regnet in Amsterdam' conveys the information that it is raining in Amsterdam only to speakers of German or those already familiar with this German sentence. In other words, for speakers of German the meaning of the sentence 'Es regnet in Amsterdam' is that it is raining in Amsterdam. To explain the meaning of the German sentence to you, I have relied on translating it into English. But what is this meaning? What characterises someone who grasps the meaning of the sentence 'Es regnet in Amsterdam'? One answer that is popular among researchers on meaning is that to understand what a sentence means, I need to be able to distinguish between situations in which the sentence is true and those in which it is false.

It is important to realise that there is a difference between understanding the meaning of a sentence – i.e. knowing under which conditions it is true – and knowing that the sentence is actually true. Whether a particular sentence, such as 'Es regnet in Amsterdam', is true right now depends on both the meaning of the sentence and the current state of affairs in the world. I characterise meaning and current state of affairs as follows.

- **The meaning of the sentence**: what counts as a situation in which the sentence is true. For the sentence in question, this includes the condition that water is falling from the sky. Conditions like this one are partly determined by the *conventions* (see Part 1 of this block) of a particular language such as German or English. In other words, the meaning of a sentence is partly constructed.

- **The current state of affairs in the world**: whether it is actually raining in Amsterdam at the time the sentence is uttered, a *fact in the real world* that can be discovered.

Whereas the meaning of a sentence can involve *knowledge construction* (by relying on human-made conventions), determining the current state of affairs involves *knowledge discovery*. Assuming we know the meaning of the words 'it is raining', whether it is raining or not is something that can be discovered – for example, by observing that raindrops are falling from the sky.

Activity 15 (self-assessment)

For a long time, the Solar system was thought to consist of nine planets: Mercury, Venus, Earth, Mars, Jupiter, Saturn, Uranus, Neptune and Pluto. In 2006, however, the General Assembly of the International Astronomical Union (IAU) gathered in Prague to decide on the definition of a planet. A committee was set up and after some very long discussions (see International Astronomical Union (2006) for details), a proposal emerged. At the closing ceremony on 24 August, the members of the IAU voted for the following definition of a planet:

> A celestial body that (a) is in orbit around the Sun, (b) has sufficient mass for its self-gravity to overcome rigid body forces so that it assumes a hydrostatic equilibrium (nearly round) shape, and (c) has cleared the neighbourhood around its orbit.

International Astronomical Union, n.d.

In other words, (a), (b) and (c) are conditions that together define the meaning of the word 'planet'. As a result, Pluto is no longer considered a planet (Figure 7); it has been demoted to 'dwarf planet' on the grounds that it does not satisfy condition (c). Pluto does not satisfy this condition because it is accompanied by a great number of similarly sized objects known as the trans-Neptunian region – in other words, it has not cleared the neighbourhood around its orbit.

Figure 7   Poor Pluto

Now, consider the sentence 'Pluto is not a planet'. Would you say that this is a fact that can be discovered or more of a human-made convention? In other words, is the knowledge expressed by this sentence something that can be discovered or something that has been constructed?

The previous activity suggests that truth is partly constructed and partly discovered. It is constructed in the sense that the meaning of the sentences we use is to some extent up to us. Above you saw an extreme example, where a committee decided on the meaning of a particular word. However, for many words in our everyday language, meaning is established in a less transparent way. Everyday words such as 'house' and 'shoe' are not defined by a committee; rather, speakers of English somehow have come to an implicit agreement about what they mean. Dictionaries make such meanings explicit, but do not establish them. In any case, provided that the meanings of the words in a sentence have been established, whether the sentence is true is up for discovery. Box 3 briefly explores the complicated relationship between knowledge and truth.

Box 3 Knowledge discovery and construction: where it gets complicated

To get an idea of the ongoing fascinating, but also highly intricate, discussion among philosophers about the construction and discovery of knowledge, I will just hint at some of the complications. I said that 'Pluto is a planet' is false according to the new definition of a planet. So if someone tells me today that Pluto is a planet, I can tell them that they are wrong. But what about someone who called Pluto a planet before 2006? They were in agreement with the encyclopaedias and textbooks of the time. Was that person wrong or not? Looking at both possibilities:

- Suppose we say that they were wrong. Does that then mean we could be wrong right now as well? After all, the IAU may decide to change the definition once more at some point in the future.

- Alternatively, suppose we say that they were right. Does that then mean we can't speak of the absolute truth of a sentence, but only of its truth relative to the time at which it was uttered?

Either way, we seem to have landed ourselves in a bit of a mess! If you don't immediately see how we can get out of this, don't despair. The best minds in philosophy have looked at this and related problems for centuries, and they have not yet come up with a universally accepted solution.

2.5 Conclusion

This session introduced information as the 'stuff' that helps us with making decisions. In the context of decision making, it explained the importance of having information on one's goals and constraints, options, and the relationship between the two. Information was distinguished from data and knowledge. The relationship between information and meaning was characterised as follows: the information some data conveys to a person is the meaning which that person extracts from the data. Finally, the example of the dwarf planet Pluto was used to discuss how knowledge can involve both construction and discovery.

This session should have helped you with the following learning outcomes.

- Compare the two perspectives on information, i.e. construction and discovery.
- Evaluate evidence relating to social, economic, political and personal issues raised by the processing and communication of information.
- Prioritise information sources according to various criteria.

3 Finding, evaluating and organising information

This session (including Figures 8–14 and Activities 16–33) is delivered online. It can be found in the resources page associated with this part on the TU100 website.

Beyond search: recommendation systems and agents

4

The aim of this session is to demonstrate the capabilities of intelligent agents for dealing with information.

This part has focused on finding, evaluating and organising information – in particular, information that is fit for purpose. This included assessing presentation, relevance and correctness of information. When it came to relevance and correctness, you saw that search engines such as Google use, among other things, the 'wisdom of crowds' to rank information sources. So far, however, the assumption has been that each search is carried out in isolation, regardless of previous searches by the same user. This final session discusses ways in which search and information navigation can be personalised for a specific user. I will discuss ways in which information can be automatically filtered to fit the preferences of individual users, and look at research on the use of computer-animated agents to make information navigation more personal and natural.

4.1 Recommendation systems

The online bookseller Amazon allows you to search for books from a huge catalogue through both keyword search and subject category-based browsing. Additionally, for registered users, it provides a *recommendation system*. Whenever I visit the Amazon home page, it provides me with numerous recommendations under various headings including 'Customers with similar searches purchased …', 'New for You' and 'Recommended for You'. Each recommendation comes with a 'Why is this recommended for you?' link, which opens up a pop-up page that shows me the item on the basis of which the recommendation was made. For example, one of my recommendations is Charles Leadbeater's book *We-Think: Mass Innovation, Not Mass Production*, and this is based on my purchase of David Weinberger's *Everything is Miscellaneous: The Power of the New Digital Disorder*. Both books deal with how the digital era is changing many existing practices in business, media and other areas.

Figure 15 is an example recommendation page. Note that the item that caused the recommendation is provided at the bottom of each recommendation.

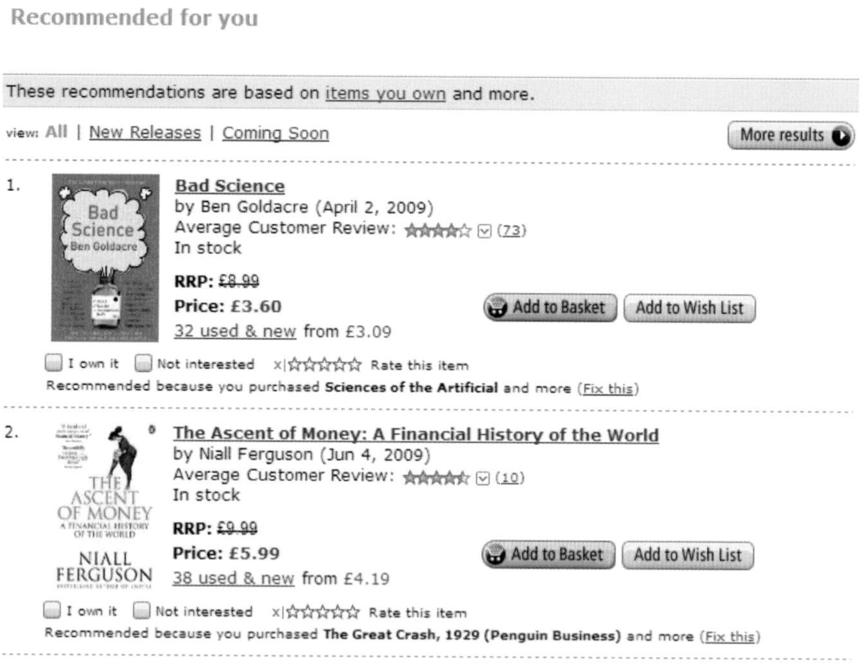

Figure 15   Example of two recommendations made by Amazon's recommendation system (taken from personal Amazon recommendations page)

Linden et al. (2003) describe the algorithm that lies behind Amazon's recommendations. The approach is called item-by-item collaborative filtering and proceeds as follows:

- First the data for an item that the customer purchased in the past is retrieved.
- A table is calculated that records which items other customers have bought together with the aforementioned item.
- From the table of aforementioned items, the most popular item (the one bought by most customers) or the item that is most correlated to the original item (that is, which most customers bought together with the original item) is recommended.

This approach can be contrasted with traditional collaborative filtering. Roughly speaking, in traditional collaborative filtering a customer is represented in terms of the set of distinct catalogue items they have bought. The algorithm then compares this representation of the customer with that of other customers and finds the most similar customers (it is beyond the scope of this part to go into precisely how the similarity is calculated). Recommended items are then chosen from the set of items that the original customer didn't buy, but which the most similar customers did buy. Often these items are ranked according to how many similar customers bought an item.

4.2   Computer-animated intelligent agents

Amazon's recommendation system can be viewed as an intelligent agent that actively helps the user to find items they desire. It is personal in the sense that it takes the user's past purchases into account. It is, however, impersonal in the sense that the recommendations are presented to the user as coming from a faceless system (or at least, they were at the time this part was written). One school of researchers in human–computer interaction believe that giving such systems a face, body and voice will improve the user experience, and there is some evidence that users do indeed find such systems more entertaining.

Dehn and van Mulken (2000) describe several studies that compare interfaces with and without an embodiment.

The following activity allows you to explore the capabilities of *computer-animated intelligent agents* such as IKEA's Anna and National Rail Enquiries' Lisa (Figure 16).

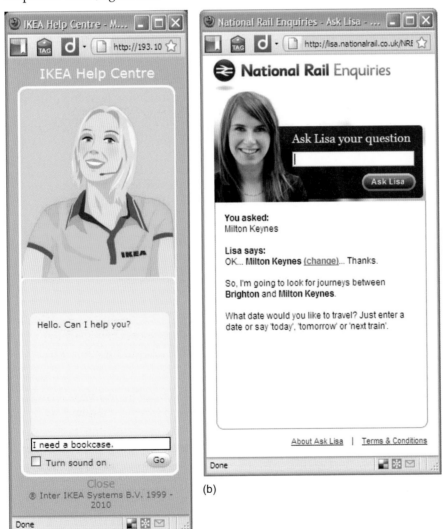

(a)

(b)

Figure 16   (a) IKEA's Anna and (b) Lisa of National Rail Enquiries

Activity 34 (exploratory)

This activity gives you the chance to try out a computer-animated intelligent agent for yourself and also introduces you to a more sophisticated type of embodied agent. You will find the instructions for it in the resources page associated with this part on the TU100 website.

4.3 Conclusion

This final session discussed two ways in which intelligent agents may be able to help us navigate information. The first one, recommendation systems, relies on combining individual and collective behaviours in an intelligent way to provide users with options that are relevant to them. The second way in which intelligent agents may change how we find information is by making our interaction with computer agents more natural. This can be achieved by giving agents embodiment and allowing them to have a conversation with the user.

This session should have helped you with the following learning outcome.

• Describe how intelligent agents can filter information and make information navigation more personal and natural.

Summary

In this part, you have studied information: what it is and how to find, evaluate and organise it. You saw that the ever-increasing amount of information has led to the 'economy of attention'. With information being ever more abundant, the thing that consumes information – our attention – has become a scarce resource.

The primary view of information in this part was as a resource for making decisions. You learned about the difference between data, information and knowledge. I linked information to data by defining it as the meaning that a person can extract from data.

The largest session of this part equipped you with knowledge and skills for finding, evaluating and organising information. You engaged in several activities that practised different aspects of this.

The final session moved beyond conventional search engines. It briefly introduced intelligent agents and how they may help us find information.

Once you have completed your work on this part, including the online session, and investigated the other resources related to Block 2 Part 4 that are provided on the TU100 website, you're ready to start Part 5, which directly follows this part in the book.

Answers to self-assessment activities

Activity 1

Since the question asks for a number in years, I first need to find out how many words I can read in a year. I know how many words I can read in a minute (200), so I need to determine how many minutes I will spend reading in a year. A year contains 365 days, and on each day I spend 12 hours reading. Each hour in turn consists of 60 minutes. Thus, an entire year gives me:

$$365 \times 12 \times 60 = 262\ 800 \text{ minutes}$$

Since I can read 200 words per minute, in a year I can read:

$$262\ 800 \times 200 = 52\ 560\ 000 \text{ words}$$

That is approximately 52.5 million words per year. Wikipedia contains one billion words, that is one thousand million words. To arrive at the number of years it would take me to read Wikipedia, I need to divide the total number of words in Wikipedia by the number of words that I can read in a year:

$$1000 \text{ million words}/52.5 \text{ million words per year} = 19 \text{ years}$$

So it would take me no less than 19 years to read Wikipedia from beginning to end!

Activity 2

An example of the information push I experience is the steady flow of unsolicited emails that fill my inbox every day. Another example is connected with the local elections we had recently where I live: each of the parties decided to send me leaflets to promote their candidates.

Examples of information pull include those occasions when I go to the website of Network Rail to consult their train timetables because I need to travel somewhere by train. Another example is the background research I did for writing this part, which involved searches on the Web, visiting the library and talking to colleagues. Of course, occasionally, colleagues would also push information my way if they thought that it was particularly relevant for this part.

Activity 4

The company spent 25% of its overall IT budget on data centres in 2009: 25% of £400 000 is £400 000 × 0.25 = £100 000.

A percentage growth of 6% in the overall IT budget means that in 2010 the overall IT budget was £400 000 × 1.06 = £424 000.

A percentage growth of 20% in the spending on data centres means that in 2010 the company was spending £100 000 × 1.20 = £120 000 on data centres.

Out of a total IT budget of £424 000 for 2010, the company was spending £120 000 on data centres – that is, (120 000/424 000) × 100% = 28.3% of the total IT budget.

Activity 6

- When the distribution of media content such as films and music moved from shipping physical carriers (CDs and DVDs) to delivery over the internet, storing and distributing the content became much cheaper. Previously, mainstream stores limited their stock to the most profitable products because of the costs of storage and shipping. This meant that the content was pre-filtered by the stores (i.e. they decided which items they thought would be most successful in the marketplace and only stocked those items).

- The decrease in cost of storage and distribution, together with a model where a distributor only pays the producer when a product is sold, made it possible for product catalogues to be virtually unlimited in size. Technologies such as recommendation systems help users to navigate and post-filter this new market of abundance.

- All this together has meant that products that would previously not have been on the mainstream market at all are now being purchased through mainstream sellers such as Apple iTunes, even if the demand is only a fraction of that of the bestsellers.

Activity 9

According to the classical definition of knowledge, I did not know that my team would win. The first and second conditions apply, but the third one doesn't: I believed that my team would win (the first condition applies), and this belief turned out to be true (the second condition also applies), but I did not have a good reason for my belief – in fact, I had a good reason (the information on past performance of my team) for not believing that my team would win (thus the third condition fails to apply).

Activity 12

Firstly, I would need to decide on my goals and constraints. Am I going to use the computer strictly at home, or do I want to be able to carry it around with me? What applications will I be running on it? Does it need to be compatible with my old computer so that I can easily move data across? What can I afford?

Secondly, I would need to explore my options. I might visit a couple of online stores and look for offers.

Finally, for each of the options, I would need to find out to what extent it meets my goals and constraints.

Of course, these three steps will often not be carried out in the strict order suggested here. For instance, as I browse for options I might learn about new features that I then include among my goals and constraints.

Activity 14

Here's how I see the relationship between the two. The IGD plan involves three components relevant to a decision: information about the goals and constraints, the options, and the relationship between the two. The problem of allocating attention can be viewed as a decision problem: the problem is to decide which available pieces of information to focus one's attention on. So, the options in the IGD plan are the alternative pieces of information that are competing for our attention.

Activity 15

I would argue that it is a bit of both. On the one hand, it obviously involves some sort of construction. The meaning of the word 'planet' was devised by a committee and voted on by an assembly. To say that the committee and the assembly discovered the meaning of the word 'planet' doesn't seem quite right – I'd prefer to say that they constructed that meaning, they created a convention. However, once the meaning of the word 'planet' was fixed, whether Pluto is a planet became a discoverable fact. The fact that Pluto is not a planet is grounded in the astronomical observation of many other objects of a similar size in its vicinity. We would, however, need to change our judgement if it turned out that these observations of similar-sized objects were based on some intricate optical or other illusion.

Glossary

artefact A human-made object, which may either be decorative or have a practical use.

computer-animated intelligent agent An intelligent agent that has a computer-animated embodiment. This can range from a cartoon-like animation of a person, animal or object to a photo-realistic full body that displays believable human behaviours. Behaviour can range from movements and gestures to use of speech.

data The sets of numbers, letters or symbols used for processing by a computer.

economy of attention A term coined by Herbert Simon to describe the problem faced by an information recipient of allocating their attention in the way that best serves their goals, given that they have a limited amount of attention and thus can focus on only a fraction of all the information that is available.

information Data that has been interpreted and placed in context so that it carries meaning.

information pull A situation in which control is entirely with the information recipient; the recipient 'pulls' information as and when it is deemed necessary.

information push A situation in which control is not with the information recipient; information is 'pushed' towards the recipient by others whose interests may not be the same as those of the recipient.

knowledge True justified belief, as defined by the Greek philosopher Plato (*c*.470–399 BC). For example, I know it is raining now if and only if (1) I believe it is raining now, (2) it is indeed raining now, and (3) my belief is justified (I have a good reason for holding it – e.g. I'm outdoors and can see/feel the raindrops).

knowledge construction The idea that our knowledge can depend on human-made conventions. For example, the meaning of the word 'planet' was determined by a committee of experts, who therefore constructed the meaning of that word.

knowledge discovery The idea that our knowledge can depend on discovering what the current state of affairs in the world is. Assuming I know what the sentence 'it is raining' means, I can discover whether it is raining now by, for example, venturing outside and seeing whether I get wet.

long tail The claim that there is demand for niche/specialist products, in particular media content, that has recently surfaced as a result of the realisation of media content product catalogues of virtually unlimited size.

meaning   A concept that may be defined indirectly by asking what characterises someone who grasps the meaning of a sentence. To understand what a sentence means, one needs to be able to distinguish between situations in which the sentence is true and those in which it is false.

post-filtering   The filtering of products that are already on the market, carried out by the consumers themselves.

pre-filtering   The filtering of products before they come to the market.

recommendation system   A system or algorithm which recommends choices or products to a user, based on various factors such as previous decisions or purchases by the user and other users.

References

Anderson, C. (2006) *The Long Tail: Why the Future of Business Is Selling Less of More*, New York, Hyperion.

Apple (2004) *iTunes Music Store Catalog Tops One Million Songs* [online], http://www.apple.com/pr/library/2004/aug/10itms.html (accessed 1 October 2010).

Brown, J.R. and Goolsbee, A. (2002) 'Does the Internet Make Markets More Competitive? Evidence from the Life Insurance Industry', *Journal of Political Economy*, vol. 110, no. 3, pp. 481–507; also available online at http://www.journals.uchicago.edu/doi/abs/10.1086/339714 (accessed 1 October 2010).

Bradbury, R. (2008 [1953]) *Fahrenheit 451*, London, Harper Voyager.

Communications Consumer Panel (2009) *Not online, not included: consumers say broadband essential for all* [online], London, Communications Consumer Panel, http://www.communicationsconsumerpanel.org.uk/downloads/not%20online%20-%20not%20included%20-%20June%202009.pdf (accessed 1 October 2010).

Competition Commission (2006) *Proposed acquisition of Ottakar's plc by HMV Group plc through Waterstone's Booksellers Ltd* [online], http://www.competition-commission.org.uk/rep_pub/reports/2006/fulltext/513.pdf (accessed 31 August 2010).

comScore (2009) *Fast Growing U.K. Online Newspaper Market Attracting Even Larger Audiences from Beyond the Pond* [online], Press Release, comScore, Inc., 13 May, http://www.comscore.com/Press_Events/Press_Releases/2009/5/U.K._Newspaper_Sites_Aattract_Visitors_from_Around_the_World (accessed 1 October 2010).

Dehn, D.M. and van Mulken, S. (2000) 'The impact of animated interface agents: a review of empirical research', *International Journal of Human–Computer Studies*, vol. 52, no. 1, pp. 1–22.

Estabrook, L., Witt, E. and Rainie, L. (2007) *Information searches that solve problems: How people use the internet, libraries, and government agencies when they need help* [online], Pew Internet & American Life Project/Graduate School of Library and Information Science, http://www.pewinternet.org/~/media//Files/Reports/2007/Pew_UI_LibrariesReport.pdf.pdf (accessed 1 October 2010).

Facebook (2010) *Statistics* [online], http://www.facebook.com/home.php#/press/info.php?statistics (accessed 1 October 2010).

Google (2010) *More Google Products* [online], http://www.google.com/intl/en/options/ (accessed 1 October 2010).

Holly-Davis, T. (2009) 'Environment pays the price for boom in laptops and mobiles', *The Times* [online], 19 April, http://business.timesonline.co.uk/tol/business/industry_sectors/technology/article6122387.ece (accessed 1 October 2010).

International Astronomical Union (2006) *The IAU draft definition of 'planet' and 'plutons'* [online], News Release IAU0601, Prague, http://www.iau.org/public_press/news/detail/iau0601/ (accessed 1 October 2010).

International Astronomical Union (n.d.) *Pluto and the Developing Landscape of Our Solar System* [online], http://www.iau.org/public_press/themes/pluto/ (accessed 1 October 2010).

Johnson, B. (2009) 'Google's power-hungry data centres', *The Guardian* [online], 3 May, http://www.guardian.co.uk/technology/2009/may/03/google-data-centres (accessed 1 October 2010).

Junee, R. (2009) 'Zoinks! 20 Hours of Video Uploaded Every Minute!', post made to *Broadcasting Ourselves: The Official YouTube Blog* [online], 21 May, http://youtubeukblog.blogspot.com/2009/05/zoinks-20-hours-of-video-uploaded-every.html (accessed 1 October 2010).

Library of Congress (2010) *About the Library: Fascinating Facts* [online], http://www.loc.gov/about/facts.html (accessed 1 October 2010).

Linden, G., Smith, B. and York, J. (2003) 'Amazon.com recommendations: item-to-item collaborative filtering', *IEEE Internet Computer*, January/February 2003, pp. 76–80.

Martin, J. (1978) *The Wired Society*, London, Prentice Hall.

Preece, W.E. (1981) 'Preface to the Fifteenth Edition' in *PROPAEDIA: Outline of Knowledge and Guide to the Britannica*, Chicago, Encyclopaedia Britannica, Inc.

Simon, H. (1969) *Designing Organizations for an Information-Rich World*, Brookings Institution Lecture, Johns Hopkins University; available online at http://diva.library.cmu.edu/webapp/simon/item.jsp?q=/box00055/fld04178/bdl0002/doc0001/ (accessed 29 August 2010).

Wikipedia (2009) 'Wikipedia: About' in *Wikipedia: the free encyclopedia* [online], http://en.wikipedia.org/wiki/Wikipedia:About (accessed 30 June 2009).

YouTube (n.d.) *About YouTube* [online], http://www.youtube.com/t/about (accessed 1 October 2010).

Acknowledgements

Grateful acknowledgement is made to the following sources.

Figures

Figure 1(a): Taken from Google Inc.

Figure 1(c): © iStockphoto.com

Figure 1(d): Nokia UK Limited

Figure 5: Originally published in THE FUTURIST. Used with permission from the World Future Society (www.wfs.org)

Figure 6: © Dale Wilkins

Figure 7: © Mathias Helmuth Pedersen

Figure 16(a): © IKEA. Reproduced by permission

Figure 16(b): © National Rail

Every effort has been made to contact copyright holders. If any have been inadvertently overlooked the publishers will be pleased to make the necessary arrangements at the first opportunity.

Author: Chris Dobbyn

Part 5
'With the tears wiped off'

Statistics are human beings with the tears wiped off.

Paul Brodeur, *Outrageous Misconduct*

Torture numbers, and they'll confess to anything.

Attributed to Gregg Easterbrook

Introduction

Have a look at the following quotation:

> A new statin drug dramatically cuts the number of heart attacks and strokes, even for people without high cholesterol.
>
> In a major trial, daily treatment with Crestor slashed the rate of heart problems and deaths by 44 per cent.
>
> [...]
>
> Heart attacks were cut by 54 per cent, strokes by 48 per cent and the need for angioplasty or bypass by 46 per cent among the group on Crestor compared to those taking a placebo or dummy pill.
>
> Those taking Crestor, also known as rosuvastatin, were actually 20 per cent less likely to die from any cause.
>
> Hope, 2008

We read this kind of thing daily. It certainly looks impressive. There are sober references to trials and placebos, and the numbers and percentages – the statistical data – lend a sense of scientific authority. The results clearly seem to justify the claim that all of us should be taking Crestor. Surely this is information of the highest quality?

Maybe, but nothing is more likely to be misleading than statistical information. Even if you discounted the writer's hilarious last sentence – can it really be true that taking Crestor may increase your chances of living forever? – you may already have thought that statistics like these have to be carefully interpreted before they can truly count as information.

Part 4 of Block 2, which you have just completed, dealt with the theme of information: what it is; how it can be unearthed; and how the immense tide of information, pseudo-information and non-information that cascades daily from the electronic media may be evaluated and organised. Much of the information with which we grapple comes to us in the form of numbers, as in the example above. So Part 5 of this block, on which you're now embarking, is concerned with making sense of statistical data – information that comes to us in the form of numbers. It is organised in three sessions:

1   We were all taught numbers at school, but in Session 1 you'll step back to look at what numbers are actually good for, i.e. as a means of understanding the complicated and chaotic world we inhabit. This comes down to five related uses: *counting* things; *comparing* them; identifying *causes*; peering into the future to look at possible *consequences*; and finally dealing with uncertainty by estimating *chances*.

For many, numbers on their own are alien and difficult to understand, so Session 1 also introduces the idea of the statistical graphic, in which numbers are translated into shapes, patterns and spaces that the eye can readily take in.

2   Session 2 is a short interlude in which you will do two activities. In the first, you will use the SenseBoard to gather some numerical information of your own. In the second, you are asked to search for information, some of it statistical, from a number of sources and combine it in a formal report.

3   Session 3 returns to the five uses of numbers and looks at how each of them can be used, deliberately or otherwise, to distort and to mislead.

Learning outcomes

Your study of this part will help you to do the following.

Knowledge and understanding
- Describe some simple statistical methods and their applicability.
- Describe some guidelines for the effective presentation of numerical information.

Cognitive skills
- Use a software application to process statistically a data set.
- Use the SenseBoard to gather some statistical information.
- Discuss the role of statistics in everyday domains such as commerce, security, weather forecasting and economics.

Key skills
- Compile a report based on statistical and other data.

1

Interpreting numbers

> Aw, people can come up with statistics to prove anything, Kent. 'Forfty' per cent of all people know that.
>
> Homer Simpson, *The Simpsons* – 'Homer the Vigilante'

Daily, we fight through a blizzard of statistics. Hourly, the information media – radio, television, newspapers and the internet – bombard us with surveys, studies, official figures, audits and analyses. Sometimes it is hard not to feel like Winston Smith, the dingy, doomed anti-hero of George Orwell's *Nineteen Eighty-Four*, listening as:

> ... The fabulous statistics continued to pour out of the telescreen. As compared with last year there was more food, more clothes, more houses, more furniture, more cooking-pots, more fuel, more ships, more helicopters, more books, more babies – more of everything except disease, crime, and insanity.
>
> George Orwell, *Nineteen Eighty-Four*

But, as you will see, just as in the nightmare of *Nineteen Eighty-Four*, a vast proportion of this storm of numerical non-information is simply valueless. So, why bother with statistics at all?

1.1 What are numbers for?

Consider two very obvious facts about our world:

1 It is *big* and *messy*, a world of over six billion people, innumerable other creatures and things, and countless ideas, opinions and motives, swirling around in apparent chaos.

2 It is *unpredictable* and *risky*: in this colossal jumble, almost nothing can be taken as certain. It is human instinct to want to foresee the future – will I get cancer? what will my pension be? – and to plan for it. But how is this possible in such a vast and confusing world?

One way – perhaps the only way – to tackle the big questions about the world is to use numbers. Many people feel an aversion to numbers, but they do bring great advantages. In this session, I want to concentrate on five related purposes that numbers are good for, all conveniently beginning with 'C'.

1 *Counts*. The most obvious use for numbers is to count things.

2 *Comparisons*. Counting different things gives us a good basis for comparing them.

3 *Causes*. Comparing one thing with another may help us understand why things are happening.

4 *Consequences*. Comparisons may also enable us to detect trends and so make predictions about the future.

5 *Chances*. Using numbers, we can estimate the likelihood of certain things happening or not happening.

These categories overlap to some extent, but they are a neat way of organising our discussion. If they seem rather vague at the moment, then I hope to make all clear with plenty of examples.

Before you start thinking about these five uses of numbers, let's consider one way we can make the struggle with them easier and slightly more appealing.

1.2 Numbers and pictures

Let's be honest: many people hate numbers. They see them as alien, incomprehensible and deceptive, and there is good evidence that none of us are born with a capacity to understand them. It is something we have to learn.

But there is one natural power most of us are born with: an ability to make sense of visual images. Humans have evolved to interpret shapes, patterns and spaces. So the best statistical work often presents numbers in forms we can understand – as images, as patterns of shape and space. Let me try to illustrate this point with two famous examples.

Dr Snow's cholera map

On 31 August 1854, at 40 Broad Street in the Soho area of London, a man known to history only as Mr G. suffered the terrible death that the disease cholera brings. Within three days, 127 more people had died; within another week, over 500. By the time the outbreak petered out, over 600 people had lost their lives.

For more information see Johnson (2006).

At the time, there were two theories on the causes of cholera. The first, and by far the most widely held, was the miasmic hypothesis – that the disease was caused by 'bad air', by the spread of noxious, evil-smelling vapours. In a city where the Thames was the only cesspool, and where people often stored their sewage in their cellars or even under their floorboards, this was easy to believe. In summer especially, the stench was unimaginable. A rival theory, however, was that cholera spread through the action of a carrier, then unknown, in the water supply.

Dr John Snow, a physician famous for his work on anaesthetics, started to visit Soho to collect data on the outbreak. Teaming up with a local clergyman, Henry Whitehead, he diligently collected statistics: numbers and locations of cases, fatalities, distances between cases, water sources,

John Snow

and so on. Buried within the detail of these numbers was the answer to that central question – what was causing the outbreak? But this answer was far from easy to see, lost as it was among the figures. However, Snow's inspired idea was to present his results visually, in the form of a map.

Figure 1 reproduces Snow's map. It shows the street plan of the area in which the epidemic raged, with each case marked on it as a black dot. Crucially also, Snow marked in the positions of the pumps from which the locals drew their drinking water. At once it was clear that the pump I've marked, the one in Broad Street, lay at the heart of the problem. But note also the dotted line. Snow drew this to mark the area within which the

Figure 1   John Snow's cholera map

people found it most convenient, because of the patterns of the streets and distance travelled, to go to the Broad Street pump rather than to any other. You can easily see that pretty well all the cases lie within that area.

On 8 September 1854, the handle of the Broad Street pump was removed, and the outbreak died away almost immediately. Cholera is a waterborne disease.

Napoleon's retreat from Moscow

On 24 June 1812, with an army of over half a million men, Napoleon Bonaparte crossed the river Neman into Russia. His goal was Moscow. Marching nearly 700 miles through trackless forests, across dirt roads, mires and fens, crushing Russian armies along the way, the French entered Moscow on 14 September 1812. There they found the city deserted and stripped of all useful supplies. Looting and arson quickly broke out and four-fifths of the city was destroyed by fire. With no other option, Napoleon's army began a long retreat through the gathering Russian winter. Temperatures dropped to around −40 °C. Frozen and starving, the French struggled back the way they had come, plagued by disease, desertions and suicides, and harried by Russian troops all the way. By 22 December, the force had been ejected from Russia completely. Fewer than 40 000 men remained.

The figures alone speak of the extent of this calamity. But are there ways of making those figures more immediate? In 1869 Charles Joseph Minard, a French engineer, presented a map depicting the progress and effect of the whole campaign that has been described as 'the best statistical graphic ever drawn'. Figure 2 reproduces Minard's map.

Spend a bit of time looking at the map and then try the following activity.

Activity 1 (exploratory)

List some of the features of the French disaster that Minard has tried to illustrate on his map. How has he used space and shape to do this? Don't spend more than about 20 minutes on this.

Comment

Minard used spaces on the surface of the map to illustrate five different sets of statistics.

1 *Geography*: the map acts just like any other map, showing cities, rivers and so on.

2 *The army's route*: the light brown path shows the army's course towards Moscow; the black path shows the retreat.

3 *Numbers* are represented by the width of the path. Note how it gets narrower and narrower, and reflect that each millimetre the width contracts represents the loss of 10 000 men!

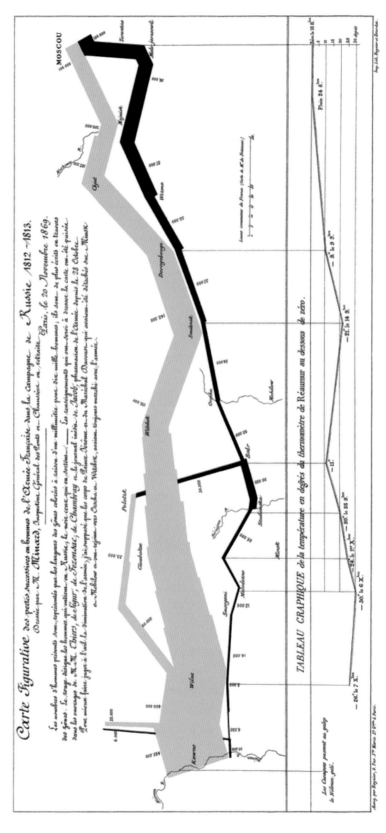

Figure 2 Minard's map of Napoleon's advance to, and retreat from, Moscow in 1812

4   *Temperature*: at the bottom, the steadily falling temperature is
     shown, using the French Réaumur scale (0° Réaumur = 0° Celsius;
     80° Réaumur = 100° Celsius).

5   *The passage of time during the retreat*: time flows from right to left below
     the temperature scale, from 24 October ('pluie' = 'rain') to 7 December
     (–27 °R = –34 °C).

A French scientist later remarked of the map: 'it defies the pen of the
historian in its brutal eloquence'.

Let's now consider how numbers help us understand the world: to count,
to compare, to pinpoint causes and consequences, and to estimate
chances.

1.3   Using numbers to cope

The world is big and messy. As I've already suggested, one way of
making sense of it is to count things, and then use the counts to make
meaningful comparisons. This whole approach is called *descriptive
statistics*.

Counts

Why and when do we need to count things? Obviously, we all do a fair bit
of counting in our daily lives. It's useful to know how much is in our bank
account, for instance, or how many children we have. But when we move
from our personal lives to questions on a larger stage, counting becomes
essential.

Consider this: maybe you think there is some kind of social or national
problem – crime, say, or poor health care? OK. But is it *really* a problem?
And if it is, how *big* a problem is it? The only way to estimate the size and
significance of any phenomenon sensibly is to start counting. It should be
easy enough; we've all learned how. Let's discuss an example, one I chose
because we are bombarded more with health statistics than with any other
kind – the question of *obesity*.

In everyday speech, 'obese ' is just another word for 'overweight' or, less
politely, 'very fat'. However, health professionals use a more technical
definition. If your body mass index (BMI) is over 25, you are overweight;
if it is over 30 you are obese. BMI is calculated by dividing a person's
weight in kilograms by the square of their height in metres.

I've simplified here. Health
professionals take into
account waist measurement
as well as BMI, and there are
various categories of obesity.

Activity 2 (self-assessment)

John Dough weighs 132 kg and is 1.91 metres tall. What is his BMI? Is he obese?

You will probably need to use a calculator for this activity.

Data from NHS Information Centre (2010).

Obesity is no joke. An obese woman is about 13 times as likely to develop diabetes, four times as likely to have high blood pressure, and nearly twice as likely to have a heart attack as a woman whose weight is satisfactory. (I'll consider the interpretation of statistics like these later in the part.) So if someone is obese they have cause to worry. But is obesity a national public health problem that politicians and concerned citizens should lose sleep over?

Really, the only way to answer this question is to count the obese people in Britain and then consider the result against the population of the whole country. Surely that's easy enough?

Samples and estimates

Not really. Reflect on the problem for a moment: how can we count the number of obese people in the country? The UK's population is about 61 million. Knocking on everyone's door would be astronomically costly and time-consuming (setting aside the fact that people might not wish to answer questions on something as personal as their weight). A local doctor or head teacher might be able to count the number of obese people in their care, but trying to get a national figure by simple counting is a non-starter.

The only way round this is to take a *sample* of the population and use it to *estimate* the figure we are after. For example, we could weigh and measure 10 000 UK citizens, count the obese individuals and then use this number to estimate the national figure by multiplying. Try this in the next activity.

Activity 3 (self-assessment)

Suppose we found 2422 obese individuals in our sample of 10 000. What would be your estimate of the number of obese people in the whole population?

In theory, this estimate should be roughly the right number for the whole population. However, we have to be very careful when we base our estimates on samples. Think about the reasons for this for a moment.

Activity 4 (self-assessment)

Why do you think we should be cautious when estimating from a sample?

I'll return to these points later. For now, let's move on to consider ways of thinking about the results we get when we count things.

Thinking about populations

So we do some counting, generally within a sample. What will the results tell us about the group as a whole? Let's introduce one or two statistical concepts.

Suppose we've assembled our sample of 10 000 people, and we calculate the BMI of each of them. Statisticians refer to each measurement as an *observation*, or sometimes just as a *statistic*, and the whole group as a *population*. Fair enough, but still all we have is a mess of numbers. However, remember that if we relate numbers to shape and space by constructing a *statistical graphic*, ideas hidden in the numbers may leap out.

Let's draw a picture in this way: for each BMI from, say, 16 to 40, count the number of people in the sample that have that BMI. We will get a set of results similar to those shown in Table 1.

Table 1   BMI measurements

BMI	Number counted
17	8
18	9
19	11
etc.	etc.

To display these results graphically, we can lay out the BMIs from 16–40 along a line known as an *axis* (see Figure 3), and over each draw a column whose height is proportional to the number of people counted for that BMI.

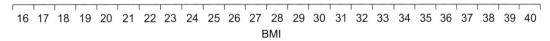

16 17 18 19 20 21 22 23 24 25 26 27 28 29 30 31 32 33 34 35 36 37 38 39 40

BMI

Figure 3   A scale of BMIs

So for BMI 21, for example, with 51 people counted, and BMI 27, with 124 people counted, we get something like Figure 4.

Notice how we can read off the number of people counted in each category on the second axis, the vertical scale on the left. However, the

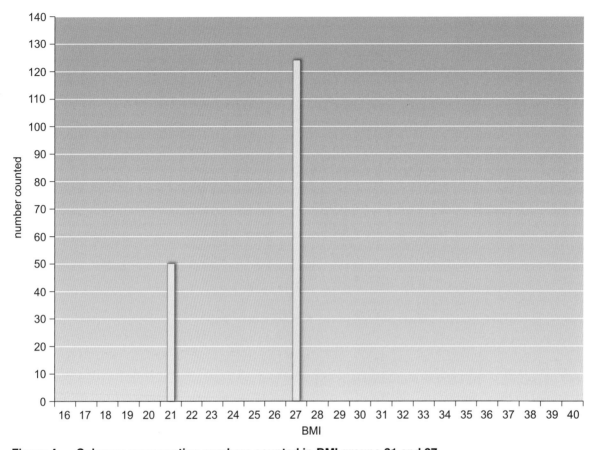

Figure 4   Columns representing numbers counted in BMI groups 21 and 27

height of the column alone, which we estimate instantly by eye, gives an excellent idea of the relative numbers counted in each BMI group.

Now, if we do that for all the BMIs in our sample, we will get something looking like Figure 5.

If we decide to measure our BMIs more accurately, counting also the half values between the whole number values (such as BMI 16½ or 21½), we get Figure 6.

It's a bit bumpy, but then the world is a messy place. However, the bigger our samples and the more accurately we calculate the BMIs, the closer the picture gets to the smooth symmetrical curve in Figure 7 – the *bell curve*.

This shape, which statisticians call the *normal distribution*, lies at the heart of all statistics. This is no place to delve too deeply into its many mysteries, but it is useful to make two observations about it.

First of all, notice the fact that the BMIs don't occur in equal numbers: there are comparatively few extremely obese and very skinny people, and much larger numbers somewhere between the two. This agrees with our everyday experience. Walk down any street and you will notice one or

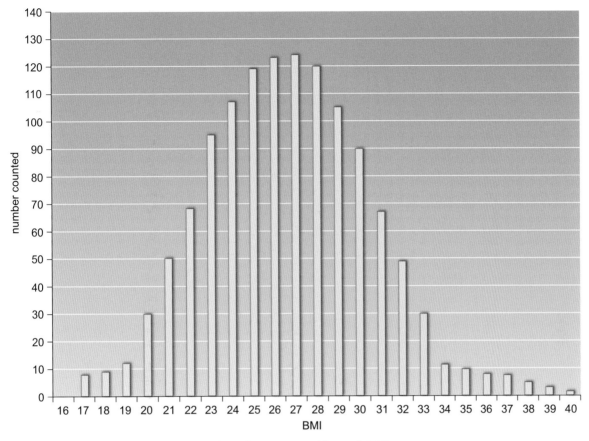

Figure 5   Column chart of full set of numbers counted in each BMI group

two featherweights and one or two heavyweights, but the majority are somewhere in the middle. So it is with many other human qualities. The overwhelming number of people we meet aren't super-intelligent or ultra-dumb, toweringly tall or vanishingly tiny, dazzlingly beautiful or hideously ugly – most are a bit on either side of average.

Statisticians are not generally very interested in the tiny minorities at either end of the bell curve (known as *outliers*). They usually focus on those many observations around the middle – what they call the *central tendency*. There are several ways of putting a value on this – but there is one we all learned at one time or another, and were taught to call the *average*.

Activity 5 (self-assessment)

Stretch your mind back to those maths lessons and calculate the average of the following set of figures:

3, 5, 7, 2, 8, 4, 4, 6, 7, 1

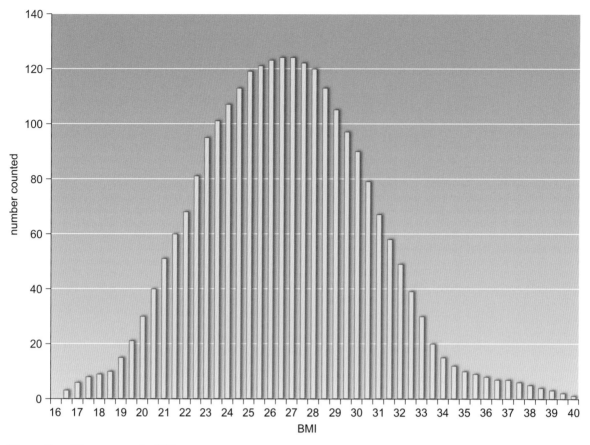

Figure 6   More accurate BMIs

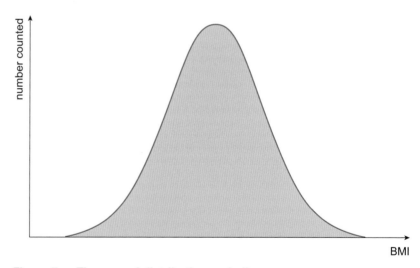

Figure 7   The normal distribution, or bell curve

In fact, there are several ways of evaluating this central tendency of a set of observations. To avoid confusion, statisticians refer to what we call the average as the *mean*. I'll look briefly at another type of average later.

Calculating the mean manually for large data sets would clearly be tedious, and professional statisticians use computer tools instead. However, just glance at the normal distribution in Figure 5 and the mean jumps out at you: it's the BMI at which the curve reaches its highest point. Note, though, that this is true for the normal distribution only. As you will learn later in the part, there are other distributions that don't have this property.

Activity 6 (self-assessment)

So what is the mean BMI of our sample above?

A second feature of the normal distribution curve for a set of observations is slightly harder to explain. It's called the *dispersion*. Think of it this way. Suppose we have two samples of BMI measurements, S1 and S2, both with the same mean. However, in S1 there are quite a lot of high and low measurements, and fewer round the middle. In S2, the observations are more tightly clustered round the mean. In other words, the values in S1 are more evenly spread out than in S2, even though the mean is identical.

This is easier to visualise if we compare the bell curves for each sample (Figure 8). Again, the difference is obvious when seen pictorially: S1 is clearly much more dispersed than S2. But note that despite the different shapes of the curves, the mean is the same in both.

As with the central tendency, there are various ways of calculating the dispersion of a set of observations. The two most common are the *variance* and the *standard deviation*. I'm not going to cover how these are calculated: all you do need to know is that a high variance, or a high standard deviation, means a large amount of dispersion.

Activity 7 (exploratory)

The tiny island state of Infomania has a population of only about 1500 souls, almost all of whom are bureaucrats, who have been collecting every kind of statistic for years. Among these is a very accurate set of weight and height statistics for the entire population.

In the resources page associated with this part on the TU100 website, you will find further information about Infomania and instructions on how to start doing statistical analyses using a spreadsheet. If you have never used a spreadsheet before, there is an introductory exercise you should go through ('Introduction to spreadsheets') that explains all the basic ideas.

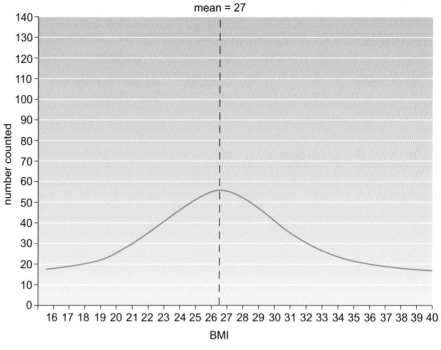

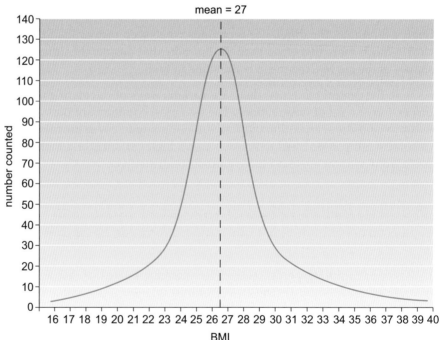

Figure 8   High and low dispersions

That's enough statistical terms. I've looked at the sort of results we get when we start counting, and noted a couple of ways to make sense of these results, but it's still hard to see that these figures are very informative. However, counts become more revealing when we start comparing things.

Comparisons

If you've paid attention to the BMI statistics so far, you've probably done a comparison in your head already, perhaps without even being aware of it. Recall that if a person has a BMI that is over 25, they are overweight. The national average BMI is 27. Comparing these two facts reveals that the UK is a nation of overweight people.

A further useful comparison we could make – it's another example of one we are hardly aware of as a comparison – is of the number of obese people against the size of the population as a whole. Calculating what *proportion* or *percentage* of the entire population some count represents should indicate the significance of the figure. If only 1% of the population is obese, it may not matter much. If it is 60% we have cause for concern.

Percentages are just fractions of 100, so 1% is one hundredth (1/100) and 60% is 60 hundredths (60/100). It was drilled into me at school that you calculate a percentage by dividing the number you've counted by the size of the population as a whole and then multiplying by 100. Mostly we just take the figure on trust, but to remind yourself, try this simple activity.

Activity 8 (self-assessment)

We've counted 57 people in an overall sample of 235 as being obese. What is the percentage of obese people? You will probably need to use your calculator for this activity.

In a study carried out by Foresight in 2007, the percentage of obese people in the UK was 24%. This is 24 hundredths – nearly a quarter. The population of the UK is 61 million, so 24% of 61 million means over 14.5 million obese people.

One way of capturing percentages in an arresting image is to use a graphic called a *pie chart*. The idea is simple: imagine a pie divided up into slices. The pie represents the whole population, and the size of each slice indicates the proportion of the population that a certain count corresponds to. This is illustrated in Figure 9 with a pie chart showing the proportions of underweight, normal, overweight and obese people in the UK.

As ever, our eye takes in the comparisons straight away. Even without the numbers on the chart, we instantly grasp the proportions involved.

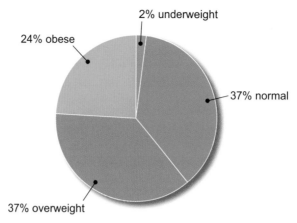

Figure 9   Pie chart showing proportions of underweight, normal, overweight and obese people in the UK population

This chart paints a depressing picture. But there are all sorts of other comparisons we might want to make. Are women worse affected than men? What about age groups: do younger people tend to have higher or lower BMIs than older? If we troubled to record the age and sex of each person in our sample then these two comparisons are easy, and we can even display the answers in the same picture, as in Figure 10.

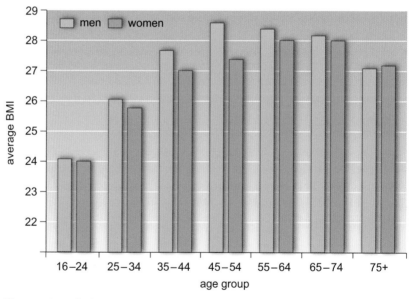

Figure 10   Column chart comparing BMIs of age groups

Once again, the height of the column shows the number of people counted in each group. So, at a glance, we can see that women tend to have slightly lower BMIs than men in all age groups except the oldest. It's also plain that average BMI seems to increase with age up to about 55, and then declines.

Take another comparison we might be interested in: region. Are people in some parts of the country more prone to obesity than others? Again, if we record where each person we measured comes from, we could depict the count for each region (of England in this case), as in Figure 11.

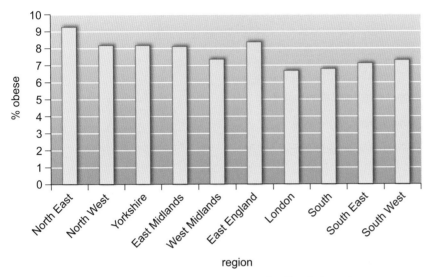

Figure 11   Column chart comparing obesity by English region

Alternatively, why not do what Minard did and present detailed results as a map, as in Figure 12? From the fairly crude classification by region that we get in Figure 11, the moral seems to be that one shouldn't live in north-east England. However, as you can see, the map reveals a more complex picture.

Activity 9 (exploratory)

Now to return to the Infomanian obesity statistics. Go to the resources page associated with this part on the TU100 website and follow the instructions for this activity on how to generate your own charts using a spreadsheet.

Causes and consequences

So, descriptive statistics – counting things and then making comparisons between the numbers we've counted – can reveal a lot about the way things are. But can we go further? Surely we are not just interested in the state of things *now*? We generally care just as much, or more, about *why* they are this way, *how* they got that way and what they are *going to be* in the future.

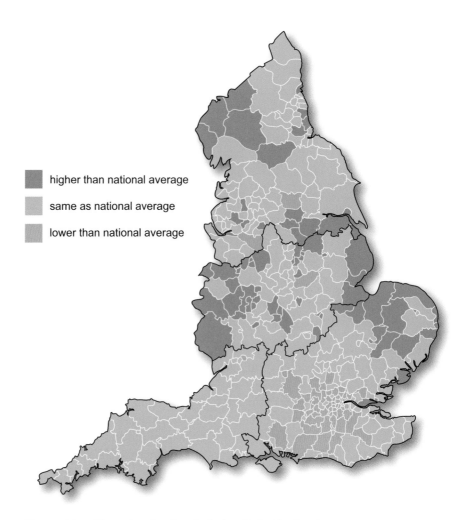

Figure 12   Map showing level of obesity in England

As I suggested earlier, comparing one count with another may uncover *trends* and so make predictions possible. Comparisons may also reveal the causes of things. Using numbers to establish causes and trends, and to make predictions, takes us into a new realm – *inferential statistics*.

Change and decay in all around I see

The world never stands still. Time flows on, and the fears of today transfer into anxieties about tomorrow. One of the deepest ironies of the human condition is that we are desperately concerned with what the future will bring, but have absolutely no way of knowing. We may get a vague feeling that things are getting better (or, much more often, worse), but without numbers this can only be a hunch. Numbers give us a way of forecasting the future that is not perfect, but is better than guesswork. They enable us to identify and project trends.

Let's stick with our obesity statistics. Are things getting better or worse? To tackle this question we obviously have to do another comparison – this time comparing the most recent count with one made in the past. Better still, we could compare the present count with a whole sequence of earlier ones, going further and further back. The obesity figures I've been quoting are based on surveys done in 2007–08. However, these are only the latest in a series of studies stretching back to 1993. Remember that the proportion of UK people counted as being obese in 2007 was 24%. Put this alongside the earlier measurements and we get Table 2.

Table 2   Proportion of obesity in the UK population by year

Year	Obese people (%)
1993	14.9
1994	15.7
1995	16.4
1996	17.5
1997	18.4
1998	19.4
1999	20.0
2000	21.2
2001	22.4
2002	22.5
2003	22.6
2004	22.9
2005	23.2
2006	23.9
2007	24.0

As usual with tables, this looks rather forbidding, although you can probably see a trend. However, presenting the results graphically once again brings it into clear focus (Figure 13).

The upward trend is unmistakable. But what about the future? Here we have to be careful. It is easy to imagine the line rising ever upwards, until there is no one left in the UK who can even climb the stairs, but things are seldom that simple. Statisticians have to use quite sophisticated techniques to project trends like this into possible futures. Nevertheless, the think-tank Foresight estimates that by 2015, 36% of men and 28% of women (aged between 21 and 60) will be obese. By 2025 the estimate is that 47% of men and 36% of women will be obese, rising to 60% of men and 50% of women in 2050 (Foresight, 2007).

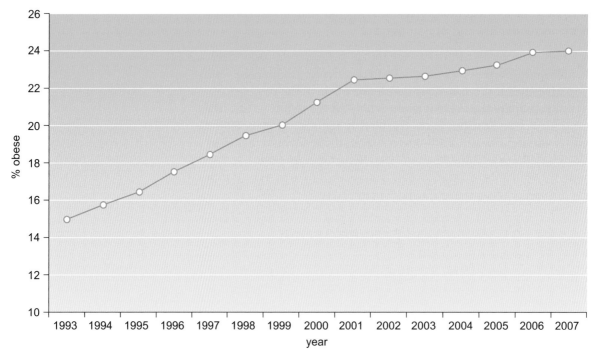

Figure 13   **Graph of UK obesity trend**

Activity 10 (exploratory)

The Infomanian health minister is worried about health trends on the island. Go to the resources page associated with this part on the TU100 website and follow the instructions for this activity to determine whether she is right to be alarmed.

Causes

So, the UK obesity picture is gloomy. Even if you are not overweight yourself, you are involved: your taxes will pay some of the extra NHS costs that will be the result, e.g. in treatment of heart attacks, stroke, diabetes, etc. But what can be done about it?

To answer this question, we first need some idea of what is causing these disturbing trends. The answer looks simple: as a people, we eat too much of the wrong things and exercise too little.

This may be true, but without numbers to back it up this explanation is no more than guesswork. So, *do* the numbers back it up? Well, in 2003 researchers counted the BMIs of individuals in three groups: those undertaking high, medium and low levels of physical activity. Figure 14 was created by calculating the percentage of individuals who were obese or overweight in each category, and then plotting the results in a column chart.

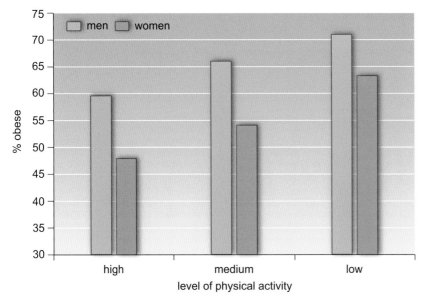

Figure 14   Column chart showing relationship between overweight/obesity and level of physical exercise

At first glance, there does seem to be a clear relationship between physical activity and obesity. In statistical jargon, we say that the two are *correlated*. By correlated, we simply mean that when one figure changes so does the other, in a predictable way. In this case, the percentage of obese individuals gets less as the level of physical activity increases, an example of what is called *negative correlation*.

We have to be careful here: a *correlation* does not necessarily mean a direct *cause*. I'll discuss this point in Session 3.

Activity 11 (self-assessment)

Given that the relationship between exercise and obesity is a negative correlation, what would a *positive correlation* be? Can you think of an example?

The 2003 figures show a similar correlation between obesity and diet – no surprises there. But so far what we have is rather superficial. It's all very well to point out that poor diet and lack of exercise are behind our current obesity problems, but that doesn't actually explain very much. What factors are causing people to behave in this way? Why now? Why is it getting worse?

These are complex sociological questions, but numbers may again be of some help. Pursuing the idea of the relationship of obesity to factors such as lifestyle, geography, poverty and ethnicity, statisticians turned up all sorts of correlations. To take one: is obesity somehow connected to low income, or outright poverty? Here the statistics tell a subtle story. Have a look at Figure 15.

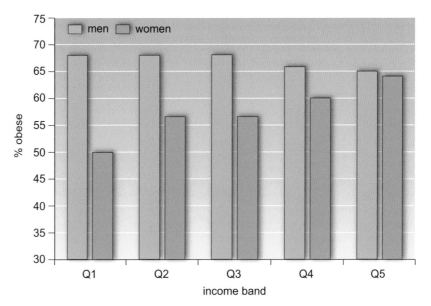

Figure 15   **Column chart showing relationship between overweight/obesity and income**

The income bands along the bottom scale, marked Q1, Q2, etc., are called *quintiles*. All this means is that the income distribution of the UK population has been divided into five equal ranges, with Q1 containing the top 20% of earners and Q5 the bottom 20%.

Things are less clear here than they were with the link between exercise and obesity. See what you think with the following activity.

Activity 12 (self-assessment)

On the evidence of Figure 15, what correlations, if any, can you see between income and obesity?

The 2003 statistics threw up all sorts of other correlations, some of which are unexpected. Obesity seems to be correlated with:

- ethnicity – Afro-Caribbean and Irish men had the highest prevalence
- marital status – stay single and stay slim
- smoking – smoke a lot and stay slim
- alcohol consumption – don't drink and stay slim.

You might wonder if staying thin is worth all the trouble.

Clinical trials

Hardly a day goes by during which we aren't hit with some new comparative health statistic. Why are comparisons so important in medicine?

Suppose a company comes up with a new drug – to cure eczema, say. Before they prescribe it, obviously doctors will want to know that it actually works. That sounds pretty easy: take two groups of people; give one group the drug and withhold it from the other; count people who get better in each group and compare. What could be simpler?

But of course it's not simple at all. Life is too chaotic for that. People get better for all sorts of reasons: illnesses clear up of their own accord, lifestyle plays a part, genetic factors matter. In fact, it is well known that just being given a pill – even a pill with no drug in it – can make people better, a phenomenon known as the *placebo effect*. So how, in such confusion, can we tell if a new drug really will cure you? Somehow we have to remove every possible other factor from the comparison, so that we are only comparing the effect of the medication with its absence – a *randomised*, *placebo-controlled*, *double-blind*, *clinical trial*.

Here is how such a trial works. Take a sample of people who are suffering from the illness we are trying to treat and divide them, at random, into two groups: the *active group* and the *control group* or *placebo group*. The active group are given the drug being tested, while the placebo group take a dummy pill that looks identical but has no drug in it (a *placebo*). Obviously subjects must not know if they are getting the drug or the placebo, but the experimenter must not know either – the test is *double-blind* – so the random assignment to groups is generally done by a computer.

'At random' here means that every individual has an equal chance of being included in one or the other group.

Activity 13 (self-assessment)

Why do you think it is important that the experimenter doesn't know who is getting the drug and who isn't?

If, at the end of the trial, more people in the active group have got better than in the placebo group, then surely the drug works? Perhaps, but it could have been mere chance. We know that people get better of their own accord, and it might just be that this simply happened more in the active group.

Here things get difficult. The experimenters now have to do a careful statistical analysis. They need to show that the result is *statistically significant*, meaning that there is a very low probability that greater rates of improvement in the active group arose from pure chance. They calculate what is known as a *p-value*; if this is below 0.05, or sometimes below 0.01, then it is considered vanishingly unlikely that the result was a matter of pure chance. How this analysis works is beyond my scope here. But I do need to underline how big a part pure chance plays in our lives, so let's now turn to questions of risk and probability.

Chances

Tom Stoppard's play *Rosencrantz and Guildenstern Are Dead* begins with the two main characters, Rosencrantz and Guildenstern, alone on stage flipping coins (Figure 16). They have evidently been doing this for some time, and it soon becomes clear that every single coin is coming down heads. Although Guildenstern seems oblivious to the oddness of this, Rosencrantz knows – and we, the audience, know too – that something strange is happening. This is not the way the world works. Flipped coins, if they are fair, do not fall heads every time.

A *fair coin* is one that genuinely has a 50:50 chance of falling heads or tails, i.e. it is not double-headed or biased in some other way.

Figure 16   Malcolm Tulip (Guildenstern), left, and Loren Bass (Rosencrantz) in *Rosencrantz and Guildenstern Are Dead*

Our world is a chancy place. Very few things will happen with absolute certainty (except death and TMAs): there is usually only some possibility or risk that an event will happen. We tend to speak of possible pleasant outcomes in terms of the *chances* that they will happen, and of unpleasant ones in terms of their *risk*; but really we are talking about the same thing – about *probability*. Flipped coins and thrown dice are our classic images of probability.

Do we just have to accept the chances and risks and hope for the best? Not entirely. We do have a way of at least estimating the likelihood of some future event happening, and thus maybe taking steps to increase or lessen it. Numbers once again come to our aid.

Reckoning probabilities

Humans generally seem to be very poor at judging and reasoning about probabilities. A weather forecaster on a US TV network is alleged once to have announced that since there was a 50 per cent chance of rain on Saturday and a 50 per cent chance of rain on Sunday, there was thus a 100 per cent chance of it raining on both Saturday and Sunday. One doesn't have to be a professional mathematician to suspect that there was something wrong with this reasoning. But to demonstrate just how bad most of us are at thinking about probabilities, here is a classic question.

Activity 14 (exploratory)

How many people would there need to be in a room together for there to be a 50:50 (50%) chance of two of them having the same birthday? Try to think carefully about this one before you look at the answer.

Comment

You may have heard this one already, but if you haven't then you might be surprised at the answer. Maybe you thought along these lines: there are 366 days in the year (counting leap years), so to be absolutely certain (100% chance) of any two people in our room having the same birthday, we would need to assemble 367 people. Quite right. So, most of us might then go on to suggest that we would need about half that number – say about 183 – for a 50:50 chance.

Wrong. In fact we would need only 23 people in the room for a 50:50 chance of two of them having the same birthday. If you are interested in how this is worked out, you'll find an explanation in the resources page associated with this part on the TU100 website.

The mathematics of probability can be tricky, and this is no place to discuss it in any depth. But, since probability plays such a large part in our lives, and since we are so bad at reasoning about it, it's worth saying just a bit more.

We can start with our familiar standby, the flipped coin. Here is an easy activity.

Activity 15 (self-assessment)

Flip a fair coin once. What are the chances of it coming down heads?

There are several ways of expressing this basic idea. For example, we might talk about:

- the *odds* of heads – 2 to 1
- the *chance* of heads – 50:50
- the *relative chance* of heads – 1 in 2
- the *percentage chance* or *risk* of heads – 50%.

But remember these are all ways of expressing the same thing: the *probability* of heads. The formal way to state the probability of any event is as a number between 0 (certain *not* to happen) and 1 (certain *to* happen), with probabilities in between as fractions of 1. So the probability of the coin landing heads is ½ or 0.5 (exactly midway between 0 and 1).

Now, a trickier question. Flip the coin twice. What are the chances of it coming down heads both times?

It should be clear at once that the weatherperson mentioned above was hopelessly wrong: on their reasoning the probability of it raining on both Saturday and Sunday was ½ + ½ = 1. But two heads in a row is obviously not a certainty. So what is the probability? The weatherperson's mistake was to *add* the probabilities; what we have to do is *multiply* them. The probability of two heads in a row is ½ × ½ = ¼ or 0.5 × 0.5 = 0.25; we could express this result as 4 to 1, 1 in 4 or 25%, depending on the context. This *multiplication principle* applies however many flips we want to consider: three heads in a row has a probability of 0.5 × 0.5 × 0.5 = 0.125 or 12.5%; four heads in a row is 0.5 × 0.5 × 0.5 × 0.5 = 0.0625 or 6.25%, and so on.

Activity 16 (self-assessment)

Let's take a slightly more complex example. Suppose I have a chest of drawers with four drawers:

- Drawer 1 contains four shirts: red, green, blue and white.
- Drawer 2 contains five pairs of trousers: black, grey, green, fawn and blue.
- Drawer 3 contains three ties: mauve, green and blue.
- Drawer 4 contains six pairs of socks: black, blue, white, pink, green and yellow.

Staggering up in the dark of a winter morning, I grope blindly into each drawer, pulling out one item from each. What are the chances of my ending up with an all-blue outfit?

An even less likely prospect is my winning the National Lottery. Like you, probably, I offer up my pound each week – the price of a little fantasy. But what is the probability that I'll win the jackpot? This is a slightly trickier calculation, although it is along similar lines. I won't rehearse it here (you can find details on the TU100 website). However, it might be sobering to reflect, when you next hand over your pound, that the probability of a jackpot is about 0.000000072 or just under 14 million to 1.

Estimating probabilities

The probabilities we are really interested in can't usually be calculated so easily – the world is far messier than the flip of a coin. Let's return to our obesity statistics for the last time. Earlier, I quoted a few risk estimates for obesity – a 13 times increased risk of diabetes, four times the risk of high blood pressure, and so on. How are these figures calculated?

There is only one way – to gather and analyse data from the past, doing comparisons and finding correlations over a long period. For years, doctors and scientists will have collected data on obese people and the illnesses they suffer, comparing health outcomes for obese and non-obese individuals. All this data will be combined and analysed in huge *meta-studies*. Gradually correlations will emerge, and the more data we collect the more precisely we can estimate the probability of certain outcomes, such as diabetes, heart attack, etc. But remember, these figures cannot represent certainties – only degrees of risk.

1.4   Conclusion

So there we have it: counts, comparisons, causes, consequences and chances.

For any problem or issue we want to investigate, we can get a grasp of its nature and size by *counting*, and counting allows us to make *comparisons*. We call this descriptive statistics. These figures then give us a basis for reasoning further about the problem – inferential statistics. Comparisons give us a starting point for understanding the problem's *causes* and *consequences*, and allow us to project the figures forward in time and so suggest how things may develop in the future. Numbers also allow us to estimate risks or *chances*. Throughout, you've seen how the numbers can be made immediately understandable by means of statistical graphics.

Time to take a break now – you'll return to these five uses of numbers in Session 3.

This session should have helped you with the following learning outcomes.

- Describe some simple statistical methods and their applicability.
- Describe some guidelines for the effective presentation of numerical information.
- Use a software application to process statistically a data set.

2

Interlude – writing a report

The previous session ended with the five uses of numbers as a source of information. In Session 3, I'll return to these five and look at some of the ways they can be abused – and are abused daily – in the name of 'information'. But now you will have a short interlude in which to practise two key skills, to prepare you for the rest of the part.

The following activity is the first in a series of exercises that will start you on the road to using the SenseBoard to gather some numerical data of your own. This data can be recorded in a file of a form that can be read by a spreadsheet such as the Google Docs software you have been using or Microsoft Excel. The spreadsheet can then be used to analyse the data, draw graphs and so on.

Activity 17 (exploratory)

Go to the Sense activities section of the 'Study resources' page on the TU100 website and follow the instructions you find there for this activity.

The next activity is more general. One requirement of a multitude of jobs, both inside and outside IT, is an ability to track down information from a number of sources and to bring it together in the shape of a formal report. This is one of the key skills that we want you to develop in TU100. Another essential skill for success in formal study, and particularly in study at the OU, is the ability to interpret the assignment feedback you receive from your tutor and to use it to improve your future work. So, in the next activity I am asking you to produce a report combining both verbal and numerical information, and then to compare your report with two marked sample answers.

I hope you will tackle this activity, as doing so should help you improve your grade in the next TMA.

Activity 18 (exploratory)

Access the resources page associated with this part on the TU100 website and follow the instructions you find there for this activity.

This session should have helped you with the following learning outcomes.

- Use a software application to process statistically a data set.
- Use the SenseBoard to gather some statistical information.
- Compile a report based on statistical and other data.

3 Deceptive numbers

Numbers may be the best way to make sense of our big and messy world, but most of the issues that really matter – unemployment, poverty, immigration, health, global warming – tend to be intensely political. More or less anyone discussing them will have some line they want to promote, so the temptation to distort the numbers to suit that agenda – or simply to twist the numbers into outright lies – is often irresistible.

It's fair to say that much of the statistical information showered over us today is a mass of distortion, hysteria, misreporting, concealment and lies. In this session, I want to take you through some of the ways we can be misled. There is only space to cover a few of the most flagrant errors and tricks here, but I hope that, at the very least, it will make you immediately suspicious whenever someone begins a sentence with 'The statistics prove …'.

Let's abandon the obesity numbers now, and revisit our five activities – counting, comparing, uncovering causes and consequences, and estimating chances – with a set of new examples that all demonstrate how, accidentally or deliberately, to make a complete mess of them.

3.1 Creative counting

> Not everything that counts can be counted, and not everything that can be counted counts.
>
> Albert Einstein, notice in his Princeton office

All statistics start with counting. It's as easy as 1, 2, 3.

Very true, but counting is easy only if you know exactly *what* you are counting. Counting the number of empty bottles on the floor, or the number of overdue library books, shouldn't present problems. But as soon as we try to count really important and interesting things, the sheer messiness of the world overwhelms us.

What to count

In the previous session you looked at a perfect example: *unemployment*. How many unemployed people are there in the UK? That doesn't sound too hard. However, as you saw, before we start we have to settle what it means to be unemployed. On the face of it, that doesn't sound hard either: surely an unemployed person is just someone not working. But what about people who don't want to work or don't need to? All right, so to be unemployed means wanting work, but not being able to find any. But what about people who want to work, but are too ill, or are carers? OK, an unemployed person is willing and able to work, but can't find any. What about older people, beyond retirement age? And what counts as work? Part-time work? Unpaid voluntary work? Housework? Hobbies? What about people who are only temporarily not working – moving between jobs, say?

You've already seen that both the UK and US governments have had to put a lot of agonised thought into a definition of what it means to be unemployed. It's obvious that things simply don't fit into neat categories, nor do they stand still. A worse problem is that unemployment numbers are another highly political matter. The government will want to present as low a figure as possible; their opponents will want the opposite. They can both achieve their aim by working from different definitions, and altering those definitions as it suits them. Between 1980 and 1988, for example, the UK government made 23 changes to the definition of unemployment, each time – surprise, surprise – resulting in a lower number than the previous one. So counting anything must be based on a definition, and some definitions are always likely to be controversial. Worse still, the definition may often not fit in at all with our everyday ideas about the thing being defined. To take another example, consider the concept of poverty.

Or 26 changes: even counting the number of changes is problematic – see *The Tiger that Isn't* (Blastland and Dilnot, 2007).

In any decent society poverty is unacceptable, and we all believe that governments should tackle it. So among a government's priorities will be to count the number of poor people, based on some agreed definition. What does the word 'poverty' suggest to you? Possibly you get mental pictures of squalid, damp rooms; of ragged, helpless children, their bellies swollen with hunger; of starvation and disease. But what does poverty mean *officially*?

Activity 19 (exploratory)

Spend a few minutes on the Web finding out how the UK government currently defines poverty. As you would expect, this is a very intricate problem, so there is no need to go into too much detail.

Comment

Governments usually distinguish between *absolute* and *relative* poverty. In 1995, the UN defined absolute poverty as:

> ... a condition characterized by severe deprivation of basic human needs, including food, safe drinking water, sanitation facilities, health, shelter, education and information.

> United Nations, 1995, p. 41

But governments generally prefer definitions based on relative poverty – that is, poverty as compared to the general standard of living in the country in question. One popular measure is based on income: households in poverty are living on less than 60% of the median national income.

This is based on one set of figures. Measuring income is pretty tricky too.

The median is just a special way of measuring averages, which I'll discuss shortly. All that matters for now is the reflection that the UK median income in 2008 was just under £21 000, so an officially 'poor' household living on 60% of that would have a yearly income of about £12 600 or below.

I certainly don't want to pretend that £12 600 a year is a lot of money, but people are sometimes surprised to learn that this is the figure at which poverty officially starts in the UK. It doesn't altogether fit with the UN definition above or the images that the word conjures up – penury, starvation, squalor. In the USA, with higher median incomes and generally lower costs, people officially classified as being in poverty may have reasonable homes, television sets and even cars.

Valerie Pegg (2005) also highlights the issue of defining binge drinking.

One final example that is maybe a little closer to home: are you a binge drinker? Well, according to official definitions you may be. But before you aim a furious slap at me, consider this: the UK government defines a binge as drinking twice the recommended maximum for a day in one session. Now, the recommended weekly alcohol intake is about 21 units; divide by seven and you get a daily figure of 3 units. Multiply by two, and a binge is 6 units. Last night I had a meal with a friend: a pint of lager before the meal – 3 units; a shared bottle of wine over the meal – 5 units. Hey presto! 8 units: a binge, although maybe not everybody's idea of one. So I'm a binge drinker too.

Two out of three doctors agree ...

... and the third couldn't make up his mind. It's an old joke, but what is it saying about counting? Well, remember that most significant counts can't be done directly: they have to be estimated on the basis of samples (Figure 17). But for the result to be of any use, certain things have to be true of the sample.

Activity 20 (self-assessment)

Try to recall what properties a sample needs for it to be a reliable basis for a count.

Figure 17 Yet another survey

Numbers, especially official numbers, give an air of grave authority. They seem precise, dignified and unchallengeable. Mighty organisations are dedicated to the simple activity of gathering them. But would it surprise you to hear that many counts based on samples are more or less complete guesswork? Let's consider four small case studies of counting from samples.

Information from National Statistics (2008).

1   According to official statistics, there were 300 000 migrants into the UK in 2008. One body responsible for collecting migration statistics is the International Passenger Survey (IPS). IPS officials, stationed on passenger ferries and at airports, armed with clipboards and a questionnaire, select passengers to ask about the purpose of their journey. About 300 000 passengers a year are interviewed, of whom about 600–700 admit to being immigrants.

2   In 2008, a major insurance company commissioned a polling organisation to conduct a survey into cycling safety. There were 2193 responses to an online questionnaire. From the responses, the pollsters concluded that 43% of adults in Britain cycle, and that there had been a 29% increase in cycling accidents in the six months of May–November 2008 compared with the previous six-month period.

3   Around 2006, Durham County Council's Education Department, troubled by poor exam performance for some time, set up a trial in which 5000 children in their GCSE year were given a daily dose of six fish oil capsules supplied by the drug company Equazen. The children's educational progress from then on was followed in the press and TV, and at the end of the year-long trial, their actual exam results were compared with the results predicted for them by their teachers. The idea was to establish whether fish oil could improve children's memory, concentration and reasoning skills.

4   The National Hedgehog Survey was set up in 2000 to report on populations of hedgehogs in the UK. Its scope was broadened to become the Mammals on Roads survey in 2002. It estimates populations of hedgehogs and other small mammals by counting the numbers of corpses found flattened by cars on UK roads. Between 2001 and 2004, it reports, populations of hedgehogs fell by about 25%, although the rate of decline may have slowed recently, as shown in Figure 18.

Data taken from Mammals Trust UK (2005).

Now, recalling the points made above about effective samples, think about the following.

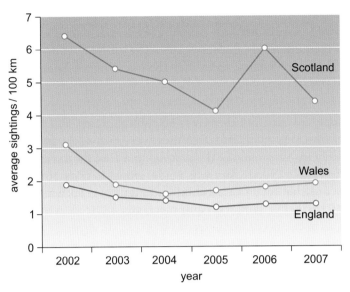

Figure 18   Dead hedgehogs

Activity 21 (exploratory)

How valuable a basis for counting do you think the samples in the case studies would be? Jot down a few ideas on each of the four.

Comment

My thoughts ran along the following lines.

1   A sample of 300 000 sounds a lot, but remember that the sample must be large in proportion to the population under scrutiny. Here, the IPS is dealing not with the population of the UK, but with the *journeys* made by individuals to and from the country. This is a staggeringly large number: to get an idea of just how large, consider the fact that over 67 million passengers passed through Heathrow *alone* in 2008. So 300 000 is, in fact, a tiny proportion of the journeys made.

There are further problems with the sample: IPS interviewers are free to choose whoever they want, and they are bound to be biased in their choice. Which would you pick, the shaven-headed youth with tattoos or the little grey-haired old lady? Moreover, as no one is obliged to answer, all sorts of further biases are likely to creep in. It is highly unlikely that the sample will be a random one.

2   A sample of 2193 is a respectable size in a survey of this kind, but the fact that it was conducted online should make us cautious. A problem with samples in online studies is that they are self-selecting: the people who respond have chosen to do so, and may have some personal axe to grind, such as having suffered an accident themselves. Therefore they are not likely to be representative of the population as a whole.

Another old joke: nine out of ten people who responded thought that surveys are a good thing.

The finding that 43% cycle is suspiciously high. The UK General Household Survey, carried out with carefully randomised samples, concludes that the number is only about 19%. The estimate of the number of cycling accidents is greater than the government figures by a factor of ten.

3   There were many fatal flaws in this experiment. The sample was probably an adequate size, but there was no control group, and the children were conscious at all times that they were in a study, and in the glare of publicity, thus making the placebo and Hawthorne effects more or less inevitable. No attempt was made, either, to filter out any of the other factors that might cause children to improve, such as new teaching initiatives, better staff and equipment, etc.

4   It would be very difficult to conclude from this sample that hedgehog populations have fallen. The sample is only of hedgehogs that have been squished, so what is being measured? Hedgehog populations may be stable, and there may simply be more cars on the road. Or hedgehogs might have developed much better road sense, so fewer of them are being flattened. Who knows?

So, whenever you see claims made on the basis of a sample, the questions you should ask yourself are these:

How big? How representative? How random?

The elusive Mr Average

From an (imaginary) estate agent's blurb concerning a new estate:

The Leafmould Estate is an area of architect-designed properties enjoying stunning rural views. The average cost of a house on the estate is £250 000, while the average council tax band is D (£68 000–£88 000) ...

No one expects estate agents' literature to be fountains of honesty, but surely there is a plain contradiction here? Council tax bands are based on the valuations of houses, so the agent seems to be claiming that the average value of a house on the estate is £250 000 (and thus that the estate is a beautiful, opulent area) and at the same time is somewhere between £68 000 and £88 000, say £78 000 (and so has quite low council tax). Which is true?

The problem is that they can both be true, because the meaning of the word 'average' is ambiguous. Remember that the average is a way of measuring the central tendency of a population. But in fact there are several, quite different, ways of doing this. Switching between them, while just blandly referring to the 'average', can be a way of telling all sorts of lies.

Let's focus on our estate agent's claims: how can an average of £250 000 and an average of about £78 000 both be right? Well, suppose there were only eleven houses on the Leafmould Estate, with values as in Table 3.

Table 3 Prices of properties on the Leafmould Estate

Property	Value (£)
Chez Nous	72 000
Mon Repos	77 982
Rivendell	76 154
Totleigh Towers	1 034 567
Dunroamin	74 568
Cartref	84 876
Fisherman's Rest	79 213
The Moorings	71 459
Lothlorien	88 126
Blandings Castle	993 456
The Laurels	78 135

No need to do the calculation yourself: the mean value of the eleven properties is £248 231. However, another measure of the average is known as the *median*, and is defined as the middle value of a group of values, with an equal number of values above and below it. Test your understanding of this definition with the following activity.

Activity 22 (self-assessment)

What is the mean of the following set of values: 1, 1, 5, 5, 6, 7, 19, 24, 36? What is the median? You will probably need to use a calculator for this activity.

So what is the median value of our eleven properties? This looks a little trickier, but start by sorting the values into ascending order:

£71 459
£72 000
£74 568
£76 154
£77 982
£78 135
£79 213
£84 876
£88 126
£993 456
£1 034 567

It is then much easier to see that £78 135 is the median, with five properties below it in value and five above. So our estate agents are telling the truth (sort of): they are using the *mean* house price to advertise the desirability of the area, and the *median* house price to draw attention to the low council tax.

What is going on here? Why are the median and the mean not the same? The answer lies in the way that the values are distributed.

Activity 23 (self-assessment)

Have another look at Table 3. What strikes you about the range of values you can see there?

Look back at Figure 7, showing the smooth, bell-shaped curve of the normal distribution (you drew similar curves in Activity 7). Note that it is perfectly symmetrical about the mean. In the case of distributions like this, the median and the mean *will* be the same. But if we were to draw the distribution of house prices on the Leafmould Estate, we would get a curve like Figure 19.

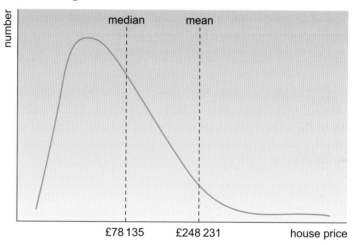

Figure 19   Distribution of house prices on the Leafmould Estate

What has happened is that the absurdly high prices of the two top properties have pulled the whole curve out of shape, distorting it towards the right-hand side and creating what statisticians call a *skewed distribution*. The mean has been dragged away from the median towards the right by the million-pound properties.

This might simply be a statistical curiosity, were it not for the fact that politicians are obsessed with the average: they love to appeal to the middle ground, forever chattering about the 'average family', the 'middle classes' and so on. For governments of the 1980s and 1990s, it was 'middle Britain'; since then it has been 'ordinary hard-working families'. Any proposed change, we are always told, will never adversely affect these 'average' people – people like us. But who are these people really?

When we think of 'middling' people, perhaps we think of homeowners with a car, possibly fairly conservative, not rich but safely employed in white-collar jobs, with a reasonable income and some savings. But the earlier example of poverty should teach us to be cautious – too often there is a gap between our picture of something and the reality. How realistic a picture is this? What do the numbers tell us?

The obvious way of putting numbers to work here is to consider income. After all, money is a key factor in determining an individual's or a family's lifestyle. So middling people must to some extent be people with middling, average incomes. But what does that mean in the UK?

Figure 20 shows the distribution of net income in the UK for 2008. You can see that it is a typically skewed distribution, with the mean income pulled away from the median by high-income earners. In fact the distribution is a great deal more skewed than the figure suggests: the bar on the furthest right represents, lumped together, the 1.2 million individuals who earn over £1500 a week – but as we know, this includes some who are so colossally rich that £1500 a week would be peanuts to them. To fit these incomes onto the diagram, the scale would have to be extended literally yards to the right.

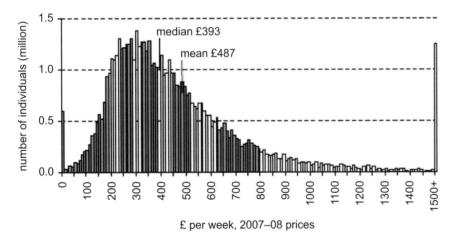

Figure 20   Income distribution in the UK, 2007–08 (Brewer et al., 2009, p. 5)

Now you can easily see that 'Mr or Ms Average' earns £393 a week (£20 436 a year – the median income). It's not poverty, but it's certainly not wealth, and may not even be a comfortable income these days. Compare this to the insurance company AXA's definition of 'middle Britain' as households with gross incomes between £40 000 and £100 000, with an average of £62 500. 'Average' earners have elsewhere been defined as paying the 40% rate of income tax.

For more details see TUC (2009).

Now if we divide the population by income into quintiles, each containing about 20% of UK adults, and focus on the 3rd quintile (about £325–£450 a week) – the middling people – then slightly surprising facts emerge. A TUC survey of the 3rd quintile, conducted in 2008, revealed that:

* fewer than 30% had a university degree, with 12% having no qualifications at all

* 32% had been unemployed in the past ten years

* 33% had no pension scheme

* 49% had no savings over £1000

* 44% read the *Sun*, *Mirror* or *Star* newspapers

* 24% described themselves as 'left-wing' politically, 30% as 'in the centre' and 17% as 'right-wing'.

This does not, perhaps, conform to AXA's view of 'middle Britain'. It is also revealing to look at how well our middle group has actually done in the past few decades, since politicians always claim to be looking after their interests. Once again, a graphic will be much more eloquent than mere words (Figure 21).

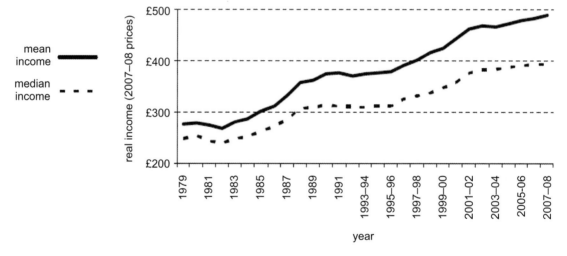

Figure 21   Changes in median and mean income, 1979–2008 (Brewer et al., 2009, p. 8)

Activity 24 (self-assessment)

What do you think Figure 21 shows us about how well the middling folk have done in the past 30 years?

The raw figures tell an even bleaker story: between 1979 and 1997, the incomes of the richest 20% of the UK grew by 2.5%, while median incomes grew by only 1.6%. Between 1997 and 2008, median incomes grew by about 1.6% again; the incomes of the richest grew by almost 2%.

Activity 25 (exploratory)

The Infomanian Ministry of Finance keeps careful records of the incomes of all Infomanian citizens. An election is forthcoming in Infomania and both government and opposition politicians are anxious to talk about wealth and tax.

Go to the resources page associated with this part on the TU100 website and follow the instructions for backing the arguments of either side.

Draw your own conclusions, but next time you hear someone talking about the 'average man' or the 'average family', ask:

Average? Which average?

3.2   Deceptive graphics (1) – chartjunk

You've already seen several examples of how images can be used to convey complicated data in vivid and striking ways. You've also now learned that it is easy to construct a pleasing graphic of your own. However, statistical graphics are as open to abuse as any other form of statistical information, and one of the most common forms of abuse is unintentional – it's called *chartjunk*.

Have a look at the chart in Figure 22. What information do you think it is trying to convey?

Most of us would agree that it's hard to tell. The diagram appears to be a graph, depicting changes in three quantities over time, but what these quantities are is mysterious. There is no scale at the side from which we could read values, as there is in Figure 4 above, say. The eye is confused by a riot of text, icons, colours and visual elements that are distracting or simply irrelevant to the information represented by the graph. The designer's whole emphasis has been on making the picture look flashy.

What is the purpose of a statistical graphic? Simply this: to convey information as clearly and immediately as possible – and to convey the information alone. So chartjunk is anything that distracts the eye from the information, or makes the information harder to discern, or adds nothing to the information message. It can appear in more innocent forms than in the example above. Have a look at the bar chart in Figure 23.

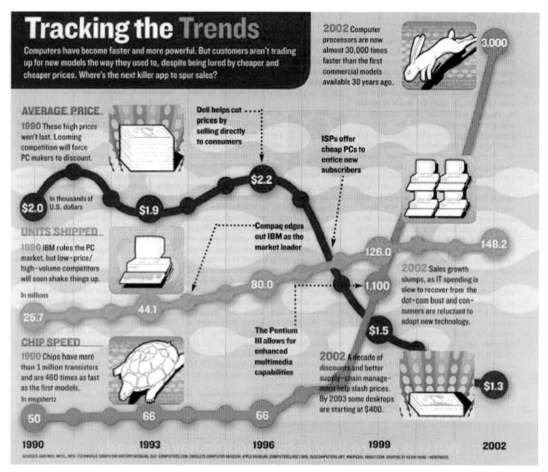

Figure 22   Chartjunk at its worst

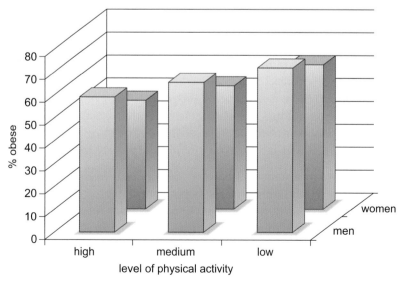

Figure 23   3D representation of Figure 14

This shows exactly the same obesity and exercise data as Figure 14 above, but has been put into a pleasing-looking 3D format.

Activity 26 (self-assessment)

Do you think this graphic is more or less informative than Figure 14?

You can see the same problem if we try to make the pie chart from Figure 9 look more interesting. A superficially more pleasing way to present it is as in Figure 24. But is this really an improvement? The 3D effect really only makes the proportions harder to judge.

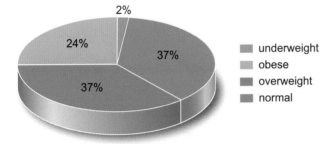

Figure 24   More chartjunk: 3D representation of Figure 9

Chartjunk also turns up in distracting crosshatching on diagrams (see Figure 25a) or garish and unnecessary colouring (see Figure 25b).

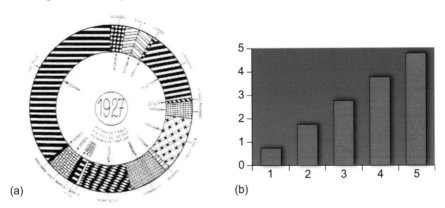

(a)   (b)

Figure 25   (a) Confusing crosshatching; (b) garish colouring

3.3   Crude comparisons

> Comparisons are odorous.
>
> Shakespeare, *Much Ado About Nothing*, III. v. 15

This is an age of league tables. From newspapers, television and the internet flows a cascade of surveys in which schools, health providers, local councils, products and companies are compared and ranked. Even

"Remember, son...money can't buy happiness,
but it pays for a lot of anti-depressants."

Figure 26   Happy now?

the relative happiness of citizens of the countries of the world has been compared (Figure 26). In a survey of 2006, the world's nations were compared on the Satisfaction with Life Index. The happiest country turned out to be Denmark, and the most miserable Burundi; the UK came 41st.

In Session 1 of this part, you learned about the importance of comparisons in statistical analysis. As an example, I compared the incidence of obesity across gender, exercise habits and region. Evaluations like this might be useful, and to compare things is only human. But just how valuable are comparisons of such things as schools, councils and nations? Are we really the 41st least grumpy country on earth?

To compare my height with yours, the number of obese people in the north with the number in the south, or the average temperatures last summer with this summer's is easy. But when it comes to comparing many interesting things, a fog of confusion descends. To compare one nation's happiness against another's, we have to know how to measure happiness in the first place. How is this possible?

Activity 27 (exploratory)

Think of ways in which happiness, or satisfaction with life, could be measured. How would it be possible to put a number on it? How would this compare with putting a number on BMI, say, or temperature?

Comment

This comes down to the problem of definition I dealt with earlier. To put a numerical value on temperature or BMI is simple: both terms refer to a single thing with a clear definition. By contrast, happiness is an exceptionally vague concept with no clear definition, which may refer to a whole set of different things, related or unrelated.

One possible way of measuring the happiness of a nation might simply be to ask a sample of its people to assess their happiness on a scale of 1–10. Or, if this seems too unscientific, we might try to measure the set of things about a country that are likely to make its citizens happy: good healthcare, effective education and governance, for instance.

The Satisfaction with Life study quoted above basically used *subjective measures*, in which people were asked to rate their own happiness. In this approach happiness, like BMI, was treated as being a single, well-defined idea. Statisticians refer to such precise concepts as being *single indicator* concepts – only one measurement is necessary to evaluate them. Alternatively, we may choose to measure happiness by putting together a whole cluster of related (and unrelated) *objective measures*, in which case we have a *composite indicator*. Comparisons of the quality of life between nations are often made in this way. The Economist Intelligence Unit (2005), for example, measures a nation's satisfaction by combining nine sets of measures:

1   material wellbeing (e.g. income)
2   health (e.g. life expectancy at birth)
3   political stability and security
4   family life (e.g. divorce rate)
5   community life (e.g. church attendance)
6   climate and geography (warmer or colder)
7   job security (e.g. unemployment rate)
8   political freedom
9   gender equality (e.g. male compared to female earnings).

Another research organisation, International Living, measures quality of life using a rather different – although to some extent overlapping – set of indicators.

Activity 28 (exploratory)

What problems do you think might arise from using subjective, single-indicator measures of happiness? What about objective, composite-indicator measures?

Comment

There are a number of possible drawbacks to the subjective approach. How realistic is it to compare a Dane's view of happiness with a Burundian's? Culturally, they may have completely different conceptions of happiness. Another objection is that responses will not reflect how people really feel about their life, only how satisfied they are expected to be – responses are entirely subjective.

But the objective, composite-indicator strategy may well have its flaws also. Why those nine indicators, rather than any others, such as quality of education, cultural activity, etc.? And why should, say, church attendance be a better measure of community life than, for example, attendance at football matches? It all seems rather arbitrary.

The unsatisfactory nature of objective, composite-indicator comparisons is revealed by the fact that a survey based on the Economist indicators rated Ireland as the happiest nation, with Zimbabwe last and the UK 29th; whereas International Living (2008), using their indicators, rated France happiest, with Iraq last and the UK 37th.

Whenever we compare any two things, the nagging doubt must be that we are not comparing like with like. Is it really fair to compare France with Iraq? To take another example, when school league tables were first introduced in 1992 they used a single indicator, GCSE passes, to measure how 'good' a school was. But obviously, comparing a private school like Eton with a comprehensive in a deprived inner-city area was unfair: they are dissimilar in a hundred ways. Worse still, schools seemed to leap or drop hundreds of places in the rankings from year to year, suggesting that it was just the ability of each year's intake that was being measured, rather than the quality of the school. Recognising this, in 2007 the UK government introduced a new rating system that took into account pupils' socio-economic background, ethnicity, special educational needs, free school meals, income deprivation, age and gender. But this appeared only to create new problems. Schools that had formerly been high in the tables dropped to near the bottom, and vice versa. Moreover, close analysis of the results showed that every school in the land was more or less as successful as any other – in other words, the tables revealed no useful information at all.

Comparisons are tricky and dangerous. So next time you see a league table or ranking of some kind, ask yourself:

What was the basis of the comparison? Does this compare like with like?

3.4 Fictitious causes

An explanation of cause is not a justification by reason.

C.S. Lewis, recalled on his death, 22 November 1963

To compare things is a human desire, but an even more pressing urge is to understand the causes of things. We need to understand why things are happening. Something has gone wrong. Why? There have been disturbing events. What is the reason for them? I have unpleasant symptoms. What is causing them?

In Session 1 of this part, I looked at statistical correlations – cases where as the number for one thing changes, so does the number for another, in a regular and predictable way. I looked at examples of correlation between obesity and diet, and obesity and exercise. I could add examples. Decades of medical data reveal a strong correlation between smoking and lung cancer, between high cholesterol and heart disease, between alcohol abuse and liver failure. There is a clear correlation between the length and quality of a person's education and their lifetime's earnings.

In most of these cases, we might feel justified in saying that one factor causes the other: bad diet causes obesity, smoking causes lung cancer and so on. But remember how messy the world is. Things are rarely that simple. Even in the examples above, there may be complications. Bad diet causes obesity? Up to a point maybe, but obesity is a complex phenomenon and is likely to have complex causes. Education and wealth? Education clearly plays a part, but there are bound to be many other factors – or maybe wealthier people are just more likely to go to university.

The fact that two things are correlated should never be taken to mean that one necessarily causes the other. Look at the following miniature case studies, in all of which two factors are correlated.

1   In May 2007, the ice cream makers Ben and Jerry ran an expensive new advertising campaign. In the next three months ice cream sales rose by over 30%.

2   Every year in US cities, a rise in ice cream sales is always accompanied by a rise in the murder rate.

3   The greater the number of police on a city's streets, the higher the crime rate in that city.

4   The graph in Figure 27 shows a very strong negative correlation between the quantity of lemons imported from Mexico into the USA and fatal road accidents on all US roads.

5   Experiments show that as the temperature of a gas is raised, the pressure of the gas increases also.

Now try the following activity.

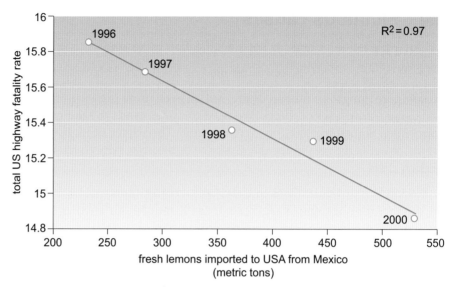

Figure 27   Correlation and coincidence (redrawn from Lowe, 2009)

Activity 29 (exploratory)

In each of these five cases, which factor is being claimed to be the cause of the other? In each case, state what alternative explanation there might be.

Comment

Case 1: the advertising campaign looks as though it might have caused the rise in sales. However, note that the three months over which sales improved were June, July and August – high summer – in which sales would have increased anyway.

Case 2: it hardly seems likely that eating ice cream actually causes people to become more murderous. Far more probable is that summer heat caused both a yearning for ice cream and more explosive tempers.

Case 3: it might be tempting to say that increasing the number of police on patrol actually increases the crime rate – after all, the two are correlated. However, it should be obvious that if there is a causal relationship, surely it goes the other way: the fact that the city is crime-ridden has caused more police to come onto the streets.

Case 4: by no stretch of the imagination could imports of lemons decrease road deaths. The two factors are clearly correlated, but the correlation must be pure coincidence.

Case 5: looks like a case of true causation. But does increase in temperature cause an increase in pressure, or is it the other way round? The truth is, increased temperature causes increased pressure; but equally, increased pressure causes increased temperature.

Statisticians refer to the mistake in Case 1 as a *history effect*. The advertising campaign probably had no effect on ice cream sales, but we expected it to do so – a self-fulfilling prophecy. As for Case 2, there seems to be some unmentioned common factor – a *common causal variable* – causing the rise in both ice cream sales and murders. In Case 3, there may well be a causal relationship between the two factors, but we have to be careful about what is causing what: the number of police and the crime rate is an example of *reverse causation*. And always remember just how messy and complicated the world is. There are bound to be millions of correlations that are simply *coincidence*, as in Case 4. In cases where there is true causation, such as Case 5, sometimes the factors are so closely intertwined that it is impossible to say which is causing which.

These examples might seem pretty trivial, but claiming that one factor is causing another when the two are correlated can often be a deadly serious business. This is especially true in the case of medical statistics, where we are looking for the causes of epidemics or the prevalence of chronic complaints such as obesity. However, let's take another even more contentious example, one where the stakes could hardly be higher. Let's step gingerly into the viper's nest of climate change.

In 2009, the overwhelming scientific consensus could be summed up in two simple points:

1   Overall global temperatures are rising, and will continue to do so.
2   The rise is mainly caused by human activity, principally the burning of fossil fuels.

Disastrous consequences may flow from this rise. The Intergovernmental Panel on Climate Change (IPCC) forecasts droughts, extinctions of species, food shortages, major flooding and increased disease as possible consequences, depending on how far temperatures actually rise in the future.

This is the consensus, and these conclusions are entirely based on numbers. At the same time, the internet swirls with contributions – many notable for their intemperance and sheer rage – from *climate change denialists*, who reject either point (1) of the IPCC's conclusions or point (2), and sometimes both. Their arguments, too, are based entirely on numbers, and often on the same numbers.

Have a look at the grossly simplified graph in Figure 28. The temperature anomaly is the difference between the actual temperature and the typical or normal temperature expected at that time.

This graph should carry a health warning, but it will do for the moment to illustrate one point. It seems to show a fairly steady increase in global temperatures since 1900. Since the period 1900 up to the present day coincides with the rapid industrialisation of the planet, it is possible to

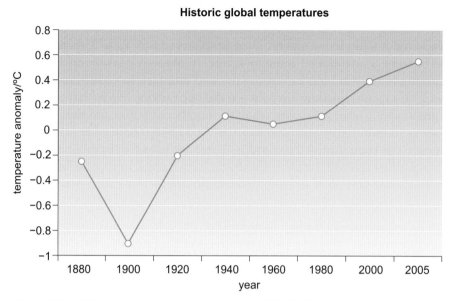

Figure 28   Global temperature anomalies, 1850–2008 (data from Brohan et al., 2006)

conclude that the rise in temperatures is caused by human industrial activity.

But is this so? This is no place to take sides in this vicious dispute, but one of the main arguments deployed by denialists is that other causal factors – a rise in the activity of the sun is a favourite – are the true cause of global temperature rise: the correlation between it and fossil fuel burning, they claim, is pure coincidence.

I'll consider the arguments over climate change a bit further in the next section. For the moment, though, when someone tries to persuade you that two factors seeming to change together means that one is causing the change in the other, remember that:

Correlation does not necessarily imply causation.

3.5 Messy consequences

In Session 1, I examined ways in which we compare present with past data, thus identifying trends and projecting them into the future. Look back at Figure 28, for instance: the upward line since 1900 looks clear. Surely we can expect global temperatures to go on rising in the future?

Once again, only maybe; and once again, remember – messy. I advised you that the graph in Figure 28 might need a health warning; and so it does, because it conceals a huge amount of information.

Activity 30 (self-assessment)

How do you think the graphic in Figure 28 conceals information?

A more honest picture is presented in Figure 29.

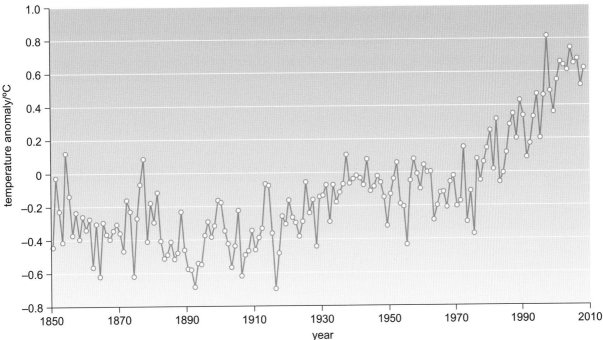

Historic global temperatures 1850–2008

Figure 29   Global temperature anomalies, 1850–2008 (data from Brohan et al., 2006)

In fact, the readings fluctuate wildly up and down. This is a perfectly recognisable portrait of the chaotic, ever-changing world we inhabit – we would see the same sort of thing in more or less any set of figures we cared to collect. There are no straight lines or smooth curves – things sway around without apparent pattern.

Activity 31 (self-assessment)

What mistake do you think one might make when investigating messy data like that in Figure 29?

Blastland and Dilnot (2007) call this phenomenon 'the frisky dog'. Picture a very dark night. A man dressed entirely in black is walking his dog along a straight path. The dog too is black, but wears a luminous collar, which is clearly visible as it romps backwards and forwards, chasing after rabbits, stopping to sniff things, jumping up to lick its master's hand. All we can see is the dog's chaotic darting to and fro; the darkness hides the man's steady progress along the path.

So how is it possible to make sense of the frisky dog of global temperature readings? Statisticians use a set of techniques referred to generally as *regression* to identify trends in chaotic data series like my example here. Details of how these techniques work are beyond the scope of this module, but Figure 30 illustrates one possible regression line indicating the trend towards higher temperatures.

Historic global temperatures 1850–2008

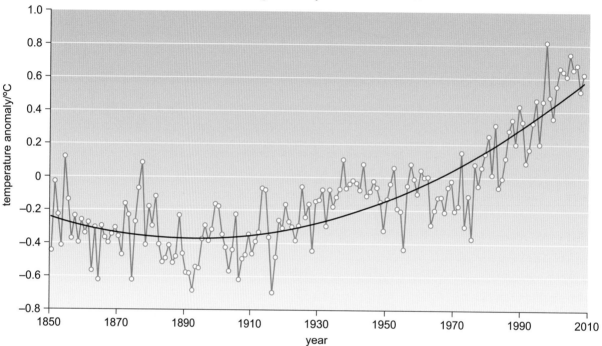

Figure 30   Global temperature anomalies, 1850–2008, with trend line

Finding trends among the chaos of the real world can be hugely controversial, and there are ample opportunities for cheating. For a start, with a bit of mathematical ingenuity it is usually possible to find regression lines that show quite opposite trends from the more obvious ones. On 6 January 2009, for example, the newspaper *The Australian* published an article containing a graph of temperature readings (from a source other than the one I am using here) showing an optimistic picture (Figure 31).

I've superimposed a trend line (dashed) on the graph to illustrate the upward trend the figures would seem to demonstrate. However, the line in *The Australian*'s article (black) tells a different story: the earth is actually cooling! The black line represents an esoteric mathematical function known as a sixth-order polynomial, the use of which has been widely

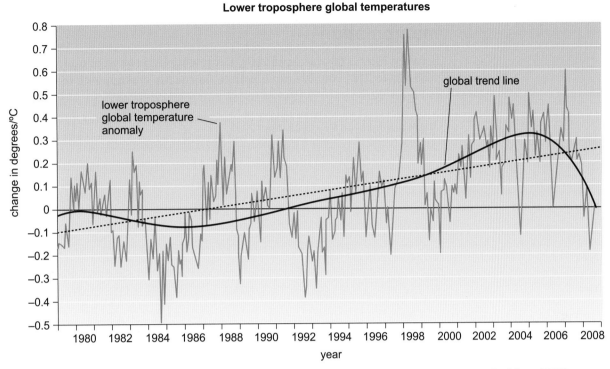

Lower troposphere global temperatures

Figure 31   Global temperature anomalies, 1978–2008, with trend lines (redrawn from Jenkins, 2009)

ridiculed by commentators and climate scientists. Right or wrong, though, this case illustrates that it is always possible to find a contrary trend.

The graph in Figure 31 also demonstrates another swindle. Note that the temperature data starts in about 1978. What about all the previous years? A very easy way to distort a trend is to carefully select a period of figures that suits one's argument. This isn't hard to do in a world where things swing wildly up and down anyway.

This strategy of selecting only the data that suits one's argument, and ignoring anything inconvenient to it, is perhaps the commonest statistical swindle of all, and is known as *cherry-picking*.

Activity 32 (self-assessment)

Have a look back at Figure 29. How might one select a period of data that would demonstrate that global temperatures are falling?

In fact, the whole business of using charts to illustrate trends and comparisons is open to chicanery of every kind. Let's look at one or two examples. Before we do, though, just remember:

In a world of chaotic change, trends can be deceptive and controversial.

3.6   Deceptive graphics (2) – political manipulation

Between May 2008 and April 2009, UK unemployment went up from 1685 000 to 2381 000. We can illustrate this neatly enough with the graph in Figure 32.

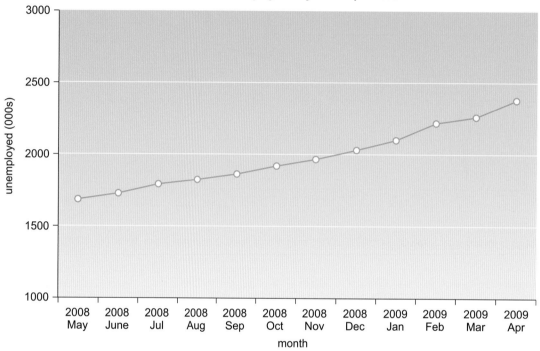

Adult unemployed May 2008–April 2009

Figure 32   Unemployment 2008–09

Now imagine that you are an opposition politician: you will want to make as much capital as you can out of the government's embarrassment. The line shows a rather menacing upward trend, but how can we make things look worse, without actually lying? Easy. Note that the scale on the vertical axis of the graph runs from 1000 000 to 3000 000. All we have to do now is to *narrow* that range, as in Figure 33, and everything looks a lot more doom-laden. Look how fast the line is rising! And we haven't falsified the figures one bit.

Have a look back at Figure 21. Can you see a similar trick there? Was the author trying to clarify or to mislead?

Of course, a government spokesman can do just the opposite: by *widening* the range, the figures can be made to look a lot less worrying, as in Figure 34.

Unemployment is more or less stable!

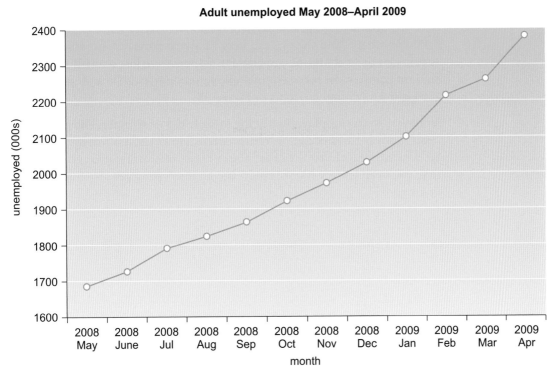

Figure 33   Scary unemployment 2008–09

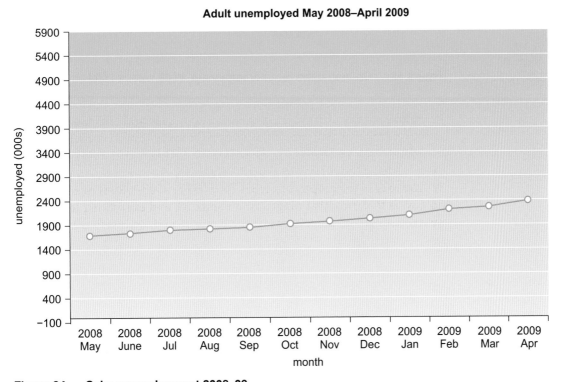

Figure 34   Calm unemployment 2008–09

These sorts of frauds arise from the fact that a statistical graphic relies on the eye's ability to judge shape, height and size partly without reference to actual numbers. And the eye can very easily be deceived, especially when various kinds of chartjunk are present. Suppose we just wanted to show a straight comparison between unemployment in May 2008 and in April 2009 using a column chart, as in Figure 35.

Note that we could play exactly the same tricks as with the line graph again, simply by altering the vertical scale. However, assume we want to be honest, but feel that the chart doesn't look interesting enough. Rather than use boring old bars, we could use an interesting graphic instead, as in Figure 36.

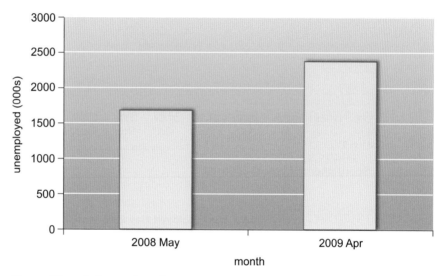

Figure 35   Column chart for unemployment, 2008 versus 2009

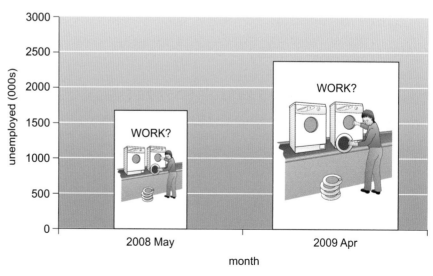

Figure 36   More chartjunk for unemployment, 2008 versus 2009

What is the problem here? Why does 2009 look so much worse than 2008? If you check on the vertical scale, you can see that the height of each 'unemployed man' graphic is about right. However, in order to keep the original shape of the 2009 graphic, the designer has also widened it, increasing its area. So, the height of 2009 is about 44% greater than 2008, but its area has doubled. The result is that 2009 looms much bigger because the eye is taking in the relative areas, not the heights.

Statistical graphics can be a wonderful way to convey complicated numbers, but it always pays to be a little suspicious of them.

Activity 33 (exploratory)

In the thick of election fever, Infomanian politicians are still hard at work. Go to the resources page associated with this part on the TU100 website and follow the instructions for helping both sides.

3.7 Improbable chances – 'stuff happens'

> As flies to wanton boys are we to the gods;
> They kill us for their sport.
>
> Shakespeare, *King Lear*, IV. i. 36–7

What will happen? What is the risk?

Human life is uncertain. Our existence is a mass of confusion and doubt, and the only way to make rational sense of it is to talk in terms of chances, odds and risks. But the trouble is that humans tend to be irrational about the whole concept of probability. Our beliefs about it are generally quite wrong. Let's illustrate that with a simple example.

In Session 1, I noted that tossing coins and throwing dice are classic emblems of probability and chance. So take a dice and throw it 30 times, noting the number that comes up each time. If you don't have the time, you can use the sequence I recorded:

4 6 6 1 2 3 4 5 6 6 6 3 1 1 3 3 4 4 5 6 6 6 5 3 5 6 2 1 3 4

At first sight, this looks fairly random. However, have a closer look at it.

Activity 34 (self-assessment)

Do any aspects of this purely random sequence look mildly unexpected to you?

When we see groupings like the run of 1 to 6 or the clusters of 6s, it's often hard to believe that these arose perfectly randomly – they look too ordered. The trouble is that randomness does not always look random, and this often causes problems for us.

The Texan sharpshooter

Earlier, I noted the danger of supposing that one thing causes another just because the two are correlated. This is largely because most events have not a single cause, but complex mixtures of causes – usually so many, and so intricately intertwined, that it's fair to say that the event was really a matter of pure chance. The vast majority of events in life come about largely by luck, good or ill. In the immortal words of Donald Rumsfeld, 'Stuff happens'. It just happens.

However, this is not the way we humans see things. We want to understand the causes of things, so that we can avoid the dangers and bring on the good times. As so many events happen mainly by chance, they will tend to happen in clusters or runs, just like the throw of the dice above. Our mistake is to see too much significance in the clusters and runs. Too often, we look for single, simple causes for these and ignore the role that chance has played.

This is perfectly illustrated by what is known as the *Texan sharpshooter's fallacy*. Here is how it goes. It's easy to prove that you are a very good shot, even if you have never fired a gun before. Take a machine gun, stand about 20 yards from the side of a barn, say, and empty the magazine in that direction. It doesn't affect the issue at all if you are blind drunk, or even blindfolded – just blaze away. When you've finished, inspect your results. In all likelihood, you will see a pattern of shots resembling Figure 37.

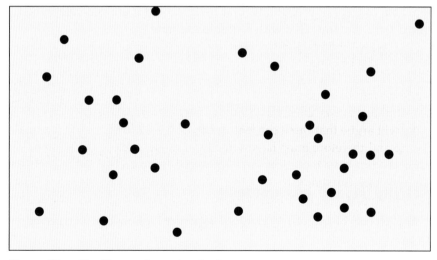

Figure 37   The Texan sharpshooter I

The sort of thing we might expect, perhaps. As you're unlikely to be an expert with a machine gun, the pattern is essentially random. But now all you have to do to prove that you are a better than average shot is walk up to the barn and draw a target, like Figure 38.

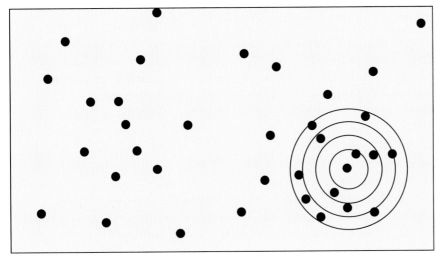

Figure 38   The Texan sharpshooter II

Look at the excellent placement! You even scored two bullseyes! (And if we then also cover up the bullet holes outside the target, labelling them as 'practice', say, you've become a first-rate marksman!)

The point is this: the pattern is essentially random. But as you've seen, random events often have a way of clustering, and it is an all too human characteristic to read significance into these clusters when in fact they have none. Because we are always looking for simple causes, we see the cause of the cluster as being excellent shooting rather than pure chance.

This is not an academic point. The problems caused by the clumpy, bunching effect of randomness are alive today, not least in the issue of *cancer clusters*. Cancer clusters are groups of cancer cases diagnosed among people living in a certain small area, often around power stations, pylons, phone masts, chemical plants, etc. Observers, and especially locals, will argue that these concentrations of cases are above the national average and therefore must have some local cause, such as radiation or chemicals. But have they? It is only human to see ourselves at the centre of things, to look for simple causes and for someone to blame. In the case of some clusters, it may be true: there may be a single identifiable cause. But sometimes it might just be plain dumb luck. Stuff happens.

So, just remember:

> **Randomness does not always look random.**

This is another example of cherry-picking. A link to information on how to avoid some other scams is given on the TU100 website.

Reckoning with risk

In Session 1 you learned how to carry out simple calculations of probabilities using the multiplication principle. This is a good way of calculating the probability of, say, winning the lottery or drawing an ace in blackjack. However, applying it blindly in a complex world of human motives and intertwined causes can lead to tragic results.

In a case that has become notorious, on 23 February 1998 solicitor Sally Clark was arrested for the double murder of her baby sons Christopher and Harry. Both children had died in their cots, Christopher at eleven weeks old and Harry at eight weeks, both apparently victims of what doctors term Sudden Infant Death Syndrome (SIDS), but which is more often called 'cot death'. At Clark's trial, the paediatrician Professor Sir Roy Meadow (Figure 39) testified that the odds against two children from the same family suffering cot death were 73 million to 1. Mainly on the basis of this evidence, Clark was convicted and sentenced to life imprisonment. Although the Royal Statistical Society immediately issued a report questioning Meadow's figures, Clark's first appeal in 2000 was rejected, and she served three years in prison before her conviction was finally overturned at a second appeal. However, although the Appeal Court recognised grave statistical flaws in Meadow's evidence, the second appeal succeeded mainly on the grounds of microbiological evidence that had originally been concealed from the defence.

The case was a disaster for all concerned. Meadow was struck off the medical register in 2005, although he was later reinstated; Sally Clark never recovered from the trauma and died in 2007 from alcohol poisoning.

Figure 39   Professor Sir Roy Meadow leaves court

What happened? Meadow had simply applied the multiplication principle you learned of earlier. There are good estimates that the chances of a child dying of SIDS are 1 in 8543. So Meadow had simply reasoned that the chances of two children in the same family dying are 8543 × 8543, which is about 1 in 73 million. So what were the flaws in Meadow's statistical reasoning?

Activity 35 (self-assessment)

On the basis of what you have now learned about correlations and causes, do you detect anything suspect in Meadow's argument?

In fact, there were two serious errors in Meadow's reasoning:

1   The multiplication principle works fine for coin tosses and dice throws, because each toss or throw is an *independent event*. Flip a coin; if it comes down heads, the chances of it coming down heads on the next flip are always 50:50. No matter how many heads you get in a row, the coin *has no memory* – each flip is entirely independent of all the others before it. Yet in the case of Clark's children, things can't have been that simple. Christopher and Harry had the same parents and lived in the same house. There could have been any number of hidden causal factors, genetic and environmental, acting on them both. Professor Meadow's assumption that the Clark's household was typical of every other household of the same kind where SIDS had not taken place, and thus ignoring the possibility of some hidden cause, is an example of what is termed the *ecological fallacy*.

2   The second mistake is much trickier and is known as the *prosecutor's fallacy*. The jury were asked to judge between two possible explanations of the children's death: SIDS and a double murder. The odds against it being SIDS were high, but *so were the odds against it being murder*. Two SIDS deaths in a family are very rare, but double murders are even rarer. So the real odds on Clark's innocence were the *relative chance* of double SIDS and double murder. One commentator tried to calculate this relative chance, and came up with 2:1 in favour of double SIDS.

This is a very subtle mistake. A link to further explanation and examples is given on the TU100 website.

Meadow had also ignored another important factor: that boys are more prone to SIDS than girls. The true odds for the SIDS deaths among boys should have been 1 in 1300, not 1 in 8543.

Human intuitions about risk are often faulty. Numbers can be a guide, but the mathematics of probability has to be applied with the greatest of care where human lives and happiness may be at stake. So remember:

> **In a world of complex causes, simple risk calculations should be applied with the greatest care.**

Scaring ourselves to death

It sometimes feels as if we live in a state of constant terror for our health, and with a desperate yearning to prolong our lives forever. The information media pour out statistics about the deadly risks of certain kinds of food and drink, and the life-enhancing effects of others. Bacon, alcohol and butter will give us cancer. Pomegranate juice, blueberries, mackerel and olive oil will make us live eternally.

These statistics are almost always stated in terms of *risk*. Smoking 50 cigarettes a day will not *definitely* give you lung cancer – some heavy smokers live to a great age – but it will certainly increase your risk of developing the disease. So health statistics talk of increased risk, often in terms of a percentage increase. Let's end where we began, by returning to the *Daily Mail* report on the Crestor study that I quoted in the introduction. There we were told that the drug cut the risk of heart attack by 54%, strokes by 48% and so on. But what do these figures actually mean?

Activity 36 (self-assessment)

Do you feel there is any information missing from figures like these that would be necessary to make sense of them?

The question we need answering is '54% lower than what?'. The 'what' here is known as the *baseline risk*. Unless I know that, the claim of a 54% reduction makes no sense – it's just a vaguely imposing-sounding number. In fact, as Goldacre (2008) points out, my baseline risk of a heart attack in the next ten years is about 3.7%, and on Crestor it is 1.7%. My risk was already tiny. Crestor makes it a bit tinier.

We can see exactly the same thing, but in reverse, in a widely reported study by the World Cancer Research Fund. Among its findings was the claim that eating bacon increases the risk of colorectal cancer by 21%. If you like bacon, that sounds pretty scary, but once again the baseline figure was omitted from most reports on the study. However, the fact is that the baseline risk of a man developing colorectal cancer in his lifetime is about 5%.

Activity 37 (self-assessment)

So what is the risk of colorectal cancer for men who love their bacon?

Health statistics of this kind are frequently reported in this misleading form – a percentage of a baseline we may or may not be told – known as a *relative risk reduction* (or *relative risk increase*). The clearer form used by Goldacre is known as an *absolute risk reduction* (or *absolute risk increase*). Relative risk is a very handy tool for people with a vested interest: politicians out to deceive us, big companies that want to sell us drugs, or journalists whose only interest is in creating health scares.

There is a deeper problem here, too, and it's this: people don't really understand percentages very well. In one survey (Paulos, 2001), in which participants were asked questions like '40% is (a) one quarter, (b) 4 out of 10 or (c) every 40th person', over a third got the answer wrong. This is not a comment on the average person's mathematical ability. The fact is that a statement like 'X will reduce your risk of cancer from 6% to 5%' means very little to most of us; it's simply not something we are good at judging. Much clearer is to put it another way: '6 people in 100 get cancer; X will reduce this risk to 5 people in 100'. This is much easier to comprehend, because it's easy enough to visualise 100 people, and it's obvious straight away that 6 in 100 is not significantly worse than 5 in 100. Expressions of percentages as 'X in 100' or 'X in 1000' are known as a *natural frequencies*. They are clearer and easier to understand than any other way of expressing a percentage.

So the next time you hear some statement such as 'X will reduce your risk of Y by 5%' or 'Government borrowing has increased by 5%', think:

5% of *what*?

3.8   Conclusion

Numbers should be clear and unambiguous. Sadly, though, they are as open to abuse as any other kind of analysis. In this session, you've learned about some of these kinds of abuse. You've seen how difficult it can be to pin down the things we are trying to count, and how ridiculous conclusions can be drawn from tiny, unrepresentative samples, misleading averages and false comparisons. You've noted that mere correlation need not imply causation and that pure randomness can easily seem like order and pattern. You've learned that much popular science reporting involves meaningless percentages. And worst of all, you've seen ways in which statistical graphics can be manipulated to suit a particular point of view.

This session should have helped you with the following learning outcomes.

* Describe some simple statistical methods and their applicability.
* Describe some guidelines for the effective presentation of numerical information.
* Discuss the role of statistics in everyday domains such as commerce, security, weather forecasting and economics.

Summary

This part has been about statistical information – about numbers. You've learned how numbers are used to:

1   *count* things

2   *compare* things, using counts as a basis

3   identify possible *causes*, by finding correlations between the things we have counted

4   find trends, and project counts into the future to reveal possible *consequences*

5   deal with the fundamental uncertainty of the world by estimating *chances*.

You've also seen how all these uses can be supported by statistical graphics, in which the bare numbers are translated into patterns of shape and space that can be easily appreciated by the eye. You have gathered some statistics and constructed several statistical graphics of your own.

However, you've also learned some of the ways in which honest statistics can be distorted in order to deceive or mislead. In particular, you've learned to beware the following:

- counting things that are essentially ill-defined

- small, self-selected or otherwise unrepresentative samples

- misleading averages

- not comparing like with like

- taking correlation to imply causation

- seeing significant patterns and simple causes in mere randomness

- quoting relative percentages with no baseline.

And you've also seen some of the ways in which these mistakes and swindles can be supported by junky or plain misleading graphics.

None of this is intended to decry the use of numbers. They are a vital tool for getting to grips with our messy, complicated and uncertain world, but they can also be slippery things. When statistical information is presented to you by an ignorant journalist, or by anyone with an axe to grind, it is always as well to be on your guard.

You have now completed your study of Block 2. Once you are satisfied that you have looked at all the resources associated with this part on the TU100 website, you can move on to Block 3, which broadens the focus of your study once more to look at the way computers can be integrated into our environments to provide us with applications as diverse as smart homes, cloud computing and location-specific information. The first three parts of Block 3 are online, so you should now go to the TU100 website and start work on Part 1.

Answers to self-assessment activities

Activity 2

Using a calculator, I got $132 \div (1.91 \times 1.91) = 132 \div 3.6481 = 36.18$. Yes, he is obese.

Activity 3

I reasoned it this way: 2422 out of 10 000 means that about a quarter (25% or 1 in 4) of the individuals in the sample are obese. So, for the whole UK population of 61 million, around a quarter will be obese – about 15 million people!

Activity 4

I thought of two reasons:

1 The size of the sample must be *sufficiently large,* i.e. a decent proportion of the population we are dealing with. One couldn't estimate UK obesity numbers from a sample of just 2, for instance. However, with a sample of 30 million one could be confident of the result.

2 The sample must be a cross section of the population. It must be *representative* of UK citizens as a whole. Taking our sample entirely from people attending health farms or from among professional athletes, for instance, would give us a hopelessly biased estimate.

You may have thought of others.

Activity 5

You probably remembered that to calculate the average, we add up the figures and divide them by the number in the set. So, in this example, we get:

$$3 + 5 + 7 + 2 + 8 + 4 + 4 + 6 + 7 + 1 = 47$$

Divide 47 by the number of figures, 10, and we get an average of 4.7.

Activity 6

The top of the curve is at BMI 27, so 27 is the mean for this sample.

Activity 8

The percentage is $(57 \div 235) \times 100\% = 24.26\%$.

Activity 11

The incidence of obesity *decreases* with *increase* in exercise. So, a positive correlation would be where one factor *increases* as the other increases.

A strong example is the correlation between smoking and lung cancer. The more you smoke and the longer you have been a smoker, the more likely you are to develop the disease.

Activity 12

There certainly does seem to be some correlation between income and obesity among women. Women in the higher income groups seem to be less prone to obesity than poorer women, so this is a negative correlation. Among men, however, there seems to be little correlation.

Activity 13

Even if the experimenter is perfectly honest, they may signal their knowledge to the subjects in all sorts of unconscious ways. It sounds incredible, but it is well established that even tiny cues such as the experimenter's body language, choice of words and facial expressions can alter the outcomes of the trial. This is known as the *Hawthorne effect*.

Activity 15

I'm sure there was nothing wrong with your intuitions here. Since there are only two possible outcomes, heads and tails, and both are equally likely, then it's a one in two chance.

Activity 16

We can apply exactly the same principles as in the coin-flipping example.

There are four shirts, so the chances of a blue shirt are one in four, or 25% or 0.25.

What about blue trousers? There are five pairs, so the chances are one in five, or 20% or 0.2. A blue tie? One in three – 33%, or 0.33. A pair of blue socks? One in six, or roughly 17% or 0.17.

OK, we now know the probability of each separate outcome. What about the probability of *all* of them happening together? Just apply the multiplication principle again. When we multiply the four probabilities together:

$$0.25 \times 0.2 \times 0.33 \times 0.17$$

we get a probability of 0.0028, about a quarter of one per cent, or a relative chance of 1 in 400. Little likelihood of a colour-coordinated me, then.

Activity 20

The sample has to be sufficiently large and it has to be representative. You may recall also that for counting complex things, such as the number of people cured by a particular drug, a control sample will be needed, and that the estimate should be made double-blind.

Activity 22

The mean is 11.56:

$$1 + 1 + 5 + 5 + 6 + 7 + 19 + 24 + 36 = 104$$

$$104 \div 9 = 11.56$$

The median is the value that divides the set in two, with an equal number of values above and below. So the median of this set is 6: there are four values greater than 6 and four less.

Activity 23

The range goes from £71 459 to £1034 567, but the peculiar thing about it is that there is a cluster of nine values that are in the range £71 459 to £88 126, and then two enormously expensive, million-pound houses at the top.

Activity 24

The most obvious point is that incomes have risen generally over this period. However, there is a clearly widening gap between median and mean earnings. The real middle Britain is being left behind.

Activity 26

Figure 23 seems to me less clear than Figure 14. Remember that we assess the size of each category by the height of its column, and we compare categories by comparing the heights of columns that are side by side. In Figure 23, this is hard to do. At best, the additional dimension adds no extra information to that in Figure 14; at worst, it obscures the columns at the back, makes comparison difficult, and makes it hard to read numbers on the scale at the side.

Activity 30

The figure conceals information because it records data for only the first year of each 20-year period. Data for all the intervening years is missing.

Activity 31

The most obvious mistake is that we might miss the overall upward trend, noticing perhaps only swings, possibly downward, that are happening now or have happened recently.

Activity 32

I chose the years 1937–76. Isolating this short period of cooler temperatures enabled me to derive a regression line (red) showing that atmospheric temperatures are dropping. It's illustrated in Figure 40.

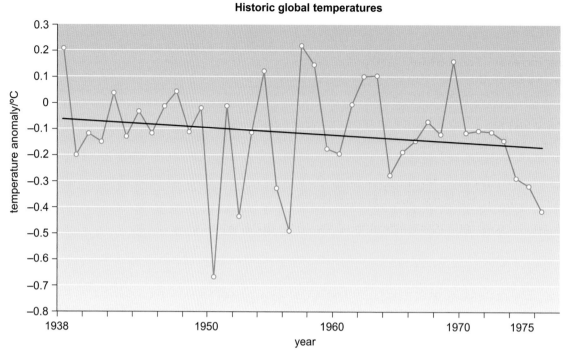

Figure 40   Global temperature anomalies, 1937–76

Activity 34

Perhaps you spotted the run 1, 2, 3, 4, 5, 6 and the two clusters of three sixes. Somehow these are not the kind of results we would expect from randomness. You might also have noted that there were 18 throws of four or over, and only 12 of three or less.

Activity 35

Although it seems unlikely that the two deaths could have been coincidence, remember that there is seldom one simple cause for any event. There may have been a hidden causal factor behind both of the deaths.

Activity 36

Cutting the risk of heart attack by 54% certainly sounds impressive, but it means nothing to me unless I know what my risk of heart attack would have been *without* the drug.

Activity 37

The additional risk is 21% of 5%, that is:

$$(5 \div 100) \times (21 \div 100) = 0.0105$$

or about 1%. So the bacon eater's risk is just over 6%. Not so scary, perhaps.

Glossary

absolute risk increase   The increase in the probability of an outcome in the presence of a factor that might influence this probability, expressed as an increase in the baseline risk of that outcome.

absolute risk reduction   The reduction in the probability of an outcome in the presence of a factor that might influence this probability, expressed as a decrease in the baseline risk of that outcome.

active group   In a clinical trial, the group of participants who are given a treatment containing the substance that is being tested.

average   A general term for various measures of the central tendency of a group of numbers. In common speech, often used to refer to the **mean**.

axis   The horizontal or vertical scale on a graph or chart.

baseline risk   The probability of some occurrence in the absence of any special influences.

bell curve   The smooth symmetrical graph that represents the relative frequency of occurrence of every observation in a set.

cancer clusters   The alleged appearance of abnormally large numbers of cancer cases in a small, well-defined area, generally around some feature such as a power station or TV mast.

central tendency   A general term describing the part of any distribution in which the most common, or average, measurements are found.

chance   One of many terms that may be used to express the idea of **probability**.

chartjunk   A term coined by the commentator Edward Tufte to describe any features of a statistical graphic that distract the eye from the meaning of the numbers that the graphic is supposed to represent.

cherry-picking   A swindle in statistical analysis that consists of focusing only on data that supports a particular hypothesis, and ignoring any data that casts doubt on it.

climate change denialism   A school of thought that insists either that climate change is not happening or that it is not caused by human activity.

clinical trial   A rigorously conducted test of some medical intervention, such as a new drug. A properly designed clinical trial should involve an **active group** and a **control group**, and be **double-blind**.

coincidence   Two events that happen to occur together but have no relationship to each other.

common causal variable Some common factor that causes two events to occur together.

composite indicator A measure of some quantity that is based on several factors.

control group In a clinical trial, the group of participants who are given a treatment that does not contain the substance that is being tested. Also known as the *placebo group*.

correlated With reference to two numbers, in a relationship such that when one changes so does the other, in a predictable way.

descriptive statistics The branch of statistics that describes the basic features of sets of numerical data, providing simple summaries of samples, measures and so on.

dispersion The degree to which the data in a set are spread out on either side of the central tendency.

double-blind A term describing a clinical trial in which neither the experimenter nor the participants know which participants are in the control group and which are in the active group.

ecological fallacy In statistics, the assumption that all individual members of a group will have the average characteristics of that group.

estimate A calculation in which some feature of a population is inferred from a sample.

Hawthorne effect In clinical trials, a tendency for subjects to improve simply because they are aware that they are being studied, rather than in response to what is being tested.

history effect A tendency for the results of a trial to be skewed by external factors occurring at the time of the trial.

independent event An outcome that is not affected or influenced by any other event.

inferential statistics The branch of statistics concerned with reaching conclusions that extend beyond the immediate data alone.

mean One way of measuring the central tendency or average of a set of numbers, calculated by adding the numbers together and dividing the result by the number in the set.

median One way of measuring the central tendency or average of a set of numbers, calculated by listing the numbers in ascending order and then taking the middle value (the one with an equal number of values above and below it).

meta-study A study that combines the results of numerous studies of the same thing.

multiplication principle   In probability theory, a means of calculating the probability that several independent events will happen together, or in sequence, by multiplying the probabilities of each individual event together.

natural frequency   A means of expressing probabilities in terms of chances in one hundred or one thousand.

negative correlation   A form of correlation in which if one quantity in the relation increases, the other quantity will decrease.

normal distribution   The smooth, bell-shaped curve that results from plotting the relative frequency of occurrence of each measurement in a large set.

obesity   A physical condition of being overweight, defined by having a body mass index of over 30.

objective measure   A measurement that is based on independently verifiable facts.

odds   One of many terms that may be used to express the idea of **probability**.

outliers   Observations that are a very long way from the central tendency of a set of data.

percentage   A standard way of expressing a comparison of some part with the whole, as a fraction of 100.

percentage chance   A term used to express the idea of probability as a fraction of 100.

pie chart   A form of statistical graphic in which the relative proportions of the parts that make up the whole are represented as slices of a circular pie.

placebo   In clinical trials, an inert medicine that contains no active ingredients, but that nevertheless may make participants feel better.

placebo effect   In clinical trials, the tendency for subjects to improve if they are given a treatment of any kind, even if it does not contain any active components.

placebo-controlled   A term describing a clinical trial in which participants are divided into a control group (which receives a placebo) and an active group (which is treated with the intervention being tested).

population   In statistics, a set of observations from which statistical inferences are to be drawn.

positive correlation   A form of correlation in which if one quantity in the relation increases, the other quantity will increase also.

probability   A measure of the chance or likelihood that some event will occur.

proportion   A number expressing the relationship between the part and the whole.

prosecutor's fallacy   A subtle mistake commonly made in criminal trials and elsewhere. If evidence is collected and the prosecution claims that the probability of finding this evidence if the accused were innocent is tiny, the fallacy is to conclude that the probability of the accused being innocent must also be tiny.

p-**value**   A mathematical measure of the probability of some event, usually expressed as a number between 1 (certain to occur) and 0 (certain not to occur).

quintile   A division containing one fifth, or 20%, of a population.

randomised   In clinical trials, a term that means participants have been assigned to the control group and the active group by purely random selection.

regression   In statistical analysis, a technique for determining the precise relationship between a variable and one or more other variables.

relative chance   The probability of one event occurring, as compared to its not occurring.

relative risk increase   The percentage increase in the probability of an outcome in the presence of a factor that might influence this probability.

relative risk reduction   The percentage reduction in the probability of an outcome in the presence of a factor that might influence this probability.

reverse causation   A situation in which although it is believed that event A causes event B, in fact B causes A.

risk   One of many terms that may be used to express the idea of **probability**.

sample   A limited quantity of something that is used to represent a much larger population of that thing.

single indicator   A measure of some quantity that is based on one factor only.

skewed distribution   A property of a set of numbers that is not distributed in the symmetrical shape of the normal distribution.

standard deviation   In statistics, a formal measure of the degree of dispersion of a set of numbers.

statistic   Any single piece of data collected for statistical purposes. Also known as an observation.

statistical graphic   Any chart, graph or picture that represents numbers in terms of shape and space.

statistically significant   In statistics, a term referring to an outcome that has an extremely low probability of having come about by pure chance.

subjective measure   A measurement that is based on individual people's personal impressions.

Texan sharpshooter's fallacy   The interpretation or manipulation of data that is essentially random or coincidental until it appears to have meaning.

trend   The general direction in which some quantity or thing is changing.

variance   In statistics, a formal measure of the degree of dispersion of a set of numbers.

References

Blastland, M. and Dilnot, A. (2007) *The Tiger That Isn't: Seeing Through a World of Numbers*, London, Profile Books.

Brewer, M., Muriel, A., Philips, D. and Sibieta, L. (2009) *Poverty and Inequality in the UK: 2009*, London, Institute for Fiscal Studies.

Brohan, P., Kennedy, J.J., Harris, I., Tett, S.F.B. and Jones, P.D. (2006) 'Uncertainty estimates in regional and global observed temperature changes: a new dataset from 1850', *Met Office Hadley Centre Observations Datasets* [online], http://hadobs.metoffice.com/hadcrut3/HadCRUT3_accepted.pdf (accessed 10 October 2010).

Economist Intelligence Unit (2005) 'The Economist Intelligence Unit's quality-of-life index', *The World in 2005* [online], *The Economist*, http://www.economist.com/media/pdf/quality_of_life.pdf (accessed 10 October 2010).

Foresight (2007) *Tackling Obesities: Future Choices*, Department for Business Innovation & Skills; also available online at http://www.bis.gov.uk/foresight/our-work/projects/current-projects/tackling-obesities (accessed 10 October 2010).

Goldacre, B. (2008) *Bad Science*, London, Fourth Estate.

Hope, J. (2008) 'The new statin drug that cuts the risk of heart attacks and strokes for EVERYONE', *The Daily Mail* [online], 10 November, http://www.dailymail.co.uk/health/article-1084345/ (accessed 10 October 2010).

International Living (2008) *2008 Quality of Life Index* [online], http://internationalliving.com/2008/01/2008-quality-of-life-index/ (accessed 10 October 2010).

Jenkins, J. (2009) 'The warmaholics' fantasy', *The Australian* [online], 6 January, http://www.theaustralian.com.au/news/the-warmaholics-fantasy/story-e6frg73o-1111118484804 (accessed 10 October 2010).

Johnson, S.B. (2006) *The Ghost Map: The Story of London's Most Terrifying Epidemic – and How it Changed Science, Cities and the Modern World*, New York, Riverhead Books.

Lowe, D. (2009) 'Mexican lemons to the rescue', *In The Pipeline* [online], blog post 1 April, http://pipeline.corante.com/archives/2009/04/01/mexican_lemons_to_the_rescue.php (accessed 10 October 2010).

Mammals Trust UK (2005) 'Mammals on roads survey: an outline of 2004's results', *Mammals on Roads Newsletter*, July, London, Mammals Trust.

National Statistics (2008) *International Passenger Survey* [online], Office for National Statistics, http://www.statistics.gov.uk/ssd/surveys/international_passenger_survey.asp (accessed 10 October 2010).

NHS Information Centre (2010) *Statistics on obesity, physical activity and diet: England, 2010* [online], Health and Social Care Information Centre, NHS, http://www.ic.nhs.uk/statistics-and-data-collections/health-and-lifestyles/obesity/statistics-on-obesity-physical-activity-and-diet-england-2010 (accessed 10 October 2010).

Paulos, J.A. (2001) *Innumeracy: Mathematical Illiteracy and Its Consequences*, New York, Hill & Wang.

Pegg, V. (2005) 'Bad statistics and binge drinking', *BBC News* [online], 31 August, http://news.bbc.co.uk/1/hi/magazine/4200056.stm (accessed 10 October 2010).

TUC (2009) 'Life in the middle – The untold story of Britain's average earners', *TUC Touchstone Pamphlet No. 6* [online], London, Trades Union Congress, http://www.touchstoneblog.org.uk/wp-content/uploads/2009/02/life-in-the-middle.pdf (accessed 10 October 2010).

United Nations (1995) 'Report of the World Summit for Social Development', *World Summit for Social Development* [online], Copenhagen, 6–12 March, http://www.un.org/esa/socdev/wssd/ (accessed 10 October 2010).

Acknowledgements

Grateful acknowledgement is made to the following sources.

Figures

John Snow (p. 288): Taken from Google Inc.

Figure 12: The NHS Information Centre (2009) 'Statistics on Obesity, Physical Activity and Diet: England'. Crown Copyright 2009. Crown copyright material is reproduced under Class Licence Number C01W0000065 with the permission of the Controller of HMSO and the Queen's Printer for Scotland

Figure 16: Taken from www.mlive.com/entertainment/ann-arbor

Figure 17: Modern Mechanix

Figure 20: © Brewer, M. et al. (2009) 'The Income Distribution in 2007–08 (UK)', Poverty and Inequality in the UK 2009, The Institute for Fiscal Studies

Figure 21: © Brewer, M. et al. (2009) 'Changes in Mean and Median Income', Poverty and Inequality in the UK 2009, The Institute for Fiscal Studies

Figure 22: Few, S. (2005) Department of Information and Knowledge Engineering at Danube University

Figure 25(a): Ransen Software

Figure 25(b): Based on en.wikipedia.org/wiki/File:Chartjunk-example.svg

Figure 26: © cartoonstock.com

Figure 39: © Graeme Robertson/Getty Images

Every effort has been made to contact copyright holders. If any have been inadvertently overlooked the publishers will be pleased to make the necessary arrangements at the first opportunity.